Table of Contents

Made in the USA
San Bernardino, CA
24 May 2019

11

Introduction

If your goal is to maintain an optimal health and to become a happier person, then you have definitely ended up in the right place!
Today, you are about to discover the method which will help your life improve in no time!
Yes, we are talking about a diet but not just any diet! We are talking about the Dash diet!

The Dash diet stands for Dietary Approaches to Stop Hypertension. This diet will lower your blood pressure and improve your overall health in no time as long as you respect its main principles.
Here are some other important health benefits brought by this amazing diet:

- It will decrease the risk of cancer
- It will lower your cholesterol
- It will decrease the risk of diabetes
- It will decrease the risk of osteoporosis
- It will help you lose the extra weight

The main thing you have to do in order to achieve all these goals is to reduce the sodium intake to no more that 2300 mg per day and to start consuming healthier products.
During this diet you can eat a lot of veggies, fruits, beans, nuts, healthy oils, low-fat dairy products, whole grains and cereals, poultry, fish, seafood and some lean meats but you have to give up most of the fat and sugar intake.
You can also use canned ingredients to make you Dash meals but make sure you opt for low-sodium or no-salt-added ones.

See? The Dash diet is not a strict one! There are many great and delicious meals you can make with the ingredients you are allowed to eat!

So, if you have decided to start this new life and to follow a dash diet, then you must really get your hands on this magnificent cookbook!
We have searched and gathered the most amazing Dash diet recipes for you to try!

So, let's start this wonderful experience!
Have fun and enjoy the Dash lifestyle!

Dash Diet Breakfast Recipes

Easy Veggie Muffins

Preparation time: 10 minutes
Cooking time: 40 minutes
Servings: 4

Ingredients:

- ¾ cup cheddar cheese, shredded
- 1 cup green onion, chopped
- 1 cup tomatoes, chopped
- 1 cup broccoli, chopped
- 2 cups non-fat milk
- 1 cup biscuit ix
- 4 eggs
- Cooking spray
- 1 teaspoon Italian seasoning
- A pinch of black pepper

Directions:
Grease a muffin tray with cooking spray and divide broccoli, tomatoes cheese and onions in each muffin cup. In a bowl, combine green onions with milk, biscuit mix, eggs, pepper and Italian seasoning, whisk well and pour into the muffin tray as well. Cook the muffins in the oven at 375 degrees F for 40 minutes, divide them between plates and serve.
Enjoy!

Nutrition: calories 212, fat 2, fiber 3, carbs 12, protein 6

Carrot Muffins

Preparation time: 10 minutes
Cooking time: 30 minutes
Servings: 5

Ingredients:

- 1 and ½ cups whole wheat flour
- ½ cup stevia
- 1 teaspoon baking powder
- ½ teaspoon cinnamon powder
- ½ teaspoon baking soda
- ¼ cup natural apple juice
- ¼ cup olive oil
- 1 egg
- 1 cup fresh cranberries
- 2 carrots, grated
- 2 teaspoons ginger, grated
- ¼ cup pecans, chopped
- Cooking spray

Directions:
In a large bowl, combine the flour with the stevia, baking powder, cinnamon and baking soda and stir well. Add apple juice, oil, egg, cranberries, carrots, ginger and pecans and stir really well. Grease a muffin tray with cooking spray, divide the muffin mix, introduce in the oven and cook at 375 degrees F for 30 minutes. Divide the muffins between plates and serve for breakfast.
Enjoy!

Nutrition: calories 212, fat 3, fiber 6, carbs 14, protein 6

Pineapple Oatmeal

Preparation time: 10 minutes
Cooking time: 25 minutes
Servings: 4

Ingredients:
- 2 cups old-fashioned oats
- 1 cup walnuts, chopped
- 2 cups pineapple, cubed
- 1 tablespoon ginger, grated
- 2 cups non-fat milk
- 2 eggs
- 2 tablespoons stevia
- 2 teaspoons vanilla extract

Directions:
In a bowl, combine the oats with the pineapple, walnuts and ginger, stir and divide into 4 ramekins. In a bowl, combine the milk with the eggs, stevia and vanilla, whisk well and pour over the oats mix. Introduce in the oven and cook at 400 degrees F for 25 minutes. Serve for breakfast.
Enjoy!

Nutrition: calories 211, fat 2, fiber 4, carbs 14, protein 6

Spinach Muffins

Preparation time: 10 minutes
Cooking time: 30 minutes
Servings: 6

Ingredients:
- 6 eggs
- ½ cup non-fat milk
- 1 cup low-fat cheese, crumbled
- 4 ounces spinach
- ½ cup roasted red pepper, chopped
- 2 ounces prosciutto, chopped
- Cooking spray

Directions:
In a bowl, combine the eggs with the milk, cheese, spinach, red pepper and prosciutto and whisk well. Grease a muffin tray with cooking spray, divide the muffin mix, introduce in the oven and bake at 350 degrees F for 30 minutes. Divide between plates and serve for breakfast.
Enjoy!

Nutrition: calories 155, fat 10, fiber 1, carbs 4, protein 10

Chia Seeds Breakfast Mix

Preparation time: 8 hours
Cooking time: 0 minutes
Servings: 4

Ingredients:
- 2 cups old-fashioned oats
- 4 tablespoons chia seeds
- 4 tablespoons coconut sugar
- 3 cups coconut milk
- 1 teaspoon lemon zest, grated
- 1 cup blueberries

Directions:
In a bowl, combine the oats with chia seeds, sugar, milk, lemon zest and blueberries, stir, divide into cups and keep in the fridge for 8 hours. Serve for breakfast.
Enjoy!

Nutrition: calories 283, fat 12, fiber 3, carbs 13, protein 8

Breakfast Fruits Bowls

Preparation time: 10 minutes
Cooking time: 0 minutes
Servings: 2

Ingredients:
- 1 cup mango, chopped
- 1 banana, sliced
- 1 cup pineapple, chopped
- 1 cup almond milk

Directions:
In a bowl, combine the mango with the banana, pineapple and almond milk, stir, divide into smaller bowls and serve for breakfast.
Enjoy!

Nutrition: calories 182, fat 2, fiber 4, carbs 12, protein 6

Pumpkin Breakfast Cookies

Preparation time: 10 minutes
Cooking time: 25 minutes
Servings: 6

Ingredients:
- 2 cups whole wheat flour
- 1 cup old-fashioned oats
- 1 teaspoon baking soda
- 1 teaspoon pumpkin pie spice
- 15 ounces pumpkin puree
- 1 cup coconut oil, melted
- 1 cup coconut sugar
- 1 egg
- ½ cup pepitas, roasted
- ½ cup cherries, dried

Directions:
In a bowl, combine the flour with the oats, baking soda, pumpkin spice, pumpkin puree, oil, sugar, egg, pepitas and cherries, stir well, shape medium cookies out of this mix, arrange them all on a lined baking sheet, introduce in the oven and bake at 350 degrees F for 25 minutes. Serve the cookies for breakfast.
Enjoy!

Nutrition: calories 281, fat 12, fiber 3, carbs 14, protein 6

Veggie Scramble

Preparation time: 10 minutes
Cooking time: 2 minutes
Servings: 1

Ingredients:
- 1 egg
- 1 tablespoon water
- ¼ cup broccoli, chopped
- ¼ cup mushrooms, chopped
- A pinch of black pepper
- 1 tablespoon low-fat mozzarella, shredded
- 1 tablespoon walnuts, chopped
- Cooking spray

Directions:
Grease a ramekin with cooking spray, add the egg, water, pepper, mushrooms and broccoli and whisk well. Introduce in the microwave and cook for 2 minutes. Add mozzarella and walnuts on top and serve for breakfast.
Enjoy!

Nutrition: calories 211, fat 2, fiber 4, carbs 12, protein 6

Mushrooms and Turkey Breakfast

Preparation time: 10 minutes
Cooking time: 1 hour and 5 minutes
Servings: 12

Ingredients:

- 8 ounces whole wheat bread, cubed
- 12 ounces turkey sausage, chopped
- 2 cups fat-free milk
- 5 ounces low-fat cheddar, shredded
- 3 eggs
- ½ cup green onions, chopped
- 1 cup mushrooms, chopped
- ½ teaspoon sweet paprika
- A pinch of black pepper
- 2 tablespoons low-fat parmesan, grated

Directions:

Spread bread cubes on a lined baking sheet, introduce in the oven and bake at 400 degrees F for 8 minutes. Meanwhile, heat up a pan over medium-high heat, add turkey sausage, stir and brown for 7 minutes. In a bowl, combine the milk with the cheddar, eggs, parmesan, black pepper and paprika and whisk well. Add mushrooms, sausage, bread cubes and green onions, stir, pour into a baking dish, introduce in the oven and bake at 350 degrees F for 50 minutes. Slice, divide between plates and serve for breakfast.
Enjoy!

Nutrition: calories 221, fat 3, fiber 6, carbs 12, protein 6

Delicious Omelet

Preparation time: 10 minutes
Cooking time: 6 minutes
Servings: 2

Ingredients:

- 2 eggs
- 2 tablespoons water
- 1 teaspoon olive oil
- ¼ cup low-fat Mexican cheese, shredded
- ¼ cup chunky salsa
- A pinch of black pepper

Directions:

In a bowl, combine the eggs with the water, cheese, salsa and pepper and whisk well. Heat up a pan with the oil over medium-high heat, add the eggs mix, spread into the pan, cook for 3 minutes, flip, cook for 3 more minutes, divide between plates and serve for breakfast.
Enjoy!

Nutrition: calories 221, fat 4, fiber 4, carbs 13, protein 7

Easy Omelet Waffles

Preparation time: 10 minutes
Cooking time: 5 minutes
Servings: 2

Ingredients:
- 4 eggs
- A pinch of black pepper
- 2 tablespoons ham, chopped
- ¼ cup low-fat cheddar, shredded
- 2 tablespoons parsley, chopped
- Cooking spray

Directions:
In a bowl, combine the eggs with pepper, ham, cheese and parsley and whisk really well. Grease your waffle iron with cooking spray, add the eggs mix, cook for 4-5 minutes, divide the waffles between plates and serve them for breakfast.
Enjoy!

Nutrition: calories 211, fat 3, fiber 6, carbs 14, protein 8

Jared Omelets

Preparation time: 10 minutes
Cooking time: 6 minutes
Servings: 2

Ingredients:
- Cooking spray
- 2/3 cup low-fat cheddar, shredded
- 4 eggs
- ½ yellow onion, chopped
- ½ cup ham, chopped
- 1 red bell pepper, chopped
- A pinch of black pepper
- 1 tablespoon chives, chopped

Directions:
In a bowl, combine the eggs with onion, ham, bell pepper and pepper and whisk well. Grease 2 mason jars with cooking spray, divide the eggs mix, introduce in the oven and bake at 350 degrees F for 6 minutes. Sprinkle the cheese all over and serve for breakfast.
Enjoy!

Nutrition: calories 221, fat 3, fiber 3, carbs 14, protein 7

Mushrooms and Cheese Omelet

Preparation time: 10 minutes
Cooking time: 15 minutes
Servings: 4

Ingredients:
- 2 tablespoons olive oil
- A pinch of black pepper
- 3 ounces mushrooms, sliced
- 1 cup baby spinach, chopped
- 3 eggs, whisked
- 2 tablespoons low-fat cheese, grated
- 1 small avocado, peeled, pitted and cubed
- 1 tablespoons parsley, chopped

Directions:
Heat up a pan with the oil over medium-high heat, add mushrooms, stir, cook them for 5 minutes and transfer to a bowl. Heat up the same pan over medium-high heat, add eggs and black pepper, spread into the pan, cook for 7 minutes and transfer to a plate. Spread mushrooms, spinach, avocado and cheese on half of the omelet, fold the other half over this mix, sprinkle parsley on top and serve.
Enjoy!

Nutrition: calories 199, fat 3, fiber 4, carbs 14, protein 6

Egg White Breakfast Mix

Preparation time: 10 minutes
Cooking time: 10 minutes
Servings: 4

Ingredients:
- 1 yellow onion, chopped
- 3 plum tomatoes, chopped
- 10 ounces spinach, chopped
- A pinch of black pepper
- 2 tablespoons water
- 12 egg whites
- Cooking spray

Directions:
In a bowl, combine the egg whites with water and pepper and whisk well. Grease a pan with cooking spray, heat up over medium heat; add ¼ of the egg whites, spread into the pan and cook for 2 minutes. Spoon ¼ of the spinach, tomatoes and onion, fold and add to a plate. Repeat with the rest of the egg whites and veggies and serve for breakfast.
Enjoy!

Nutrition: calories 235, fat 4, fiber 7, carbs 14, protein 7

Pesto Omelet

Preparation time: 10 minutes
Cooking time: 6 minutes
Servings: 2

Ingredients:
- 2 teaspoons olive oil
- A handful cherry tomatoes, chopped
- 3 tablespoons pistachio pesto
- A pinch of black pepper
- 4 eggs

Directions:
In a bowl, combine the eggs with cherry tomatoes, black pepper and pistachio pesto and whisk well. Heat up a pan with the oil over medium-high heat, add eggs mix, spread into the pan, cook for 3 minutes, flip, cook for 3 minutes more, divide between 2 plates and serve for breakfast. Enjoy!

Nutrition: calories 199, fat 2, fiber 4, carbs 14, protein 7

Quinoa Bowls

Preparation time: 10 minutes
Cooking time: 20 minutes
Servings: 2

Ingredients:
- 1 peach, sliced
- 1/3 cup quinoa, rinsed
- 2/3 cup low-fat milk
- ½ teaspoon vanilla extract
- 2 teaspoons brown sugar
- 12 raspberries
- 14 blueberries

Directions:
In a small pan, combine the quinoa with the milk, sugar and vanilla, stir, bring to a simmer over medium heat, cover the pan, cook for 20 minutes and flip with a fork. Divide this mix into 2 bowls, top each with raspberries and blueberries and serve for breakfast. Enjoy!

Nutrition: calories 177, fat 2, fiber 4, carbs 9, protein 8

Strawberry Sandwich

Preparation time: 10 minutes
Cooking time: 0 minutes
Servings: 4

Ingredients:

- 8 ounces low-fat cream cheese, soft
- 1 tablespoon stevia
- 1 teaspoon lemon zest, grated
- 4 whole wheat English muffins, halved and toasted
- 2 cups strawberries, sliced

Directions:
In your food processor, combine the cream cheese with the stevia and lemon zest and pulse well. Spread 1 tablespoon of this mix on 1 muffin half and top with some of the sliced strawberries. Repeat with the rest of the muffin halves and serve for breakfast.
Enjoy!

Nutrition: calories 211, fat 3, fiber 4, carbs 8, protein 4

Apple Quinoa Muffins

Preparation time: 10 minutes
Cooking time: 35 minutes
Servings: 4

Ingredients:

- ½ cup natural, unsweetened applesauce
- 1 cup banana, peeled and mashed
- 1 cup quinoa
- 2 and ½ cups old-fashioned oats
- ½ cup almond milk
- 2 tablespoons stevia
- 1 teaspoon vanilla extract
- 1 cup water
- Cooking spray
- 1 teaspoon cinnamon powder
- 1 apple, cored, peeled and chopped

Directions:
Put the water in a small pan, bring to a simmer over medium heat, add quinoa, cook for 15 minutes, and fluff with a fork and transfer to a bowl. Add banana, applesauce, oats, almond milk, stevia, vanilla, cinnamon and apple, stir, divide into a muffin pan greases with cooking spray, introduce in the oven and bake at 375 degrees F for 20 minutes. Serve for breakfast.
Enjoy!

Nutrition: calories 200, fat 3, fiber 4, carbs 14, protein 7

Amazing Quinoa Hash Browns

Preparation time: 10 minutes
Cooking time: 25 minutes
Servings: 2

Ingredients:
- 1/3 cup quinoa
- 2/3 cup water
- 1 and ½ cups potato, peeled and grated
- 1 eggs
- A pinch of black pepper
- 1 tablespoon olive oil
- 2 green onions, chopped

Directions:
Put the water in a small pan, bring to a simmer over medium heat, add quinoa, stir, cover, cook for 15 minutes and fluff with a fork. IN a bowl, combine the quinoa with potato, egg, green onions, pepper, and stir well. Heat up a pan with the oil over medium-high heat, add quinoa hash browns, cook for 5 minutes on each side, divide between 2 plates and serve for breakfast. Enjoy!

Nutrition: calories 191, fat 3, fiber 8, carbs 14, protein 7

Quinoa Breakfast Bars

Preparation time: 2 hours
Cooking time: 0 minutes
Servings: 6

Ingredients:
- ½ cup fat-free peanut butter
- 2 tablespoons coconut sugar
- 1 teaspoon vanilla extract
- ½ teaspoon cinnamon powder
- 1 cup quinoa flakes
- 1/3 cup coconut, flaked
- 2 tablespoons unsweetened chocolate chips

Directions:
In a large bowl, combine the peanut butter with sugar, vanilla, cinnamon, quinoa, coconut and chocolate chips, stir well, spread on the bottom of a lined baking sheet, press well, cut in 6 bars, keep in the fridge for 2 hours, divide between plates and serve.
Enjoy!

Nutrition: calories 182, fat 4, fiber 4, carbs 13, protein 11

Quinoa Quiche

Preparation time: 10 minutes
Cooking time: 45 minutes
Servings: 4

Ingredients:
- 1` cup quinoa, cooked
- 3 ounces spinach, chopped
- 1 cup fat-free ricotta cheese
- 3 eggs
- 1 and ½ teaspoons garlic powder
- 2/3 cup low-fat parmesan, grated

Directions:
In a bowl, combine the quinoa with the spinach, ricotta, eggs, garlic powder and parmesan, whisk well, pour into a lined pie pan, introduce in the oven and bake at 355 degrees F for 45 minutes. Cool the quiche down, slice and serve for breakfast.
Enjoy!

Nutrition: calories 201, fat 2, fiber 4, carbs 12, protein 7

Quinoa Breakfast Parfaits

Preparation time: 10 minutes
Cooking time: 20 minutes
Servings: 4

Ingredients:
For the crumble:
- 1 tablespoon coconut oil, melted
- ½ cup rolled oats
- 2 teaspoons coconut sugar
- 1 tablespoon walnuts, chopped
- 1 teaspoon cinnamon powder

For the apple mix:
- 4 apples, cored, peeled and chopped
- 1 teaspoon vanilla extract
- 1 teaspoon cinnamon powder
- 1 tablespoon coconut sugar
- 2 tablespoons water

For the quinoa mix:
- 1 cup quinoa, cooked
- 1 teaspoon cinnamon powder
- 2 cups nonfat yogurt

Directions:
In a bowl, combine the coconut oil with the rolled water, 2 teaspoons coconut sugar, walnuts and 1 teaspoon cinnamon, stir, spread on a lined baking sheet, cook at 350 degrees F , bake for 10 minutes and leave aside to cool down. In a small pan, combine the apples with the vanilla, 1-teaspoon cinnamon, 1-tablespoon coconut sugar and the water, stir, cook over medium heat for 10 minutes and take off heat. In a bowl, combine the quinoa with 1-teaspoon cinnamon and 2 cups yogurt and stir. Divide the quinoa mix into bowls, then divide the apple compote and top with the crumble mix. Serve for breakfast.
Enjoy!

Nutrition: calories 188, fat 3, fiber 6, carbs 12, protein 7

Breakfast Quinoa Cakes

Preparation time: 10 minutes
Cooking time: 30 minutes
Servings: 4

Ingredients:
- 1 cup quinoa
- 2 cups cauliflower, chopped
- 1 and ½ cups chicken stock
- ½ cup low-fat cheddar, shredded
- ½ cup low-fat parmesan, grated
- 1 egg
- A pinch of black pepper
- 2 tablespoons canola oil

Directions:
In a pot, combine the quinoa with the cauliflower, stock and pepper, stir, bring to a simmer over medium heat and cook for 20 minutes. Add cheddar and the eggs, stir well, shape medium cakes out of this mix and dredge them in the parmesan. Heat up a pan with the oil over medium-high heat, add the quinoa cakes. Cook for 4-5 minutes on each side, divide between plates and serve for breakfast.
Enjoy!

Nutrition: calories 199, fat 3, fiber 4, carbs 8, carbs 14, protein 6

Easy Quinoa Pancakes

Preparation time: 10 minutes
Cooking time: 6 minutes
Servings: 8

Ingredients:
- ½ cup unsweetened applesauce
- 2 tablespoons coconut sugar
- ½ cup nonfat milk
- 1 tablespoon lemon juice
- 1 teaspoon baking soda
- 1 and ½ cups quinoa flour

Directions:
In your food processor, combine the applesauce with the sugar, milk, lemon juice, baking soda and quinoa and pulse well. Heat up a pan over medium heat, spoon some of the pancake batter, spread into the pan, cook for 3 minutes on each side and transfer to a plate. Repeat with the rest of the pancake batter, divide the pancakes between plates and serve for breakfast.
Enjoy!

Nutrition: calories 188, fat 3, fiber 6, carbs 13, protein 6

Quinoa and Egg Muffins

Preparation time: 10 minutes
Cooking time: 30 minutes
Servings: 3

Ingredients:

- 1/3 cup quinoa, cooked
- 1 zucchini, chopped
- 2 eggs
- 4 egg whites
- ½ cup low-fat feta cheese, shredded
- A pinch of black pepper
- A splash of hot sauce
- Cooking spray

Directions:
In a bowl, combine the quinoa with the zucchini, eggs, egg whites, cheese, black pepper and hot sauce, whisk well and divide into 6 muffin cups greased with the cooking spray. Bake the muffins in the oven at 350 degrees F for 30 minutes. Divide the muffins between plates and serve for breakfast.
Enjoy!

Nutrition: calories 221, fat 7, fiber 2, carbs 13, protein 14

Apple and Quinoa Breakfast Bake

Preparation time: 10 minutes
Cooking time: 10 minutes
Servings: 6

Ingredients:

- 1 cup quinoa, cooked
- ¼ teaspoon olive oil
- 2 teaspoons coconut sugar
- 2 apples, cored, peeled and chopped
- 1 teaspoon cinnamon powder
- ½ cup almond milk

Directions:
Grease a ramekin with the oil, add quinoa, apples, sugar, cinnamon and almond milk, and stir, introduce in the oven, bake at 350 degrees F for 10 minutes, divide into bowls and serve.
Enjoy!

Nutrition: calories 199, fat 2, fiber 7, carbs 14, protein 8

Quinoa Patties

Preparation time: 10 minutes
Cooking time: 20 minutes
Servings: 6

Ingredients:

- 2 and ½ cups quinoa, cooked
- A pinch of black pepper
- 4 eggs, whisked
- 1 yellow onion, chopped
- ¼ cup chives, chopped
- 1/3 cup low-fat parmesan, grated
- 3 garlic cloves, minced
- 1 cup whole wheat bread crumbs
- 1 tablespoon olive oil

Directions:
In a large bowl, combine the quinoa with black pepper, eggs, onion, chives, parmesan, garlic and breadcrumbs, stir well and shape medium patties out of this mix. Heat up a pan with the oil over medium-high heat, add quinoa patties, cook them for 10 minutes on each side, divide them between plates and serve for breakfast.
Enjoy!

Nutrition: calories 201, fat 3, fiber 4, carbs 14, protein 8

Peanut Butter Smoothie

Preparation time: 10 minutes
Cooking time: 0 minutes
Servings: 2

Ingredients:

- 2 tablespoons peanut butter
- 2 cups non-fat milk
- 2 bananas, peeled and chopped

Directions:
In your blender, combine the peanut butter with the milk and bananas, pulse well, divide into 2 glasses and serve.
Enjoy!

Nutrition: calories176, fat 4, fiber 6, carbs 14, protein 7€

Yogurt Peanut Butter Mix

Preparation time: 10 minutes
Cooking time: 0 minutes
Servings: 3

Ingredients:

- 6 ounces nonfat yogurt
- 2 tablespoons red grapes, halved
- 4 teaspoons grape jelly
- 1 tablespoon fat-free peanut butter
- 1 teaspoons peanuts, chopped

Directions:
In a bowl, combine the yogurt with the grapes, grape jelly, peanut butter and peanuts, toss well, divide into small cups and serve for breakfast.
Enjoy!

Nutrition: calories 187, fat 2, fiber 3, carbs 6, protein 8

Slow Cooked Oatmeal

Preparation time: 10 minutes
Cooking time: 8 hours
Servings: 3

Ingredients:

- 4 cups nonfat milk
- 2 cups steel cut pats
- 4 cups water
- 1/3 cup raisins
- 1/3 cup cherries, dried
- 1/3 cup apricots, dried and chopped
- 1 teaspoon cinnamon powder

Directions:
In your slow cooker, combine the milk with the oats, water, raisins, cherries, apricots and cinnamon, stir, cover, cook on Low for 8 hours, divide into bowls and serve for breakfast.
Enjoy!

Nutrition: calories 171, fat 3, fiber 6, carbs 15, protein 7

Strawberry and Quinoa Porridge

Preparation time: 10 minutes
Cooking time: 15 minutes
Servings: 4

Ingredients:

- 1 cup quinoa
- 2 cups almond milk
- 1 tablespoon coconut sugar
- 1 teaspoon cinnamon powder
- ¼ teaspoon vanilla extract
- 1 cup strawberries, sliced

Directions:
In a small pan, combine the quinoa with the milk, stir, bring to a simmer over medium heat and cook for 10 minutes. Add sugar, cinnamon and vanilla, stir, cook for 5 minutes more, divide into bowls, top with strawberries and serve.
Enjoy!

Nutrition: calories 177, fat 4, fiber 7, carbs 14, protein 7

Delicious Breakfast Grain Salad

Preparation time: 10 minutes
Cooking time: 10 minutes
Servings: 3

Ingredients:

- 3 cups water
- ¾ cup brown rice
- ¾ cup bulgur
- 1 green apple, cored, peeled and cubed
- 1 red apple, cored, peeled and cubed
- 1 orange, peeled and cut into segments
- 1 cup raisins
- 8 ounces low-fat yogurt

Directions:
Put the water in a pan, bring to a simmer over high heat, add bulgur and rice, stir, cover, reduce heat to medium-low, cook for 10 minutes, spread on a lined baking sheet and leave aside to cool down. In a bowl, combine the grains with the apples, orange, raisins and yogurt, toss and serve for breakfast.
Enjoy!

Nutrition: calories 181, fat 3, fiber 8, carbs 16, protein 8

Colored Quinoa Salad

Preparation time: 10 minutes
Cooking time: 20 minutes
Servings: 4

Ingredients:
- 1 cup red quinoa
- 2 cups water
- Juice of 1 lime
- 2 tablespoons stevia
- 2 tablespoons mint, chopped
- 1 and ½ cups blueberries
- 1 and ½ cups strawberries, sliced
- 1 and ½ cups mango, chopped

Directions:
Put the water in a pot, bring to a boil over medium-high heat, add quinoa, stir, cover, reduce heat to medium-low, cook for 20 minutes, and fluff with a fork and transfer to a salad bowl. Add blueberries, strawberries, mango, and toss. In a bowl, combine the stevia with mint and lime juice, whisk well, pour over the salad, toss, divide into small bowls and serve for breakfast. Enjoy!

Nutrition: calories 161, fat 2, fiber 4, carbs 10, protein 8

Moroccan Breakfast Mix

Preparation time: 10 minutes
Cooking time: 20 minutes
Servings: 4

Ingredients:
- 1 cup quinoa
- 1 and ¾ cups water
- 1 tablespoon lime zest, grated
- 3 tablespoons olive oil
- 2 tablespoons lime juice
- 1 teaspoon chili powder
- 1 and ½ teaspoons cumin, ground
- 1 teaspoon coriander, ground
- 14 ounces canned black beans, no-salt-added, drained and rinsed
- 1 cup cilantro, chopped
- A pinch of black pepper

Directions:
Put the water in a pot, bring to a boil over medium heat, add quinoa, lime zest, chili powder, cumin and coriander, cover, cook for 20 minutes, fluff with a fork and transfer to a salad bowl. Add limejuice, olive oil, black beans, cilantro and black pepper, toss and serve for breakfast. Enjoy!

Nutrition: calories 201, fat 3, fiber 4, carbs 14, protein 8

Chickpeas Breakfast Salad

Preparation time: 10 minutes
Cooking time: 0 minutes
Servings: 4

Ingredients:
- 1 tablespoon parsley, chopped
- 1 tablespoon mint, chopped
- 1 tablespoon chives, chopped
- 2 ounces radishes, chopped
- 2 beets, peeled and grated
- 1 apple, cored, peeled and cubed
- 1 teaspoon cumin, ground
- 2 ounces quinoa, cooked
- 3 tablespoons olive oil
- 7 ounces canned chickpeas, no-salt-added, drained and rinsed
- 7 ounces canned green chilies, chopped
- Juice of 2 lemons

Directions:
In a bowl, combine the parsley with the mint, chives, radishes, beets, apple, cumin, quinoa, oil, chickpeas, chilies and lemon juice, toss well, divide into small bowls and serve for breakfast. Enjoy!

Nutrition: calories 251, fat 8, fiber 8, carbs 14, protein 14

Delicious Blueberry Breakfast Salad

Preparation time: 10 minutes
Cooking time: 0 minutes
Servings: 4

Ingredients:
- 2 pounds salad greens, torn
- 4 cups blueberries
- 3 cups orange, peeled and cut into segments
- 2 cups granola

For the vinaigrette:
- 1 cup blueberries
- 1 cup olive oil
- 2 tablespoons coconut sugar
- 2 teaspoons shallot, minced
- ½ teaspoon sweet paprika
- A pinch of black pepper

Directions:
In your food processor, combine 1-cup blueberries with the oil, sugar, shallot, paprika, black pepper, and pulse well. In a salad, bowl, combine 4 cups blueberries with salad greens, granola and oranges and toss. Add the blueberry vinaigrette, toss and serve for breakfast. Enjoy!

Nutrition: calories 171, fat 2, fiber 4, carbs 8, protein 8

Kale Breakfast Salad

Preparation time: 10 minutes
Cooking time: 0 minutes
Servings: 4

Ingredients:
- 6 cups kale, chopped
- ¼ cup lemon juice
- ½ cup olive oil
- 1 teaspoon mustard
- 1 and ½ cups quinoa, cooked
- 1 and ½ cups cherry tomatoes, halved
- A pinch of black pepper
- 3 tablespoons pine nuts, toasted

Directions:
In a large salad bowl, combine the kale with quinoa and cherry tomatoes. Add lemon juice, oil, mustard, black pepper and pine nuts, toss well, divide between plates and serve for breakfast. Enjoy!

Nutrition: calories 165, fat 5, fiber 7, carbs 14, protein 6

Salmon Breakfast Salad

Preparation time: 10 minutes
Cooking time: 0 minutes
Servings: 2

Ingredients:
- 3 tablespoons nonfat yogurt
- 1 teaspoon horseradish sauce
- 1 tablespoon dill, chopped
- 1 teaspoon lemon juice
- 4 ounces smoked salmon, boneless, skinless and torn
- 3 ounces salad greens
- 2 ounces cherry tomatoes, halved
- 2 ounces black olives, pitted and sliced

Directions:
In a salad bowl, combine the salmon with salad greens, tomatoes and black olives. In another bowl, combine the yogurt with horseradish, dill and lemon juice, whisk well, pour over the salad, toss well and serve for breakfast.
Enjoy!

Nutrition: calories 177, fat 4, fiber 7, carbs 14, protein 8

Banana and Pear Breakfast Salad

Preparation time: 10 minutes
Cooking time: 0 minutes
Servings: 2

Ingredients:
- 1 banana, peeled and sliced
- 1 Asian pear, cored and cubed
- Juice of ½ lime
- ½ teaspoon cinnamon powder
- 2 ounces pepitas, toasted

Directions:
In a bowl, combine the banana with the pear, limejuice, cinnamon and pepitas, toss, divide between small plates and serve for breakfast.
Enjoy!

Nutrition: calories 188, fat 2, fiber 3, carbs 5, protein 7

Simple Plum and Avocado Salad

Preparation time: 10 minutes
Cooking time: 0 minutes
Servings: 3

Ingredients:
- 2 avocados, peeled, pitted and cubed
- 4 plums, stones removed and cubed
- 1 cup cilantro, chopped
- 1 garlic clove, minced
- Juice of 1 lemon
- A drizzle of olive oil
- 1 red chili pepper, minced

Directions:
In a salad bowl, combine the avocados with plums, cilantro, garlic, lemon juice, oil and chili pepper, toss well, divide between plates and serve for breakfast.
Enjoy!

Nutrition: calories 212, fat 2, fiber 4, carbs 14, protein 11

Cherries Oatmeal

Preparation time: 10 minutes
Cooking time: 15 minutes
Servings: 6

Ingredients:

- 2 cups old-fashioned oats
- 6 cups water
- 1 cup almond milk
- 1 teaspoon cinnamon powder
- 1 teaspoon vanilla extract
- 2 cups cherries, pitted and sliced

Directions:
In a small pot, combine the oats with the water, milk, cinnamon, vanilla and cherries, toss, bring to a simmer over medium-high heat, cook for 15 minutes, divide into bowls and serve for breakfast.
Enjoy!

Nutrition: calories 180, fat 4, fiber 4, carbs 9, protein 7

Orange and Apricots Oatmeal

Preparation time: 10 minutes
Cooking time: 15 minutes
Servings: 4

Ingredients:

- 1 and ½ cups water
- 1 cup steel cut oats
- 1 cup orange juice
- 2 tablespoons apricots, dried and chopped
- 2 tablespoons coconut sugar
- 2 tablespoons pecans, chopped
- ¼ teaspoon cinnamon powder

Directions:
In a small pot, combine the oats with the water, orange juice, apricots, sugar, cinnamon and pecans, stir, bring to a simmer over medium heat, cook for 15 minutes, divide into bowls and serve for breakfast.
Enjoy!

Nutrition: calories 190, fat 3, fiber 6, carbs 8, protein 5

Cinnamon Pear Oatmeal

Preparation time: 10 minutes
Cooking time: 15 minutes
Servings: 3

Ingredients:
- 3 cups water
- 1 cup steel cut oats
- 1 tablespoon cinnamon powder
- 1 cup pear, cored, peeled and cubed

Directions:
In a small pot, combine the water with the oats, cinnamon and pear, toss, bring to a simmer over medium heat, cook for 15 minutes, divide into bowls and serve for breakfast.
Enjoy!

Nutrition: calories 171, fat 2, fiber 5, carbs 11, protein 6

Banana and Walnuts Bowls

Preparation time: 10 minutes
Cooking time: 15 minutes
Servings: 4

Ingredients:
- 2 cups water
- 1 cup steel cut oats
- 1 cup almond milk
- ¼ cup walnuts, chopped
- 2 tablespoons chia seeds
- 2 bananas, peeled and mashed
- 1 teaspoon vanilla extract

Directions:
In a small pot, combine the water with the oats, milk, walnuts, chia seeds, bananas and vanilla, toss, bring to a simmer over medium heat, cook for 15 minutes, divide into bowls and serve for breakfast.
Enjoy!

Nutrition: calories 162, fat 4, fiber 6, carbs 11, protein 4

Parsley Omelet

Preparation time: 10 minutes
Cooking time: 6 minutes
Servings: 6

Ingredients:
- 2 tablespoons almond milk
- A pinch of black pepper
- 6 eggs, whisked
- 2 tablespoons parsley, chopped
- 1 tablespoon low-fat cheddar cheese, shredded
- 2 teaspoons olive oil

Directions:
In a bowl, mix the eggs with the milk, black pepper, parsley and cheese and whisk well. Heat up a pan with the oil over medium-high heat, add the eggs mix, spread into the pan, cook for 3 minutes, flip, cook for 3 minutes more, divide between plates and serve for breakfast.
Enjoy!

Nutrition: calories 200, fat 4, fiber 6, carb 13, protein 9

Cheddar Baked Eggs

Preparation time: 10 minutes
Cooking time: 15 minutes
Servings: 4

Ingredients:
- 4 eggs
- 4 slices low-fat cheddar
- 2 spring onions, chopped
- 1 tablespoon olive oil
- A pinch of black pepper
- 1 tablespoon cilantro, chopped

Directions:
Grease 4 ramekins with the oil, sprinkle green onions in each, crack an egg in each ramekins and top with cilantro and cheddar cheese. Introduce in the oven and bake at 375 degrees F for 15 minutes. Serve for breakfast.
Enjoy!

Nutrition: calories 199, fat 3, fiber 7, carbs 11, protein 5

Hash Brown Mix

Preparation time: 10 minutes
Cooking time: 30 minutes
Servings: 6

Ingredients:
- Cooking spray
- 6 eggs
- 2 cups hash browns
- ¼ cup non-fat milk
- ½ cup fat-free cheddar cheese, shredded
- 1 small yellow onion, chopped
- A pinch of black pepper
- ½ green bell pepper, chopped
- ½ red bell pepper, chopped

Directions:
Heat up a pan greased with cooking spray over medium-high heat, add onions, green and red bell pepper, stir and cook for 4-5 minutes. Add hash browns and black pepper, stir and cook for 5 minutes more. In a bowl, combine the eggs with milk and cheese, whisk well, pour over the mix from the pan, introduce in the oven and bake at 380 degrees F for 20 minutes. Slice, divide between plates and serve.
Enjoy!

Nutrition: calories 221, fat 4, fiber 5, carbs 14, protein 6

Peaches Mix

Preparation time: 10 minutes
Cooking time: 5 minutes
Servings: 4

Ingredients:
- 6 small peaches, cored and cut into wedges
- ¼ cup coconut sugar
- 2 tablespoons non-fat butter
- ¼ teaspoon almond extract

Directions:
In a small pan, combine the peaches with sugar, butter and almond extract, toss, cook over medium-high heat for 5 minutes, divide into bowls and serve for breakfast.
Enjoy!

Nutrition: calories 198, fat 2, fiber 6, carbs 11, protein 8

Cinnamon Brown Rice Pudding

Preparation time: 10 minutes
Cooking time: 25 minutes
Servings: 4

Ingredients:

- 1 cup brown rice
- 1 and ½ cups water
- 1 tablespoon vanilla extract
- 1 tablespoon cinnamon powder
- 1 tablespoon non-fat butter
- ½ cup coconut cream, unsweetened

Directions:
In a pot, combine the rice with the water, vanilla, cinnamon, butter and cream, stir, bring to a simmer over medium heat, cook for 25 minutes, divide into bowls and serve for breakfast.
Enjoy!

Nutrition: calories 182, fat 4, fiber 7, carbs 11, protein 6

Cream Basmati Rice Pudding

Preparation time: 10 minutes
Cooking time: 25 minutes
Servings: 6

Ingredients:

- 2 cups coconut milk
- 1 and ¼ cups water
- 1 cup basmati rice
- 2 tablespoons coconut sugar
- ¾ cup coconut cream
- 1 teaspoon vanilla extract

Directions:
In a pot, combine the coconut milk with the water, rice, sugar, cream and vanilla, toss, bring to a simmer over medium heat, cook for 25 minutes, stirring often, divide into bowls and serve for breakfast.
Enjoy!

Nutrition: calories 191, fat 4, fiber 7, carbs 11, protein 6

Zucchini and Sweet Potato Bowl

Preparation time: 10 minutes
Cooking time: 10 minutes
Servings: 2

Ingredients:
- 1 big zucchini, cut with the spiralizer
- Salt and black pepper to the taste
- ¼ cup extra virgin olive oil
- ½ avocado, peeled, pitted and cubed
- 2 tablespoons green onions, chopped
- 2 garlic cloves, chopped
- 2 sweet potatoes, peeled and cubed

Directions:
Heat up a pan with half of the olive oil over medium-high heat, add potatoes, stir and cook for 8 minutes. In your food processor, mix avocado with the rest of the oil, garlic, salt and pepper and blend well. Put zucchini noodles in a bowl, add avocado cream and sweet potatoes and toss to coat. Sprinkle green onions and serve for breakfast.
Enjoy!

Nutrition: calories 171, fat 3, fiber 3, carbs 11, protein 4

Nuts Porridge

Preparation time: 7 hours
Cooking time: 7 minutes
Servings: 4

Ingredients:
- ¼ cup walnuts, raw
- ½ cup almonds, raw
- ½ cup cashews, raw
- 1/3 cup coconut flakes
- 1 egg yolk
- 1 banana, chopped
- 1 tablespoon low-fat butter
- 1 apple, chopped
- 14 ounces coconut milk
- 2 teaspoons vanilla extract
- 2 teaspoons cinnamon, powder

Directions:
Put almonds, cashews, walnuts and coconut flakes in a bowl, add filtered water to cover, cover, leave aside for 7 hours, drain, transfer to your food processor, add coconut flakes, egg yolk and banana and pulse. Heat up a pan with the butter over medium heat, add apple, vanilla, coconut milk, cinnamon and nut mix, stir well, bring to a simmer, cook for 5 minutes, divide into bowls and serve for breakfast.
Enjoy!

Nutrition: calories 180, fat 2, fiber 1, carbs 8, protein 14

Eggs, Sausage and Veggies Salad

Preparation time: 10 minutes
Cooking time: 10 minutes
Servings: 4

Ingredients:

- 9 eggs, hard-boiled, peeled and cut into small wedges
- 1 pound breakfast pork sausage, casings removed
- 3 cups cherry tomatoes, halved
- 2 avocados, chopped
- ¼ cup onion, chopped
- ½ cup cilantro, chopped
- A pinch of black pepper
- Juice of 2 lemons

Directions:
Shape sausage mix into small meatballs. Heat up a pan over medium-high heat, add meatballs, brown for 3-4 minutes on each side, transfer to a plate and leave them to cool down. In a salad bowl, combine the meatballs with eggs, onion, tomatoes, avocado, pepper, cilantro and lemon juice, toss and serve for breakfast.
Enjoy!

Nutrition: calories 180, fat 4, fiber 4, carbs 14, protein 11

Cashews and Blueberries Salad

Preparation time: 10 minutes
Cooking time: 0 minutes
Servings: 2

Ingredients:

- ¼ cup cashews, raw
- ¼ cup blueberries
- 1 banana, peeled and sliced
- 1 tablespoon almond butter
- 1 teaspoon cinnamon powder

Directions:
In a bowl, combine the banana with cashews, blueberries, almond butter and cinnamon, toss and serve for breakfast.
Enjoy!

Nutrition: calories 120, fat 0.3, fiber 1, carbs 7, protein 5

Sweet Potatoes and Apples Mix

Preparation time: 10 minutes
Cooking time: 1 hour and 10 minutes
Servings: 1

Ingredients:
- 2 pounds sweet potatoes
- 2 tablespoons water
- ½ pound apples, cored and chopped
- 1 tablespoon low-fat butter

Directions:
Arrange the potatoes on a lined baking sheet, bake in the oven at 400 degrees F for 1 hour, peel them and mash them in your food processor. Put apples in a pot, add the water, bring to a boil over medium heat, reduce temperature, cook for 10 minutes, transfer to a bowl, add mashed potatoes, stir well and serve for breakfast.
Enjoy!

Nutrition: calories 140, fat 1, fiber 4, carbs 8, protein 6

Pear Breakfast Salad

Preparation time: 10 minutes
Cooking time: 0 minutes
Servings: 4

Ingredients:
- 3 big pears, cored and cut with a spiralizer
- ¾ cup pomegranate seeds
- 5 ounces arugula
- ¾ cup walnuts, roughly chopped

For the vinaigrette:
- 2 tablespoons olive oil
- 1 tablespoon coconut sugar
- 1 teaspoon white sesame seeds
- 2 tablespoons apple cider vinegar
- 1 garlic clove, minced
- Black pepper to the taste

Directions:
In a bowl, combine the olive oil with sugar, sesame seeds, vinegar, garlic and pepper and whisk well. In a salad bowl, mix pear with arugula, walnuts and pomegranate seeds, toss, add the vinaigrette, toss and serve for breakfast.
Enjoy!

Nutrition: calories 182, fat 2, fiber 7, carbs 11, protein 7

Breakfast Bulgur Salad

Preparation time: 15 minutes
Cooking time: 0 minutes
Servings: 6
Ingredients:

- 1 and ½ cups hot water
- 1 cup bulgur
- Juice of 1 lime
- 4 tablespoons cilantro, chopped
- ½ cup cranberries, dried
- 1 and ½ teaspoons curry powder
- 1/3 cup almonds, sliced
- ¼ cup green onions, chopped
- ½ cup red bell peppers, chopped
- ½ cup carrots, grated
- 4 tablespoons pepitas
- 1 tablespoon olive oil
- Black pepper to the taste

Directions:
Put bulgur into a bowl, add boiling water, cover, and leave aside for 15 minutes, fluff bulgur with a fork and transfer to a salad bowl. Add limejuice, cilantro, cranberries, almonds, bell peppers, onions, carrots, curry powder, pepitas, black pepper and the oil, toss and serve for breakfast. Enjoy!
Nutrition: calories 190, fat 3, fiber 3, carbs 13, protein 10

Black Bean Breakfast Salad

Preparation time: 15 minutes
Cooking time: 0 minutes
Servings: 4
Ingredients:

- 1 and ½ cups canned black beans, no-salt-added, drained and rinsed
- ½ teaspoon garlic powder
- ½ teaspoon smoked paprika
- 2 teaspoons chili powder
- Black pepper to the taste
- 1 teaspoon cumin, ground
- 1 and ½ cups canned chickpeas, no-salt-added, drained and rinsed
- ¼ teaspoon cinnamon powder
- 1 lettuce head, chopped
- 1 red bell pepper, chopped
- 2 tomatoes, chopped
- 1 avocado, pitted, peeled and chopped
- 1 cup corn kernels, chopped

For the salad dressing:

- 2 tablespoons lemon juice
- ¾ cup cashews, soaked and drained
- ½ cup water
- 1 garlic clove, minced
- 1 tablespoon apple cider vinegar
- ½ teaspoon onion powder
- 1 teaspoon chives, chopped
- ½ teaspoon oregano, dried
- 1 teaspoon dill, dried
- 1 teaspoon cumin, ground
- ½ teaspoon smoked paprika

Directions:
In your blender, mix cashews with water, 2 tablespoons lemon juice, 1 tablespoon vinegar, 1 garlic clove, ½ teaspoon onion powder, dill, oregano, chives, cumin and ½ teaspoon paprika, blend really well and leave aside for now. In a salad bowl, mix black beans with chili powder, ½ teaspoon garlic powder, ½ teaspoon paprika, chickpeas, cinnamon and black pepper to the taste and stir really well. Add lettuce leaves, tomatoes, corn, avocado and bell peppers, toss everything, drizzle the salad dressing, mix everything again and serve for breakfast.
Nutrition: calories 190, fat 4, fiber 10, carbs 11, protein 11

Chickpeas Breakfast Salad

Preparation time: 10 minutes
Cooking time: 0 minutes
Servings: 2

Ingredients:

- 16 ounces canned chickpeas, no-salt-added, drained and rinsed
- 1 handful baby spinach leaves
- ½ tablespoon lemon juice
- 4 tablespoons olive oil
- 1 teaspoon cumin, ground
- Black pepper to the taste
- ½ teaspoon chili flakes

Directions:

In a bowl, mix lemon juice, oil, cumin, black pepper and chili flakes and whisk well. In a salad bowl, mix chickpeas with spinach, add salad dressing, toss to coat and serve for breakfast. Enjoy!

Nutrition: calories 220, fat 3, fiber 6, carbs 12, protein 8

Mediterranean Breakfast Salad

Preparation time: 10 minutes
Cooking time: 0 minutes
Servings: 4

Ingredients:

- 1 handful kalamata olives, pitted and sliced
- 1-pint cherry tomatoes, halved
- 4 tomatoes, chopped
- 1 and ½ cucumbers, sliced
- 1 red onion, chopped
- 2 tablespoons oregano, chopped
- 1 tablespoon mint, chopped

For the salad dressing:

- 1 teaspoon coconut sugar
- 2 tablespoons balsamic vinegar
- ¼ cup olive oil
- 1 garlic clove, minced
- 2 teaspoons Italian herbs, dried
- Black pepper to the taste

Directions:

In a salad bowl, mix cherry tomatoes with tomatoes, olives, cucumbers, onion, mint and oregano and toss. In another bowl, mix sugar with vinegar, oil, garlic, dried Italian herbs and black pepper, whisk well, add to your salad, toss to coat and serve for breakfast. Enjoy!

Nutrition: calories 180, fat 2, fiber 3, carbs 6, protein 9

Dash Diet Lunch Recipes

Delicious Veggie Quesadillas

Preparation time: 10 minutes
Cooking time: 4 minutes
Servings: 3

Ingredients:

- 1 cup black beans, cooked
- ½ red bell pepper, chopped
- 4 tablespoons cilantro, chopped
- ½ cup corn
- 1 cup low-fat cheddar, shredded
- 6 whole wheat tortillas
- 1 carrot, shredded
- 1 small jalapeno pepper, chopped
- 1 cup non-fat yogurt
- Juice of ½ lime

Directions:
Divide black beans, red bell pepper, 2 tablespoons cilantro, corn, carrot, jalapeno and the cheese on half of the tortillas and cover with the other ones. Heat up a pan over medium-high heat, add one quesadilla, cook for 3 minutes on one side, flip, cook for 1 more minute on the other and transfer to a plate. Repeat with the rest of the quesadillas. In a bowl, combine 2 tablespoons cilantro with yogurt and lime juice, whisk well and serve next to the quesadillas.
Enjoy!

Nutrition: calories 200, fat 3, fiber 4, carbs 13, protein 7

Chicken Wraps

Preparation time: 10 minutes
Cooking time: 10 minutes
Servings: 4

Ingredients:

- 8 ounces chicken breast, cubed
- ½ cup celery, chopped
- 2/3 cup mandarin oranges, chopped
- ¼ cup onion, chopped
- A drizzle of olive oil
- 2 tablespoons mayonnaise
- ¼ teaspoon garlic powder
- A pinch of black pepper
- 4 whole wheat tortillas
- 4 lettuce leaves

Directions:
Heat up a pan with the oil over medium-high heat, add chicken cubes, and cook for 5 minutes on each side and transfer to a bowl. Divide the chicken on each tortilla, also divide celery, oranges, onion, mayo, garlic powder, black pepper and lettuce leaves, wrap and serve for lunch.
Enjoy!

Nutrition: calories 200, fat 3, fiber 4, carbs 13, protein 7

Black Bean Patties

Preparation time: 10 minutes
Cooking time: 10 minutes
Servings: 4

Ingredients:
- 2 whole wheat bread slices, torn
- 3 tablespoons cilantro, chopped
- 2 garlic cloves, minced
- 15 ounces canned black beans, no-salt-added, drained and rinsed
- 6 ounces canned chipotle peppers, chopped
- 1 teaspoon cumin, ground
- 1 egg
- Cooking spray
- ½ avocado, peeled, pitted and mashed
- 1 tablespoon lime juice
- 1 cherry tomato, chopped

Directions:
Put the bread in your food processor, pulse well and transfer breadcrumbs to a bowl. Combine them with cilantro, garlic, black beans, chipotle peppers, cumin and egg, stir well and shape 4 patties out of this mix. Heat up a pan over medium-high heat, grease with cooking spray, add beans patties, cook them for 5 minutes on each side and transfer to plates. In a bowl, combine the avocado with tomato and lime juice, stir well, add over the patties and serve for lunch.
Enjoy!

Nutrition: calories 200, fat 4, fiber 4, carbs 12, protein 8

Lunch Rice Bowls

Preparation time: 10 minutes
Cooking time: 5 minutes
Servings: 2

Ingredients:
- 1 teaspoon olive oil
- 1 cup mixed bell peppers, onion, zucchini and corn, chopped
- 1 cup chicken meat, cooked and shredded
- 1 cup brown rice, cooked
- 3 tablespoons salsa
- 2 tablespoons low-fat cheddar, shredded
- 2 tablespoons low-fat sour cream

Directions:
Heat up a pan with the oil over medium-high heat, add mixed veggies, stir and cook them for 5 minutes. Divide the rice and the chicken meat into 2 bowls, add mixed veggies and top each with salsa, cheese and sour cream. Serve for lunch.
Enjoy!

Nutrition: calories 199, fat 4, fiber 4, carbs 12, protein 7

Lunch Salmon Salad

Preparation time: 10 minutes
Cooking time: 0 minutes
Servings: 3

Ingredients:

- 1 cup canned salmon, flaked
- 1 tablespoon lemon juice
- 3 tablespoons fat-free yogurt
- 2 tablespoons red bell pepper, chopped
- 1 teaspoon capers, drained and chopped
- 1 tablespoon red onion, chopped
- 1 teaspoon dill, chopped
- A pinch of black pepper
- 3 whole wheat bread slices

Directions:
In a bowl, combine the salmon with the lemon juice, yogurt, bell pepper, capers, onion, dill and black pepper and stir well. Spread this on each bread slice and serve for lunch.
Enjoy!

Nutrition: calories 199, fat 2, fiber 4, carbs 14, protein 8

Stuffed Mushrooms Caps

Preparation time: 10 minutes
Cooking time: 15 minutes
Servings: 2

Ingredients:

- 2 Portobello mushroom caps
- 2 tablespoons pesto
- 2 tomato, chopped
- ¼ cup low-fat mozzarella, shredded

Directions:
Divide pesto, tomato and mozzarella in each mushroom cap, arrange them on a lined baking sheet, introduce in the oven and bake at 400 degrees F for 15 minutes. Serve for lunch.
Enjoy!

Nutrition: calories 198, fat 3, fiber 4, carbs 14, protein 9

Lunch Tuna Salad

Preparation time: 10 minutes
Cooking time: 0 minutes
Servings: 3

Ingredients:
- 5 ounces canned tuna in water, drained
- 1 tablespoon red vinegar
- 1 tablespoon olive oil
- ¼ cup green onions, chopped
- 2 cups arugula
- 1 tablespoon low-fat parmesan, grated
- A pinch of black pepper
- 2 ounces whole wheat pasta, cooked

Directions:
In a bowl, combine the tuna with the vinegar, oil, green onions, arugula, pasta and black pepper and toss. Divide between 3 plates, sprinkle parmesan on top and serve for lunch.
Enjoy!

Nutrition: calories 200, fat 4, fiber 4, carbs 14, protein 7

Shrimp Lunch Rolls

Preparation time: 10 minutes
Cooking time: 0 minutes
Servings: 4

Ingredients:
- 12 rice paper sheets, soaked for a few seconds in warm water and drained
- 1 cup cilantro, chopped
- 12 basil leaves
- 12 baby lettuce leaves
- 1 small cucumber, sliced
- 1 cup carrots, shredded
- 20 ounces shrimp, cooked, peeled and deveined

Directions:
Arrange all rice papers on a working surface, divide cilantro, bay leaves, baby lettuce leaves, cucumber, carrots and shrimp, wrap, seal edges and serve for lunch.
Enjoy!

Nutrition: calories 200, fat 4, fiber 4, carbs 14, protein 8

Turkey Sandwich

Preparation time: 10 minutes
Cooking time: 3 minutes
Servings: 2

Ingredients:

- 2 whole wheat bread slices
- 2 teaspoons mustard
- 2 sliced smoked turkey
- 1 pear, cored and sliced
- ¼ cup low-fat mozzarella, shredded

Directions:
Spread the mustard on each bread slice, divide turkey slices on one bread slice, add pear slices and mozzarella, top with the other bread slice, introduce in preheated broiler for 3 minutes, cut the sand which in halves and serve.
Enjoy!

Nutrition: calories 171, fat 2, fiber 4, carbs 9, protein 9

Veggie Soup

Preparation time: 10 minutes
Cooking time: 16 minutes
Servings: 6

Ingredients:

- 2 teaspoons olive oil
- 1 and ½ cups carrot, shredded
- 6 garlic cloves, minced
- 1 cup yellow onion, chopped
- 1 cup celery, chopped
- 32 ounces low-sodium chicken stock
- 4 cups water
- 1 and ½ cups whole wheat pasta
- 2 tablespoons parsley, chopped
- ¼ cup low-fat parmesan, grated

Directions:
Heat up a pot with the oil over medium-high heat, add garlic, stir and cook for 1 minute. Add onion, carrot and celery, stir and cook for 7 minutes. Add stock, water and pasta, stir, bring to a boil over medium heat and cook for 8 minutes more. Divide into bowls, top each with parsley and parmesan and serve.
Enjoy!

Nutrition: calories 212, fat 4, fiber 4, carbs 13, protein 8

Melon and Avocado Lunch Salad

Preparation time: 10 minutes
Cooking time: 0 minutes
Servings: 4

Ingredients:
- 2 tablespoons stevia
- 2 tablespoon red vinegar
- 2 tablespoons mint, chopped
- A pinch of black pepper
- 1 avocado, peeled, pitted and sliced
- 4 cups baby spinach
- ½ small cantaloupe, peeled and cubed
- 1 and ½ cups strawberries, sliced
- 2 teaspoons sesame seeds, toasted

Directions:
In a salad bowl, combine the avocado with baby spinach, cantaloupe and strawberries and toss. In another bowl, combine the stevia with vinegar, mint and black pepper, whisk, add to your salad, toss, sprinkle sesame seeds on top and serve.
Enjoy!

Nutrition: calories 199, fat 3, fiber 4, carbs 12, protein 8

Spaghetti Squash and Sauce

Preparation time: 10 minutes
Cooking time: 25 minutes
Servings: 4

Ingredients:
- 1 pound beef, ground
- ½ cup yellow onion, chopped
- ½ cup green bell pepper, chopped
- 2 garlic cloves, minced
- 14 ounces canned tomatoes, no-salt-added, chopped
- 2 tablespoons tomato paste
- 8 ounces tomato sauce
- 1 teaspoon Italian seasoning
- ¼ cup low-fat parmesan, shredded
- 2 pounds spaghetti squash, pricked with a knife

Directions:
Put the spaghetti squash on a lined baking sheet, introduce in the oven, bake at 400 degrees F for 10 minutes, cut into halves, shred and separate squash pulp into spaghetti and put into a bowl. Heat up a pan over medium-high heat, add the beef, stir and brown for 5 minutes. Add onion, bell pepper, garlic, tomatoes, tomato paste, tomato sauce and Italian seasoning, stir and cook for 10 minutes. Divide the squash spaghetti between plates, top each with beef mix, sprinkle parmesan on top and serve.
Enjoy!

Nutrition: calories 231, fat 4, fiber 5, carbs 14, protein 9

Sausage and Potatoes Mix

Preparation time: 10 minutes
Cooking time: 22 minutes
Servings: 6

Ingredients:

- ½ pound smoked sausage, cooked and chopped
- 3 tablespoons olive oil
- 1 and ¾ pounds red potatoes, cubed
- 2 yellow onions, chopped
- 1 teaspoon thyme, dried
- 2 teaspoons cumin, ground
- A pinch of black pepper

Directions:
Heat up a pan with the oil over medium-high heat, add potatoes and onions, stir and cook for 12 minutes. Add sausage, thyme, cumin and black pepper, stir, cook for 10 minutes more, divide between plates and serve for lunch.
Enjoy!

Nutrition: calories 199, fat 2, fiber 4, carbs 14, protein 8

Beef Soup

Preparation time: 10 minutes
Cooking time: 20 minutes
Servings: 4

Ingredients:

- 1 tablespoon olive oil
- 1 yellow onion, chopped
- 1 pound beef sirloin, ground
- 32 ounces low-sodium beef stock
- 1/3 cup whole wheat flour
- 1 pound mixed carrots and celery, chopped

Directions:
Heat up a pot with the oil over medium-high heat, add beef and flour, stir well and brown for 5 minutes. Add onion, carrots, celery and stock, stir, bring to a simmer, reduce heat to medium, cook the soup for 15 minutes, ladle into bowls and serve for lunch.
Enjoy!

Nutrition: calories 281, fat 3, fiber 5, carbs 14, protein 11

Lunch Shrimp Salad

Preparation time: 10 minutes
Cooking time: 8 minutes
Servings: 4

Ingredients:

- 12 ounces asparagus spears, trimmed and halved
- 8 ounces baby corn
- 12 endive leaves, torn
- 12 baby lettuce leaves
- 12 spinach leaves
- 12 ounces shrimp, cooked, peeled and deveined
- 2 and ½ cups red raspberries
- ¼ cup olive oil
- ¼ cup raspberry vinegar
- 1 tablespoon cilantro, chopped
- 2 teaspoons stevia

Directions:
Put some water in a pot, bring to a boil over medium-high heat, add asparagus, cook for 8 minutes, transfer to a bowl filled with ice water, cool down, drain well and put in a salad bowl. Add corn, endive leaves, spinach, lettuce, shrimp and raspberries. In another bowl, combine the oil with the vinegar, stevia and cilantro, whisk well, add to your salad, toss and serve for lunch. Enjoy!

Nutrition: calories 199, fat 2, fiber 3, carbs 14, protein 8

Watercress, Asparagus and Shrimp Salad

Preparation time: 10 minutes
Cooking time: 4 minutes
Servings: 4

Ingredients:

- 12 ounces asparagus spears, trimmed
- 16 ounces shrimp, cooked, peeled and deveined
- 4 cups watercress, torn
- 2 cups cherry tomatoes, halved
- ¼ cup raspberry vinegar
- ¼ cup olive oil

Directions:
Put the asparagus in a pot, add water to cover, cook over medium heat for 4 minutes, drain, transfer to a bowl filled with ice water, cool down, drain again and transfer to a salad bowl. Add shrimp, watercress, tomatoes, raspberry vinegar and oil, toss well and serve for lunch. Enjoy!

Nutrition: calories 212, fat 4, fiber 7, carbs 14, protein 9

Lunch Chicken Tacos

Preparation time: 10 minutes
Cooking time: 0 minutes
Servings: 2

Ingredients:

- 4 mini taco shells
- 2 tablespoons celery, chopped
- 1 tablespoon light mayonnaise
- 1 tablespoon salsa
- 1 tablespoon low-fat cheddar, shredded
- 1/3 cup chicken, cooked and shredded

Directions:
In a bowl, combine the celery with the mayo, salsa, cheddar and chicken and toss well. Spoon this into mini taco shells and serve for lunch.
Enjoy!

Nutrition: calories 221, fat 3, fiber 8, carbs 14, protein 9

Millet Cakes

Preparation time: 10 minutes
Cooking time: 55 minutes
Servings: 4

Ingredients:

- 1 tablespoon olive oil
- 1 cup millet
- ¼ cup yellow onion, chopped
- 1 garlic clove, minced
- 3 and ½ cups water
- A pinch of black pepper
- 1/3 cup zucchini, shredded
- 1/3 cup carrot, shredded
- 1/3 cup low-fat parmesan, grated
- 1 and ½ teaspoon thyme, chopped
- 1 teaspoon lemon zest, grated
- Cooking spray

Directions:
Heat up a pan with 1-tablespoon olive oil over medium heat, add onion, stir and cook for 4 minutes. Add garlic and millet, stir and cook for 1 more minute. Add the water and a pinch of black pepper, stir, cover, reduce heat to low and cook for 20 minutes stirring once. Add carrot, zucchini, thyme, parmesan and lemon zest, stir and cook for 10 minutes more. Leave the millet mix to cool down, shape 12 millet cakes using damp hands and put them on a working surface. Heat up a pan with cooking spray over medium-high heat, add millet cakes, cook them for 5 minutes on each side, divide them between plates and serve.
Enjoy!

Nutrition: calories 211, fat 4, fiber 4, carbs 14, protein 6

Lentils Dal

Preparation time: 10 minutes
Cooking time: 10 minutes
Servings: 4

Ingredients:

- 1 and ½ teaspoons olive oil
- 1 yellow onion, chopped
- 2 teaspoons curry powder
- 14 ounces canned lentils, no-salt-added, drained and rinsed
- 14 ounces canned tomatoes, chopped
- 2 pounds chicken, roasted, and chopped
- A pinch of black pepper
- ¼ cup low-fat yogurt

Directions:
Heat up a pot with the oil over medium-high heat, add onion, stir and brown for 4 minutes. Add curry powder, stir and cook for 1 more minute. Add lentils, tomatoes, chicken and black pepper, stir, cook for 5 minutes more, take off heat, add the yogurt, toss, divide into bowls and serve for lunch.
Enjoy!

Nutrition: calories 199, fat 3, fiber 7, carbs 17, protein 8

Lunch Quinoa and Spinach Salad

Preparation time: 10 minutes
Cooking time: 25 minutes
Servings: 4

Ingredients:

- 1 cup quinoa
- 2 teaspoons olive oil
- ½ cup apricots, dried and chopped
- 2 garlic cloves, minced
- 2 cups water
- A pinch of black pepper
- 1 cup cherry tomatoes, halved
- 1 red onion, chopped
- 8 cups baby spinach
- ¼ cup almonds, sliced

For the salad dressing:
- ½ teaspoon lemon zest, grated
- 2 tablespoons lemon juice
- 1 teaspoon coconut sugar
- ½ teaspoon Dijon mustard
- 4 tablespoons olive oil

Directions:
Heat up a pan over medium heat, add quinoa, toast for 5 minutes and transfer to a bowl. Heat up a pan with the oil over medium heat, add garlic, stir and cook for 1 minute. Add quinoa and apricots, stir and cook for 4 minutes more. Add water, bring to a boil and simmer for 15 minutes more. In a salad bowl, combine the tomatoes with the onion, spinach, almonds, quinoa and apricots. In another bowl, combine the lemon zest with the lemon juice, sugar, mustard and oil, whisk well, add to the quinoa salad, toss and serve for lunch.
Enjoy!

Nutrition: calories 199, fat 3, fiber 4, carbs 16, protein 8

Italian Pasta Mix

Preparation time: 10 minutes
Cooking time: 20 minutes
Servings: 4

Ingredients:

- 1 pound whole wheat penne pasta, cooked
- 3 garlic cloves, minced
- 2 tablespoons olive oil
- 3 carrots, sliced
- 1 bunch asparagus, trimmed and cut into medium pieces
- 1 red bell pepper, chopped
- 1 yellow bell pepper, chopped
- 1 cup cherry tomatoes, halved
- A pinch of black pepper
- 2/3 cup coconut cream
- 2 tablespoons low-fat parmesan, grated

Directions:

Heat up a pan with the oil over medium-high heat, add the garlic, stir and cook for 2 minutes. Add carrots, stir and cook for 4 minutes more. Add asparagus, stir, cover the pan and cook for 8 minutes more. Add yellow and red bell peppers, stir and cook for 5 minutes. Add cherry tomatoes, black pepper, cream, parmesan and pasta, toss, divide between plates and serve. Enjoy!

Nutrition: calories 221, fat 4, fiber 4, carbs 15, protein 9

Glazed Ribs

Preparation time: 10 minutes
Cooking time: 1 hour and 20 minutes
Servings: 4

Ingredients:

- 1 rack pork ribs, ribs separated
- 1 and ¼ cups tomato sauce
- ¼ cup white vinegar
- 3 tablespoons spicy mustard
- 2 tablespoons coconut sugar
- 3 tablespoons water
- ¼ teaspoon hot sauce
- 1 teaspoon onion powder
- Cooking spray

Directions:

Put the ribs in a baking dish, cover with tin foil and bake in the oven at 400 degrees F for 1 hour. Heat up a pan with the tomato sauce, mustard, sugar, vinegar, water, onion powder and hot sauce, stir, cook for 10 minutes and take off heat. Baste the ribs with half of this sauce, place them on preheated grill over medium-high heat, grease them with cooking spray, cook for 4 minutes on each side, divide between plates and serve with the rest of the sauce on the side. Enjoy!

Nutrition: calories 287, fat 5, fiber 8, carbs 16, protein 15

Pork Chops and Sauce

Preparation time: 10 minutes
Cooking time: 9 hours
Servings: 6

Ingredients:
- 6 pork loin chops
- 1 tablespoon olive oil
- 2 tablespoons tapioca, crushed
- 1 yellow onion, chopped
- 10 ounces low-sodium cream of mushroom soup
- ½ cup apple juice
- 2 teaspoons thyme, chopped
- 1 and ½ cups mushrooms, sliced
- ¼ teaspoon garlic powder

Directions:
Heat up a pan with the oil over medium-high heat, add pork chops, brown them for 4 minutes on each side and transfer to a slow cooker. Add crushed tapioca, onion, cream of mushroom soup, apple juice, thyme, mushrooms and garlic powder, toss, cover and cook on Low for 9 hours. Divide the pork chops and sauce between plates and serve.
Enjoy!

Nutrition: calories 229, fat 4, fiber 9, carbs 16, protein 17

Shrimp and Pomegranate Sauce

Preparation time: 10 minutes
Cooking time: 50 minutes
Servings: 4

Ingredients:
- 1
- -quart pomegranate juice
- ½ cup coconut sugar
- ¼ cup lemon juice
- 1 pound shrimp, peeled and deveined
- ½ teaspoon cumin, ground
- ¾ teaspoon coriander, ground
- ¼ teaspoon cinnamon powder
- 1 and ½ tablespoons olive oil
- A pinch of black pepper
- 4 cups baby arugula

Directions:
In a pan, combine the pomegranate juice with lemon juice and sugar, stir, bring to a simmer over medium heat and cook for 45 minutes. In a bowl, combine the shrimp with the cumin, cinnamon, coriander, black pepper and the oil and toss well. Heat up a pan over medium heat, add shrimp, and cook for 2 minutes on each side and transfer to a bowl. Add arugula and the pomegranate sauce, toss and serve for lunch.
Enjoy!

Nutrition: calories 281, fat 5, fiber 8, carbs 17, protein 14

Eggplants and Tomatoes Mix

Preparation time: 10 minutes
Cooking time: 25 minutes
Servings: 4

Ingredients:

- 1 purple eggplant, cubed
- 2 garlic cloves, minced
- 2 tablespoons olive oil
- 1 teaspoon cumin, ground
- 1 teaspoon sweet paprika
- ½ cup cilantro, chopped
- 14 ounces low-sodium canned tomatoes, chopped

Directions:
Heat up a pan with the oil over medium-high heat, add eggplant, stir and cook for 1 minute. Add garlic, stir, cook for 1 minute, cover the pan, reduce heat to medium-low and cook everything for 10 minutes. Add paprika, cilantro and cumin, stir and cook for 1 minute. Add tomatoes, cover the pan and cook everything for 10 minutes more. Divide into bowls and serve.
Enjoy!

Nutrition: calories 233, fat 3, fiber 7, carbs 16, protein 7

Peas with Rice and Cheese

Preparation time: 10 minutes
Cooking time: 10 minutes
Servings: 4

Ingredients:

- 1 and ¼ cups low-sodium chicken stock
- ¾ cup brown rice
- 1 and ½ cups peas
- ¼ cup low-fat feta cheese, crumbled
- ¾ cup scallions, chopped
- ¼ cup mint, chopped
- Black pepper to the taste

Directions:
Put the stock in a small pot, bring to a simmer over medium-high heat, add rice, stir, cover and simmer for 4 minutes. Add peas, stir and simmer for 6 minutes more. Take off heat, add mint, scallions, black pepper and cheese, toss, divide between plates and serve.
Enjoy!

Nutrition: calories 187, fat 3, fiber 6, carbs 16, protein 9

Smoked Turkey Salad

Preparation time: 10 minutes
Cooking time: 0 minutes
Servings: 4

Ingredients:

- 2 mangoes, peeled and cubed
- 4 cups salad greens
- 1 cup smoked turkey, sliced
- ¼ cup cilantro, chopped
- 2 tablespoons olive oil
- 2 tablespoons water
- ¼ teaspoon lime peel, grated
- 2 tablespoons lime juice
- ¼ teaspoon ginger, grated

Directions:

In a salad bowl, combine the mangoes with salad greens, turkey and cilantro and toss. In another bowl, combine the oil with the water, lime peel, limejuice and ginger, whisk well, add to the salad, toss and serve for lunch.
Enjoy!

Nutrition: calories 199, fat 3, fiber 4, carbs 16, protein 8

Pork Salad

Preparation time: 10 minutes
Cooking time: 35 minutes
Servings: 4

Ingredients:

- 1 pound pork tenderloin, cut into small slices
- 1 tablespoon lemon peel, grated
- 6 sage leaves, chopped
- A pinch of black pepper
- ½ teaspoon cumin, ground
- 1 tablespoon olive oil
- 1 green lettuce head, torn
- 1 and ½ cups tomatoes, chopped
- 1 avocado, peeled, pitted and cubed
- 1 cup canned black beans, no-salt-added, drained and rinsed
- ½ cup green onions, chopped

For the vinaigrette:

- 1 red sweet pepper, halved
- 1 jalapeno, halved
- 2 tablespoons lime juice
- 2 tablespoons white vinegar
- 2 tablespoons olive oil

Directions:

In a bowl, combine the pork slices with lemon peel, sage, cumin and black pepper, toss and leave aside to 10 minutes. Heat up a pan with 1-tablespoon oil over medium-high heat, add pork slices, cook them for 5 minutes on each side and transfer them to a plate. Arrange sweet pepper halves and jalapeno on a lined baking sheet, introduce in the oven, bake at 425 degrees F for 25 minutes, cool them down, peel and put them in your food processor. Add 2 tablespoons lime juice, vinegar and 2 tablespoons oil and pulse well. In a salad bowl, combine the lettuce with avocado, tomatoes, black beans and green onions, toss and divide between plates. Top this mix with pork slices, drizzle the vinaigrette all over and serve for lunch.
Enjoy!

Nutrition: calories 229, fat 4, fiber 8, carbs 17, protein 18

Veggie Lunch Salad

Preparation time: 10 minutes
Cooking time: 15 minutes
Servings: 4

Ingredients:

- 1 pound firm tofu, drained and cubed
- ¾ cup low-fat Italian dressing
- 1 tablespoon olive oil
- 12 ounces yellow squash, cubed
- 2 orange sweet peppers, chopped
- ½ cup cooked quinoa
- ½ cup sorrel leaves, torn

Directions:
Heat up your kitchen grill over medium-high heat, add tofu, grill for 5 minutes and transfer to a salad bowl. Heat up a pan with the oil over medium-high heat, add squash, peppers and quinoa, stir and cook for 10 minutes. Transfer to the bowl with the tofu, add sorrel leaves and Italian dressing, toss and serve for lunch.
Enjoy!

Nutrition: calories 276, fat 4, fiber 7, carbs 16, protein 14

Spring Lunch Salad

Preparation time: 2 hours
Cooking time: 0 minutes
Servings: 6

Ingredients:

- 4 cups green cabbage, shredded
- 2 carrots, shredded
- ¾ cup mixed red, green and yellow bell peppers, chopped
- ½ cup radishes, chopped
- ¼ cup cilantro, chopped
- ¼ cup green onions, chopped
- 3 tablespoons rice vinegar
- 3 tablespoons olive oil
- 3 tablespoons coconut sugar
- 2 teaspoons ginger, grated
- ½ teaspoon dry mustard
- ¼ teaspoon red pepper, crushed

Directions:
In a salad bowl, combine the green cabbage with the carrots, bell peppers, radishes, cilantro and green onions and toss. In another bowl, combine the vinegar with the oil, sugar, ginger, mustard and red pepper, whisk well, add to your salad, toss, cover and keep in the fridge for 2 hours before serving for lunch.
Enjoy!

Nutrition: calories 200, fat 4, fiber 7, carbs 16, protein 9

Beef Stew

Preparation time: 10 minutes
Cooking time: 10 hours
Servings: 6

Ingredients:

- 1 and ½ pounds beef chuck pot roast, cubed
- 1 pound butternut squash, cubed
- 2 yellow onions, chopped
- 2 garlic cloves, minced
- 14 ounces low-sodium beef stock
- 8 ounces tomato sauce
- 1 teaspoon dry mustard
- A pinch of black pepper
- A pinch of allspice, ground
- 9 ounces green beans
- 1.5 LBS BABY DUTCH YELLOW POT.

Directions:
In your slow cooker, combine the beef with squash, onions, garlic, stock, and tomato sauce, mustard, black pepper, green beans and allspice, toss, cover and cook on Low for 10 hours.
Divide into bowls and serve for lunch.
Enjoy!

Nutrition: 271, fat 4, fiber 8, carbs 18, protein 18

Black Bean Soup

Preparation time: 10 minutes
Cooking time: 20 minutes
Servings: 4

Ingredients:

- 2 teaspoons olive oil
- 1 yellow onion, chopped
- 1 teaspoon cinnamon powder
- 38 ounces canned black beans, no-salt-added, drained and rinsed
- 32 ounces low-sodium chicken stock
- 1 sweet potato, chopped

Directions:
Heat up a pot with the oil over medium heat, add onion and cinnamon, stir and cook for 6 minutes. Add black beans, stock and sweet potato, stir, cook for 14 minutes, puree using an immersion blender, divide into bowls and serve for lunch.
Enjoy!

Nutrition: calories 221, fat 3, fiber 7, carbs 15, protein 7

Easy Tofu Salad

Preparation time: 10 minutes
Cooking time: 0 minutes
Servings: 3

Ingredients:
- 2 tablespoons low-fat mayonnaise
- 3 tablespoons non-fat yogurt
- 2 tablespoons mango, chopped
- 2 teaspoons curry powder
- A pinch of black pepper
- 14 ounces firm tofu, pressed, drained and cubed
- 2 celery stalks, chopped
- 1 cup red grapes, halved
- ½ cup scallions, chopped
- ¼ cup walnuts, chopped

Directions:
In a salad bowl, combine the mango with mayo, yogurt, curry powder, black pepper, tofu, celery, grapes, scallions and walnuts, toss and serve for lunch.
Enjoy!

Nutrition: calories 198, fat 3, fiber 6, carbs 16, protein 14

Curry Carrot Soup

Preparation time: 10 minutes
Cooking time: 22 minutes
Servings: 4

Ingredients:
- 3 tablespoons olive oil
- 8 carrots, peeled and sliced
- 2 teaspoons curry powder
- 4 celery stalks, chopped
- 1 yellow onion, chopped
- 5 cups low-sodium chicken stock
- 1 tablespoon lemon juice
- A pinch of black pepper

Directions:
Heat up a pot with the oil and the curry powder over medium heat for 2 minutes, add onion, celery and carrots, stir and cook for 10 minutes. Add stock, stir, bring to a simmer and cook everything for 10 minutes more. Blend the soup using an immersion blender, add lemon juice and a pinch of salt, stir, ladle into bowls and serve for lunch.
Enjoy!

Nutrition: calories 221, fat 4, fiber 7, carbs 16, protein 9

Red Bean Soup

Preparation time: 10 minutes
Cooking time: 1 hour and 45 minutes
Servings: 4

Ingredients:

- 1 pound red kidney beans, soaked overnight and drained
- 8 cups water
- ¾ cup low-sodium beef stock
- 1 green bell pepper, chopped
- 1 tomato, chopped
- 1 yellow onion, chopped
- 3 garlic cloves, minced
- 1 chili pepper, chopped
- 1 pound beef brisket, cubed
- 1 potato, cubed
- A pinch of black pepper

Directions:
Put the water and the stock in a pot and heat up over medium heat. Add beans, bell pepper, tomato, onion, garlic, chili pepper and beef, stir and simmer for 1 hour and 30 minutes. Add potato and a pinch of black pepper, stir, cook for 15 minutes more, divide into bowls and serve for lunch.
Enjoy!

Nutrition: calories 221, fat 7, fiber 8, carbs 18, protein 8

Beef Lunch Bowls

Preparation time: 10 minutes
Cooking time: 20 minutes
Servings: 6

Ingredients:

- 8 ounces beef sirloin steak, trimmed, fat removed and cut into cubes
- ½ cup red onion, chopped
- ¼ cup tomatoes, chopped
- ¾ cup fat-free cheddar, grated
- 2 tablespoons low-fat sour cream
- 7 tablespoons salsa
- 1 tablespoon olive oil
- 2 tablespoons cilantro, chopped

Directions:
Heat up a pan with the oil over medium-high heat, add the steak cubes, stir and brown them for 4 minutes on each side. Add onion, tomatoes and cream, toss, cover, cook for 10 minutes more, divide into bowls, sprinkle cheese, salsa and cilantro on top and serve.
Enjoy!

Nutrition: calories 251, fat 4, fiber 7, carbs 16, protein 7

Creamy Chicken Breast

Preparation time: 10 minutes
Cooking time: 20 minutes
Servings: 4

Ingredients:

- 1 tablespoon olive oil
- A pinch of black pepper
- 2 pounds chicken breasts, skinless, boneless and cubed
- 4 garlic cloves, minced
- 2 and ½ cups low-sodium chicken stock
- 2 cups coconut cream
- ½ cup low-fat parmesan, grated
- 1 tablespoon basil, chopped

Directions:
Heat up a pan with the oil over medium-high heat add chicken cubes and brown them for 3 minutes on each side. Add garlic, black pepper, stock and cream, toss, cover the pan and cook everything for 10 minutes more. Add cheese and basil, toss, divide between plates and serve for lunch.
Enjoy!

Nutrition: calories 221, fat 6, fiber 9, carbs 14, protein 7

Indian Chicken Stew

Preparation time: 1 hour
Cooking time: 20 minutes
Servings: 4

Ingredients:

- 1 pound chicken breasts, skinless, boneless and cubed
- 1 tablespoon garam masala
- 1 cup fat-free yogurt
- 1 tablespoon lemon juice
- A pinch of black pepper
- ¼ teaspoon ginger, ground
- 15 ounces tomato sauce, no-salt-added
- 5 garlic cloves, minced
- ½ teaspoon sweet paprika

Directions:
In a bowl, mix the chicken with garam masala, yogurt, lemon juice, black pepper and ginger, toss well, cover and leave in the fridge for 1 hour. Heat up a pan over medium heat, add chicken mix, toss and cook for 5-6 minutes. Add tomato sauce, garlic and paprika, toss, cook for 15 minutes, divide between plates and serve for lunch.
Enjoy!

Nutrition: calories 221, fat 6, fiber 9, carbs 14, protein 16

Chicken, Bamboo and Chestnuts Mix

Preparation time: 10 minutes
Cooking time: 20 minutes
Servings: 4

Ingredients:
- 1 pound chicken thighs, boneless, skinless and cut into medium chunks
- 1 cup low-sodium chicken stock
- 1 tablespoon olive oil
- 2 tablespoons coconut aminos
- 1-inch ginger, grated
- 1 carrot, sliced
- 2 garlic cloves, minced
- 8 ounces canned bamboo shoots, no-salt-added and drained
- 8 ounces water chestnuts

Directions:
Heat up a pan with the oil over medium-high heat, add chicken, stir and brown for 4 minutes on each side. Add the stock, aminos, ginger, carrot, garlic, bamboo and chestnuts, toss, cover the pan and cook everything over medium heat for 12 minutes. Divide everything between plates and serve.
Enjoy!

Nutrition: calories 281, fat 7, fiber 9, carbs 14, protein 14

Chuck Roast and Veggies

Preparation time: 10 minutes
Cooking time: 1 hour and 30 minutes
Servings: 6

Ingredients:
- 4 pounds lean chuck roast, fat removed
- 2 yellow onions, roughly chopped
- 1 cup low-sodium beef stock
- 1 tablespoon thyme, chopped
- 2 celery sticks, chopped
- 2 carrots, sliced
- 3 garlic cloves, minced
- A pinch of black pepper

Directions:
In a roasting pan, combine the roast with the onions, stock, thyme, celery, carrots, garlic and a pinch of pepper, introduce in the oven and roast at 400 degrees F for 1 hour and 30 minutes. Slice the roast, divide it and the veggies from the pot between plates and serve for lunch.
Enjoy!

Nutrition: calories 321, fat 7, fiber 11, carbs 14, protein 11

Salsa Chicken

Preparation time: 10 minutes
Cooking time: 25 minutes
Servings: 4

Ingredients:

- 1 cup mild salsa, no-salt-added
- ½ teaspoon cumin, ground
- Black pepper to the taste
- 1 tablespoon chipotle paste
- 1 pound chicken thighs, skinless and boneless
- 2 cups corn
- Juice of 1 lime
- ½ tablespoon olive oil
- 2 tablespoons cilantro, chopped
- 1 cup cherry tomatoes, halved
- 1 small avocado, pitted, peeled and cubed

Directions:
In a pot, combine the salsa with the cumin, black pepper, chipotle paste, chicken thighs and corn, toss, bring to a simmer and cook over medium heat for 25 minutes. Add limejuice, oil, cherry tomatoes and avocado, toss, divide into bowls and serve for lunch.
Enjoy!

Nutrition: calories 269, fat 6, fiber 9, carbs 18, protein 7

Rice with Chicken

Preparation time: 10 minutes
Cooking time: 30 minutes
Servings: 4

Ingredients:

- ½ cup coconut aminos
- 1/3 cup rice wine vinegar
- 2 tablespoons olive oil
- 1 chicken breast, skinless, boneless and cubed
- ½ cup red bell pepper, chopped
- A pinch of black pepper
- 2 garlic cloves, minced
- ½ teaspoon ginger, grated
- ½ cup carrots, grated
- 1 cup white rice
- 2 cups water

Directions:
Heat up a pan with the oil over medium-high heat, add the chicken, stir and brown for 4 minutes on each side. Add aminos, vinegar, bell pepper, black pepper, garlic, ginger, carrots, rice and stock, stock, cover the pan and cook over medium heat for 20 minutes. Divide everything into bowls and serve for lunch.
Enjoy!

Nutrition: calories 221, fat 12, fiber 6, carbs 14, protein 14

Tomato Soup

Preparation time: 10 minutes
Cooking time: 20 minutes
Servings: 4

Ingredients:

- 3 garlic cloves, minced
- 1 yellow onion, chopped
- 3 carrots, chopped
- 15 ounces tomato sauce, no-salt-added
- 1 tablespoon olive oil
- 15 ounces roasted tomatoes, no-salt-added
- 1 cup low-sodium veggie stock
- 1 tablespoon tomato paste, no-salt-added
- 1 tablespoon basil, dried
- ¼ teaspoon oregano, dried
- 3 ounces coconut cream
- A pinch of black pepper

Directions:
Heat up a pot with the oil over medium heat, add garlic and onion, stir and cook for 5 minutes. Add carrots, tomato sauce, tomatoes, stock, tomato paste, basil, oregano and black pepper, stir, bring to a simmer, cook for 15 minutes, add cream, blend the soup using an immersion blender, divide into bowls and serve for lunch.
Enjoy!

Nutrition: calories 261, fat 6, fiber 9, carbs 15, protein 7

Easy Pork Chops

Preparation time: 10 minutes
Cooking time: 20 minutes
Servings: 4

Ingredients:

- 4 pork chops, boneless
- 1 tablespoon olive oil
- 1 cup chicken stock, low-sodium
- A pinch of black pepper
- 1 teaspoon sweet paprika

Directions:
Heat up a pan with the oil over medium-high heat, add pork chops, brown them for 5 minutes on each side, add paprika, black pepper and stock, toss, cook for 15 minutes more, divide between plates and serve with a side salad.
Enjoy!

Nutrition: calories 272, fat 4, fiber 8, carbs 14, protein 17

Cod Soup

Preparation time: 10 minutes
Cooking time: 25 minutes
Servings: 4

Ingredients:
- 1 yellow onion, chopped
- 12 cups low-sodium fish stock
- 1 pound carrots, sliced
- 1 tablespoon olive oil
- Black pepper to the taste
- 2 tablespoons ginger, minced
- 1 cup water
- 1 pound cod, skinless, boneless and cut into medium chunks

Directions:
Heat up a pot with the oil over medium-high heat, add onion, stir and cook for 4 minutes. Add water, stock, ginger and carrots, stir and cook for 10 minutes more. Blend soup using an immersion blender, add the fish and pepper, stir, cook for 10 minutes more, ladle into bowls and serve.
Enjoy!

Nutrition: calories 261, fat 6, fiber 2, carbs 11, protein 9

Easy Beef Stew

Preparation time: 10 minutes
Cooking time: 1 hour and 20 minutes
Servings: 6

Ingredients:
- 2 and ½ pounds beef brisket, fat removed
- 2 bay leaves
- 4 cups low-sodium beef stock
- 4 carrots, chopped
- 3 garlic cloves, chopped
- 1 green cabbage head, shredded
- Black pepper to the taste

Directions:
Put the beef brisket in a pot, add stock, pepper, garlic and bay leaves, bring to a simmer over medium heat and cook for 1 hour. Add carrots and cabbage, stir, cook for 30 minutes more, divide into bowls and serve for lunch.
Enjoy!

Nutrition: calories 271, fat 8, fiber 3, carbs 16, protein 9

Sweet Potato Soup

Preparation time: 10 minutes
Cooking time: 1 hour and 40 minutes
Servings: 6

Ingredients:
- 4 big sweet potatoes
- 28 ounces veggie stock
- A pinch of black pepper
- ¼ teaspoon nutmeg, ground
- 1/3 cup low-sodium heavy cream

Directions:
Arrange the sweet potatoes on a lined baking sheet, bake them at 350 degrees F for 1 hour and 30 minutes, cool them down, peel, roughly chop them and put them in a pot. Add stock, nutmeg, cream and pepper, pulse really well using an immersion blender; heat the soup over medium heat, cook for 10 minutes, ladle into bowls and serve.
Enjoy!

Nutrition: calories 235, fat 4, fiber 5, carbs 16, protein 8

Sweet Potatoes and Zucchini Soup

Preparation time: 10 minutes
Cooking time: 20 minutes
Servings: 8

Ingredients:
- 4 cups veggie stock
- 2 tablespoons olive oil
- 2 sweet potatoes, peeled and cubed
- 8 zucchinis, chopped
- 2 yellow onions, chopped
- 1 cup coconut milk
- A pinch of black pepper
- 1 tablespoon coconut aminos
- 4 tablespoons dill, chopped
- ½ teaspoon basil, chopped

Directions:
Heat up a pot with the oil over medium heat, add onion, stir and cook for 5 minutes. Add zucchinis, stock, basil, potato and pepper, stir and cook for 15 minutes more. Add milk, aminos and dill, pulse using an immersion blender, ladle into bowls and serve for lunch.
Enjoy!

Nutrition: calories 283, fat 3, fiber 4, carbs 14, protein 9

Lemongrass and Chicken Soup

Preparation time: 10 minutes
Cooking time: 25 minutes
Servings: 4

Ingredients:
- 4 lime leaves, torn
- 4 cups veggie stock, low-sodium
- 1 lemongrass stalk, chopped
- 1 tablespoon ginger, grated
- 1 pound chicken breast, skinless, boneless and cubed
- 8 ounces mushrooms, chopped
- 4 Thai chilies, chopped
- 13 ounces coconut milk
- ¼ cup lime juice
- ¼ cup cilantro, chopped
- A pinch of black pepper

Directions:
Put stock into a pot, bring to a simmer over medium heat, add lemongrass, ginger and lime leaves, stir, cook for 10 minutes, strain into another pot and heat up again over medium heat again. Add chicken, mushrooms, milk, cilantro, black pepper, chilies and lime juice, stir, simmer for 15 minutes, ladle into bowls and serve.
Enjoy!

Nutrition: calories 150, fat 4, fiber 4, carbs 6, protein 7

Easy Lunch Salmon Steaks

Preparation time: 10 minutes
Cooking time: 20 minutes
Servings: 4

Ingredients:
- 1 big salmon fillet, cut into 4 steaks
- 3 garlic cloves, minced
- 1 yellow onion, chopped
- Black pepper to the taste
- 2 tablespoons olive oil
- ¼ cup parsley, chopped
- Juice of 1 lemon
- 1 tablespoon thyme, chopped
- 4 cups water

Directions:
Heat up a pan with the oil over medium-high heat, add onion and garlic, stir and cook for 3 minutes. Add black pepper, parsley, thyme, water and lemon juice, and stir, bring to a gentle boil, add salmon steaks, cook them for 15 minutes, drain, divide between plates and serve with a side salad for lunch.
Enjoy!

Nutrition: calories 203, fat 3, fiber 6, carbs 8, protein 10

Simple Summer Beef Salad

Preparation time: 10 minutes
Cooking time: 16 minutes
Servings: 4

Ingredients:
- 2 tomatoes, chopped
- 2 avocados, pitted and chopped
- 6 cups lettuce leaves, chopped
- 1 small red onion, chopped
- 1 tablespoon olive oil
- 1 teaspoon chili powder
- Juice of 2 limes
- 1 yellow onion, chopped
- 1 pound beef, ground
- 2 garlic cloves, minced
- 1 teaspoon cumin, ground
- Black pepper to the taste
- 1 bunch cilantro, chopped

Directions:
Heat up a pan with the oil over medium-high heat, add the yellow onion, stir and cook for 5 minutes. Add garlic, pepper, cumin and chili powder, stir and cook for 1 minute. Add beef, stir and cook for 10 minutes and take off heat. In a salad bowl, mix lettuce with avocados, tomatoes, red onion and cilantro and stir. Add beef mix and lime juice, toss to coat and serve for lunch. Enjoy!

Nutrition: calories 143, fat 6, fiber 4, carbs 12, protein 6

Sausage Skillet

Preparation time: 10 minutes
Cooking time: 13 minutes
Servings: 2

Ingredients:
- 1 pound sausage, sliced
- ½ red bell pepper, chopped
- 1 yellow onion, chopped
- 1 bunch kale, chopped
- 1 tomato, chopped
- Black pepper to the taste

Directions:
Heat up a pan over medium-high heat, add sausage, stir and brown on all sides for 3 minutes. Add onions, tomato, bell pepper, black pepper and kale, stir, cook for 10 minutes, divide between plates and serve.
Enjoy!

Nutrition: calories 220, fat 3, fiber 4, carbs 11, protein 9

Light Balsamic Salad

Preparation time: 10 minutes
Cooking time: 0 minutes
Servings: 3

Ingredients:

- 1 orange, cut into segments
- 2 green onions, chopped
- 1 romaine lettuce head, torn
- 1 avocado, pitted, peeled and cubed
- ¼ cup almonds, sliced

For the salad dressing:

- 1 teaspoon mustard
- ¼ cup olive oil
- 2 tablespoons balsamic vinegar
- Juice of ½ orange
- Salt and black pepper

Directions:
In a salad bowl, mix oranges with avocado, lettuce, almonds and green onions. In another bowl, mix olive oil with vinegar, mustard, orange juice, salt and pepper, whisk well, and add this to your salad, toss and serve.
Enjoy!

Nutrition: calories 120, fat 2, fiber 2, carbs 4, protein 8

Cauliflower Soup

Preparation time: 10 minutes
Cooking time: 50 minutes
Servings: 4

Ingredients:

- 3 pounds cauliflower, florets separated
- 1 yellow onion, chopped
- 1 tablespoon coconut oil
- Black pepper to the taste
- 2 garlic cloves, minced
- 2 carrots, chopped
- 2 cups beef stock
- 1 cup water
- ½ cup coconut milk
- 1 teaspoon olive oil
- 2 tablespoons parsley, chopped

Directions:
Heat up a pot with the coconut oil over medium-high heat, add carrots, onion and garlic, stir and cook for 5 minutes. Add cauliflower, water and stock, stir, bring to a boil, cover and cook for 45 minutes. Transfer soup to your blender and pulse well, add coconut milk, pulse well again, ladle into bowls, drizzle the olive oil over the soup, sprinkle parsley and serve for lunch.
Enjoy!

Nutrition: calories 190, fat 2, fiber 1, carbs 16, protein 4

Purple Potato Soup

Preparation time: 10 minutes
Cooking time: 1 hour and 15 minutes
Servings: 6

Ingredients:

- 6 purple potatoes, chopped
- 1 cauliflower head, florets separated
- Black pepper to the taste
- 4 garlic cloves, minced
- 1 yellow onion, chopped
- 3 tablespoons olive oil
- 1 tablespoon thyme, chopped
- 1 leek, chopped
- 2 shallots, chopped
- 4 cups chicken stock, low-sodium

Directions:

In a baking dish, mix potatoes with onion, cauliflower, garlic, pepper, thyme and half of the oil, toss to coat, introduce in the oven and bake for 45 minutes at 400 degrees F. Heat up a pot with the rest of the oil over medium-high heat, add leeks and shallots, stir and cook for 10 minutes Add roasted veggies and stock, stir, bring to a boil, cook for 20 minutes, transfer soup to your food processor, blend well, divide into bowls and serve.
Enjoy!

Nutrition: calories 200, fat 8, fiber 6, carbs 15, protein 8

Broccoli Soup

Preparation time: 10 minutes
Cooking time: 1 hour
Servings: 4

Ingredients:

- 2 pounds broccoli, florets separated
- 1 yellow onion, chopped
- 1 tablespoon olive oil
- Black pepper to the taste
- 1 cup celery, chopped
- 2 carrots, chopped
- 3 and ½ cups low-sodium chicken stock
- 1 tablespoon cilantro chopped

Directions:

Heat up a pot with the oil over medium-high heat, add the onion, celery and carrots, stir and cook for 5 minutes. Add broccoli, black pepper and stock, stir and cook over medium heat for 1 hour. Pulse using an immersion blender, add cilantro, stir the soup again, divide into bowls and serve.
Enjoy!

Nutrition: calories 170, fat 2, fiber 1, carbs 10, protein 9

Leeks Soup

Preparation time: 10 minutes
Cooking time: 1 hour and 15 minutes
Servings: 6

Ingredients:
- 2 gold potatoes, chopped
- 1 cup cauliflower florets
- Black pepper to the taste
- 5 leeks, chopped
- 4 garlic cloves, minced
- 1 yellow onion, chopped
- 3 tablespoons olive oil
- A handful parsley, chopped
- 4 cups low-sodium chicken stock

Directions:
Heat up a pot with the oil over medium-high heat, add onion and garlic, stir and cook for 5 minutes. Add potatoes, cauliflower, black pepper, leeks and stock, stir, bring to a simmer, cook over medium heat for 30 minutes, blend using an immersion blender, add parsley, stir, ladle into bowls and serve.
Enjoy!

Nutrition: calories 150, fat 8, fiber 6, carbs 7, protein 8

Cauliflower Lunch Salad

Preparation time: 2 hours
Cooking time: 10 minutes
Servings: 4

Ingredients:
- 1/3 cup low-sodium veggie stock
- 2 tablespoons olive oil
- 6 cups cauliflower florets, grated
- Black pepper to the taste
- ¼ cup red onion, chopped
- 1 red bell pepper, chopped
- Juice of ½ lemon
- ½ cup kalamata olives, pitted and cut into halves
- 1 teaspoon mint, chopped
- 1 tablespoon cilantro, chopped

Directions:
Heat up a pan with the oil over medium-high heat, add cauliflower, pepper and stock, stir, cook for 10 minutes, transfer to a bowl and keep in the fridge for 2 hours. Mix cauliflower with olives, onion, bell pepper, black pepper, mint, cilantro and lemon juice, toss to coat and serve.
Enjoy!

Nutrition: calories 185, fat 12, fiber 6, carbs 11, protein 8

Shrimp Soup

Preparation time: 10 minutes
Cooking time: 15 minutes
Servings: 6

Ingredients:
- 46 ounces low-sodium chicken stock
- 3 cups shrimp, peeled and deveined
- A pinch of black pepper
- 2 tablespoons green onions, chopped
- 1 teaspoon dill, chopped

Directions:
Put the stock in a pot, bring to a simmer over medium heat, add black pepper, onion and shrimp, stir and simmer for 8-10 minutes. Add dill, stir, cook for 5 minutes more, ladle into bowls and serve.
Enjoy!

Nutrition: calories 190, fat 7, fiber 2, carbs 12, protein 8

Shrimp Mix

Preparation time: 10 minutes
Cooking time: 10 minutes
Servings: 4

Ingredients:
- 1 and ½ pounds shrimp, peeled and deveined
- 1 tablespoon olive oil
- 1 teaspoon sesame seeds
- 24 ounces broccoli florets
- 1 green onion, chopped
- 1 tablespoon balsamic vinegar
- 2 garlic cloves, minced
- 1 tablespoon ginger, grated

Directions:
In a bowl, mix oil with vinegar, garlic and ginger and whisk. Transfer this to a pan, heat up over medium heat, add shrimp, stir and cook for 3 minutes. Add broccoli, stir, cook for 4 minutes more, Add sesame seeds and green onions, toss, divide everything between plates and serve.
Enjoy!

Nutrition: calories 265, fat 2, fiber 1, carbs 10, protein 20

Spinach and Lentils Stew

Preparation time: 10 minutes
Cooking time: 23 minutes
Servings: 3

Ingredients:

- 1 teaspoon olive oil
- 1/3 cup brown lentils
- 1 teaspoon ginger, grated
- 4 garlic cloves, minced
- 1 green chili pepper, chopped
- 2 tomatoes, chopped
- ½ teaspoon turmeric powder
- 2 potatoes, cubed
- A pinch of black pepper
- ¼ teaspoon cinnamon powder
- 1 cup low-sodium veggie stock
- 6 ounces spinach leaves

Directions:
Heat up a pot with the oil over medium heat, add chili pepper, ginger and garlic, stir and cook for 3 minutes. Add tomatoes, pepper, cinnamon, turmeric, lentils, potatoes, stock and spinach, stir and cook for 20 minutes. Divide into bowls and serve.
Enjoy!

Nutrition: calories 220, fat 3, fiber 11, carbs 16, protein 11

Sweet Potato Mix

Preparation time: 10 minutes
Cooking time: 25 minutes
Servings: 4

Ingredients:

- 1 small yellow onion, chopped
- 1 tablespoon olive oil
- 2 garlic cloves, minced
- 4 sweet potatoes, chopped
- 1 red bell pepper, chopped
- 14 ounces canned tomatoes, chopped
- 2 teaspoons curry powder
- A pinch of black pepper
- 2 tablespoons red curry paste
- 14 ounces coconut milk
- Juice of 3 limes
- 1 tablespoon cilantro, chopped

Directions:
Heat up a pot with the oil over medium heat, add onion, stir and cook for 5 minutes. Add garlic, ginger, sweet potatoes, red bell pepper, tomatoes, curry powder, and black pepper, curry paste, coconut milk, limejuice and cilantro, stir and simmer over medium heat for 20 minutes. Divide into bowls and serve for lunch.
Enjoy!

Nutrition: calories 270, fat 7, fiber 4, carbs 12, protein 7

Pea Stew

Preparation time: 10 minutes
Cooking time: 25 minutes
Servings: 4

Ingredients:
- 1 carrot, cubed
- 1 yellow onion, chopped
- 1 and ½ tablespoons olive oil
- 1 celery stick, chopped
- 5 garlic cloves, minced
- 2 cups yellow peas
- 1 and ½ teaspoons cumin, ground
- 1 teaspoon sweet paprika
- ¼ teaspoon chili powder
- A pinch of black pepper
- ¼ teaspoon cinnamon powder
- ½ cup tomatoes, chopped
- Juice of ½ lemon
- 1-quart low-sodium veggie stock
- 1 tablespoon chives, chopped

Directions:
Heat up a pot with the oil over medium heat, add carrots, onion and celery, stir and cook for 5-6 minutes. Add garlic, peas, cumin, paprika, chili powder, pepper, cinnamon, tomatoes, lemon juice, peas and stock, stir, bring to a simmer, cook over medium heat for 20 minutes, add chives, toss, divide into bowls and serve.
Enjoy!

Nutrition: calories 272, fat 6, fiber 7, carbs 14, protein 9

Green Beans Stew

Preparation time: 10 minutes
Cooking time: 25 minutes
Servings: 4

Ingredients:
- 2 tablespoons olive oil
- 2 carrots, chopped
- 1 yellow onion, chopped
- 20 ounces green beans
- 2 garlic cloves, minced
- 7 ounces canned tomatoes, chopped
- 5 cups low-sodium veggie stock
- A pinch of black pepper
- 1 tablespoon parsley, chopped

Directions:
Heat up a pot with the oil, over medium heat, add onion, stir and cook for 5 minutes. Add carrots, green beans, garlic, tomatoes, black pepper and stock, stir, cover and simmer over medium heat for 20 minutes. Add parsley, divide into bowls and serve for lunch.
Enjoy!

Nutrition: calories 281, fat 5, fiber 1, carbs 14, protein 11

Mushroom and Veggie Soup

Preparation time: 10 minutes
Cooking time: 25 minutes
Servings: 4

Ingredients:

- 1 yellow onion, chopped
- A pinch of black pepper
- 1 tablespoon olive oil
- 1 red chili pepper, chopped
- 2 carrots, sliced
- 4 garlic cloves, minced
- 12 mushrooms, chopped
- 2 ounces kale leaves, roughly chopped
- 4 cups low-sodium veggie stock
- 1 cup tomatoes, chopped
- ½ tablespoon lemon zest, grated
- ½ tablespoon parsley, chopped

Directions:
Heat up a pot with the oil, over medium heat, add onion, garlic, chili and carrots, stir and sauté for 5 minutes. Add black pepper, mushrooms, kale, tomatoes, stock and lemon zest, stir, cover and cook over medium heat for 20 minutes. Add parsley, toss, divide into bowls and serve for lunch.
Enjoy!

Nutrition: calories 200, fat 6, fiber 6, carbs 9, protein 10

Jackfruit and Chili Stew

Preparation time: 10 minutes
Cooking time: 25 minutes
Servings: 4

Ingredients:

- 40 ounces canned jackfruit
- 14 ounces canned red chili puree
- 1 yellow onion, chopped
- 8 garlic cloves, minced
- 1 tablespoon olive oil
- 6 cups low-sodium veggie stock
- 1 tablespoon oregano, chopped
- 1 tablespoon cilantro, chopped

Directions:
Heat up a pot with the oil, over medium-high heat, add onion and garlic stir and cook for 4-5 minutes. Add jackfruit, chili puree and stock, stir, cover and cook over medium heat for 15 minutes. Add oregano and cilantro, stir, cook for 5 minutes more, divide into bowls and serve.
Enjoy!

Nutrition: calories 263, fat 6, fiber 7, carbs 13, protein 11

Mushroom Lunch Salad

Preparation time: 10 minutes
Cooking time: 20 minutes
Servings: 4

Ingredients:

- 7 garlic cloves, minced
- 2 red chili peppers, chopped
- 1 teaspoon olive oil
- 1 yellow onion, chopped
- 1 teaspoon cumin, ground
- ½ teaspoon oregano, dried
- ½ teaspoon smoked paprika
- A pinch of black pepper
- ¼ teaspoon cinnamon powder
- 1 cup low sodium veggie stock
- 8 ounces white mushrooms, sliced
- 3 teaspoons lime juice

Directions:
Heat up a pot with the oil over medium-high heat, add garlic and chili, stir and cook for 5 minutes. Add onion, cumin, oregano, paprika, black pepper and cinnamon, stir and cook for 5 minutes. Add mushrooms, limejuice and stock, stir, cook for 10 minutes, divide between plates and serve.
Enjoy!

Nutrition: calories 221, fat 5, fiber 8, carbs 12, protein 8

Chickpeas Stew

Preparation time: 10 minutes
Cooking time: 40 minutes
Servings: 4

Ingredients:

- 1 teaspoon olive oil
- 1 cup chickpeas, soaked for 8 hours and drained
- 4 garlic cloves, minced
- 1 yellow onion, chopped
- 1 green chili pepper, chopped
- 1 teaspoon coriander, ground
- ½ teaspoon cumin, ground
- ½ teaspoon sweet paprika
- 2 tomatoes, chopped
- 1 and ½ cups low-sodium veggie stock
- A pinch of black pepper
- 3 cups spinach leaves
- 1 tablespoon lemon juice

Directions:
Heat up a pot with the oil over medium heat, add garlic, onion and chili pepper, stir and cook for 5 minutes. Add coriander, cumin, paprika and black pepper, stir and cook for 5 minutes more. Add chickpeas, tomatoes, stock and lemon juice, stir, cover the pot, cook over medium heat for 25 minutes, add spinach, cook for 5 minutes more, divide into bowls and serve.
Enjoy!

Nutrition: calories 270, fat 7, fiber 6, carbs 14, protein 9

Eggplant Stew

Preparation time: 10 minutes
Cooking time: 20 minutes
Servings: 4

Ingredients:

- ½ teaspoon cumin seeds
- 1 tablespoon coriander seeds
- ½ teaspoon mustard seeds
- 1 tablespoon olive oil
- 1 tablespoon ginger, grated
- 2 garlic cloves, minced
- 1 green chili pepper, chopped
- A pinch of cinnamon powder
- ½ teaspoon cardamom, ground
- ½ teaspoon turmeric powder
- 1 teaspoon lime juice
- 4 baby eggplants, cubed
- 1 cup low-sodium veggie stock
- 1 tablespoon cilantro, chopped

Directions:
Heat up a pot with the oil over medium-high heat, add cumin, coriander and mustard seeds, stir and cook them for 5 minutes. Add ginger, garlic, chili, cinnamon, cardamom and turmeric, stir and cook for 5 minutes more. Add limejuice, eggplants and stock, stir, cover and cook over medium heat for 15 minutes. Add cilantro, stir, divide into bowls and serve for lunch. Enjoy!

Nutrition: calories 270, fat 4, fiber 6, carbs 12, protein 9

Black Eyed Peas Chili

Preparation time: 10 minutes
Cooking time: 40 minutes
Servings: 6

Ingredients:

- 1 red bell pepper, chopped
- 1 green bell pepper, chopped
- 1 tablespoon olive oil
- 2 yellow onions, chopped
- 6 garlic cloves, minced
- 24 ounces black-eyed peas, soaked overnight and drained
- 4 cups veggie stock
- 2 tablespoons chili powder, mild
- 2 teaspoons cumin, ground
- ½ teaspoon chipotle powder
- 2 teaspoons smoked paprika
- 30 ounces canned tomatoes, no-salt-added, chopped
- 2 cups corn
- A pinch of black pepper

Directions:
Heat up a pot with the oil over medium heat, add the onions and the garlic, stir and cook for 5 minutes. Add red and green bell pepper, chili powder, cumin, chipotle powder, smoked paprika and black pepper, stir and cook for 5 minutes more. Add peas, stock, tomatoes and corn, stir, cover the pot and cook over medium heat for 30 minutes. Divide into bowls and serve for lunch. Enjoy!

Nutrition: calories 270, fat 2, fiber 10, carbs 13, protein 12

Dash Diet Side Dish Recipes

Simple Carrots Mix

Preparation time: 10 minutes
Cooking time: 40 minutes
Servings: 6

Ingredients:

- 15 carrots, halved lengthwise
- 2 tablespoons coconut sugar
- ¼ cup olive oil
- ½ teaspoon rosemary, dried
- ½ teaspoon garlic powder
- A pinch of black pepper

Directions:
In a bowl, combine the carrots with the sugar, oil, rosemary, garlic powder and black pepper, toss well, spread on a lined baking sheet, introduce in the oven and bake at 400 degrees F for 40 minutes. Divide between plates and serve as a side dish.
Enjoy!

Nutrition: calories 211, fat 2, fiber 6, carbs 14, protein 8

Tasty Grilled Asparagus

Preparation time: 10 minutes
Cooking time: 6 minutes
Servings: 4

Ingredients:

- 2 pounds asparagus, trimmed
- 2 tablespoons olive oil
- A pinch of salt and black pepper

Directions:
In a bowl, combine the asparagus with salt, pepper and oil and toss well. Place the asparagus on preheated grill over medium-high heat, cook for 3 minutes on each side, divide between plates and serve as a side dish.
Enjoy!

Nutrition: calories 172, fat 4, fiber 7, carbs 14, protein 8

Easy Roasted Carrots

Preparation time: 10 minutes
Cooking time: 30 minutes
Servings: 4

Ingredients:
- 2 pounds carrots, quartered
- A pinch of black pepper
- 3 tablespoons olive oil
- 2 tablespoons parsley, chopped

Directions:
Arrange the carrots on a lined baking sheet, add black pepper and oil, toss, introduce in the oven and cook at 400 degrees F for 30 minutes. Add parsley, toss, divide between plates and serve as a side dish.
Enjoy!

Nutrition: calories 177, fat 3, fiber 6, carbs 14, protein 6

Oven Roasted Asparagus

Preparation time: 10 minutes
Cooking time: 25 minutes
Servings: 4

Ingredients:
- 2 pounds asparagus spears, trimmed
- 3 tablespoons olive oil
- A pinch of black pepper
- 2 teaspoons sweet paprika
- 1 teaspoon sesame seeds

Directions:
Arrange the asparagus on a lined baking sheet, add oil, black pepper and paprika, toss, introduce in the oven and bake at 400 degrees F for 25 minutes. Divide the asparagus between plates, sprinkle sesame seeds on top and serve as a side dish.
Enjoy!

Nutrition: calories 190, fat 4, fiber 8, carbs 11, protein 5

Baked Potato Mix

Preparation time: 10 minutes
Cooking time: 1 hour and 15 minutes
Servings: 8

Ingredients:

- 6 potatoes, peeled and sliced
- 2 garlic cloves, minced
- 2 tablespoons olive oil
- 1 and ½ cups coconut cream
- ¼ cup coconut milk
- 1 tablespoon thyme, chopped
-
- ¼ teaspoon nutmeg, ground
- A pinch of red pepper flakes
- 1 and ½ cups low-fat cheddar, shredded
- ½ cup low-fat parmesan, grated

Directions:
Heat up a pan with the oil over medium heat, add garlic, stir and cook for 1 minute. Add coconut cream, coconut milk, thyme, nutmeg and pepper flakes, stir, bring to a simmer, reduce heat to low and cook for 10 minutes. Arrange 1/3 of the potatoes in a baking dish, add 1/3 of the cream, repeat with the rest of the potatoes and the cream, sprinkle the cheddar on top, cover with tin foil, introduce in the oven and cook at 375 degrees F for 45 minutes. Uncover the dish, sprinkle the parmesan, bake everything for 20 minutes, divide between plates and serve as a side dish. Enjoy!

Nutrition: calories 224, fat 8, fiber 9, carbs 16, protein 15

Spicy Brussels Sprouts

Preparation time: 10 minutes
Cooking time: 20 minutes
Servings: 6

Ingredients:

- 2 pounds Brussels sprouts, halved
- 2 tablespoons olive oil
- A pinch of black pepper
- 1 tablespoon sesame oil
- 2 garlic cloves, minced
- ½ cup coconut aminos
- 2 teaspoons apple cider vinegar
- 1 tablespoon coconut sugar
- 2 teaspoons chili sauce
- A pinch of red pepper flakes
- Sesame seeds for serving

Directions:
Spread the sprouts on a lined baking dish, add the olive oil, the sesame oil, black pepper, garlic, aminos, vinegar, coconut sugar, chili sauce and pepper flakes, toss well, introduce in the oven and bake at 425 degrees F for 20 minutes. Divide the sprouts between plates, sprinkle sesame seeds on top and serve as a side dish.
Enjoy!

Nutrition: calories 176, fat 3, fiber 6, carbs 14, protein 9

Baked Cauliflower

Preparation time: 10 minutes
Cooking time: 30 minutes
Servings: 4

Ingredients:

- 3 tablespoons olive oil
- 2 tablespoons chili sauce
- Juice of 1 lime
- 3 garlic cloves, minced
- 1 cauliflower head, florets separated
- A pinch of black pepper
- 1 teaspoon cilantro, chopped

Directions:
In a bowl, combine the oil with the chili sauce, lime juice, garlic and black pepper and whisk. Add cauliflower florets, toss, spread on a lined baking sheet, introduce in the oven and bake at 425 degrees F for 30 minutes. Divide the cauliflower between plates, sprinkle cilantro on top and serve as a side dish.
Enjoy!

Nutrition: calories 188, fat 4, fiber 7, carbs 14, protein 8

Baked Broccoli

Preparation time: 10 minutes
Cooking time: 15 minutes
Servings: 4

Ingredients:

- 1 tablespoon olive oil
- 1 broccoli head, florets separated
- 2 garlic cloves, minced
- ½ cup coconut cream
- ½ cup low-fat mozzarella, shredded
- ¼ cup low-fat parmesan, grated
- A pinch of pepper flakes, crushed

Directions:
In a baking dish, combine the broccoli with oil, garlic, cream, pepper flakes and mozzarella and toss. Sprinkle the parmesan on top, introduce in the oven and bake at 375 degrees F for 15 minutes. Divide between plates and serve as a side dish.
Enjoy!

Nutrition: calories 188, fat 4, fiber 7, carbs 14, protein 7

Easy Slow Cooked Potatoes

Preparation time: 10 minutes
Cooking time: 6 hours
Servings: 6

Ingredients:

- Cooking spray
- 2 pounds baby potatoes, quartered
- 3 cups low-fat cheddar cheese, shredded
- 2 garlic cloves, minced
- 8 bacon slices, cooked and chopped
- ¼ cup green onions, chopped
- 1 tablespoon sweet paprika
- A pinch of black pepper

Directions:
Spray a slow cooker with the cooking spray, add baby potatoes, cheddar, garlic, bacon, green onions, paprika and black pepper, toss, cover and cook on High for 6 hours. Divide between plates and serve as a side dish.
Enjoy!

Nutrition: calories 200, fat 4, fiber 6, carbs 12, protein 7

Mashed Potatoes

Preparation time: 10 minutes
Cooking time: 20 minutes
Servings: 6

Ingredients:

- 3 pounds potatoes, peeled and cubed
- 2 tablespoons non-fat butter
- ½ cup coconut milk
- A pinch of salt and black pepper
- ½ cup low-fat sour cream

Directions:
Put the potatoes in a pot, add water to cover, add a pinch of salt and pepper, bring to a boil over medium heat, and cook for 20 minutes and drain. Add butter, milk and sour cream, mash well, stir everything, divide between plates and serve as a side dish.
Enjoy!

Nutrition: calories 188, fat 3, fiber 7, carbs 14, protein 8

Squash Side Salad

Preparation time: 10 minutes
Cooking time: 30 minutes
Servings: 6

Ingredients:

- 1 cup orange juice
- 3 tablespoons coconut sugar
- 1 and ½ tablespoons mustard
- 1 tablespoon ginger, grated
- 1 and ½ pounds butternut squash, peeled and roughly cubed
- Cooking spray
- A pinch of black pepper
- 1/3 cup olive oil
- 6 cups salad greens
- 1 radicchio, sliced
- ½ cup pistachios, roasted

Directions:

In a bowl, combine the orange juice with the sugar, mustard, ginger, black pepper and squash, toss well, spread on a lined baking sheet, spray everything with cooking oil, introduce in the oven and bake at 400 degrees F for 30 minutes. In a salad bowl, combine the squash with salad greens, radicchio, pistachios and oil, toss well, divide between plates and serve as a side dish. Enjoy!

Nutrition: calories 275, fat 3, fiber 4, carbs 16, protein 6

Colored Iceberg Salad

Preparation time: 10 minutes
Cooking time: 0 minutes
Servings: 4

Ingredients:

- 1 iceberg lettuce head, leaves torn
- 6 bacon slices, cooked and halved
- 2 green onions, sliced
- 3 carrots, shredded
- 6 radishes, sliced
- ¼ cup red vinegar
- ¼ cup olive oil
- 3 garlic cloves, minced
- A pinch of black pepper

Directions:

In a large salad bowl, combine the lettuce leaves with the bacon, green onions, carrots, radishes, vinegar, oil, garlic and black pepper, toss, divide between plates and serve as a side dish.
Enjoy!

Nutrition: calories 235, fat 4, fiber 4, carbs 10, protein 6

Fennel Side Salad

Preparation time: 10 minutes
Cooking time: 0 minutes
Servings: 4

Ingredients:
- 2 fennel bulbs, trimmed and shaved
- 1 and ¼ cups zucchini, sliced
- 2/3 cup dill, chopped
- ¼ cup lemon juice
- ¼ cup olive oil
- 6 cups arugula
- ½ cups walnuts, chopped
- 1/3 cup low-fat feta cheese, crumbled

Directions:
In a large bowl, combine the fennel with the zucchini, dill, lemon juice, arugula, oil, walnuts and cheese, toss, divide between plates and serve as a side dish.
Enjoy!

Nutrition: calories 188, fat 4, fiber 5, carbs 14, protein 6

Corn Mix

Preparation time: 10 minutes
Cooking time: 0 minutes
Servings: 4

Ingredients:
- ½ cup cider vinegar
- ¼ cup coconut sugar
- A pinch of black pepper
- 4 cups corn
- ½ cup red onion, chopped
- ½ cup cucumber, sliced
- ½ cup red bell pepper, chopped
- ½ cup cherry tomatoes, halved
- 3 tablespoons parsley, chopped
- 1 tablespoon basil, chopped
- 1 tablespoon jalapeno, chopped
- 2 cups baby arugula leaves

Directions:
In a large bowl, combine the corn with onion, cucumber, bell pepper, cherry tomatoes, parsley, basil, jalapeno and arugula and toss. Add vinegar, sugar and black pepper, toss well, divide between plates and serve as a side dish.
Enjoy!

Nutrition: calories 100, fat 2, fiber 3, carbs 14, protein 4

Persimmon Side Salad

Preparation time: 10 minutes
Cooking time: 0 minutes
Servings: 4

Ingredients:

- Seeds from 1 pomegranate
- 2 persimmons, cored and sliced
- 5 cups baby arugula
- 6 tablespoons green onions, chopped
- 4 navel oranges, peeled and cut into segments
- ¼ cup white vinegar
- 1/3 cup olive oil
- 3 tablespoons pine nuts
- 1 and ½ teaspoons orange zest, grated
- 2 tablespoons orange juice
- 1 tablespoon coconut sugar
- ½ shallot, chopped
- A pinch of cinnamon powder

Directions:
In a salad bowl, combine the pomegranate seeds with persimmons, arugula, green onions and oranges and toss. In another bowl, combine the vinegar with the oil, pine nuts, orange zest, orange juice, sugar, shallot and cinnamon, whisk well, add to the salad, toss and serve as a side dish.
Enjoy!

Nutrition: calories 188, fat 4, fiber 4, carbs 14, protein 4

Avocado Side Salad

Preparation time: 10 minutes
Cooking time: 0 minutes
Servings: 4

Ingredients:

- 4 blood oranges, peeled and cut into segments
- 2 tablespoons olive oil
- A pinch of red pepper, crushed
- 2 avocados, peeled, pitted and cut into wedges
- 1 and ½ cups baby arugula
- ¼ cup almonds, toasted and chopped
- 1 tablespoon lemon juice

Directions:
In a bowl, combine the oranges with the oil, red pepper, avocados, arugula, almonds and lemon juice, toss, divide between plates and serve as a side dish.
Enjoy!

Nutrition: calories 231, fat 4, fiber 8, carbs 16, protein 6

Classic Side Dish Salad

Preparation time: 10 minutes
Cooking time: 0 minutes
Servings: 4

Ingredients:
- 3 garlic cloves, minced
- Juice of ½ lemon
- 6 ounces coconut cream
- 2 lettuce hearts, torn
- 1 cup corn
- 4 ounces green beans, halved
- 1 cup cherry tomatoes, halved
- 1 cucumber, chopped
- 1/3 cup chives, chopped
- 1 avocado, peeled, pitted and halved
- 6 bacon slices, cooked and chopped

Directions:
In a bowl, combine the lettuce with corn, green beans, cherry tomatoes, cucumber, chives, avocado and bacon and toss. In another bowl, combine the garlic with lemon juice and coconut cream, whisk well, add to the salad, toss and serve as a side dish.
Enjoy!

Nutrition: calories 175, fat 12, fiber 4, carbs 13, protein 6

Easy Kale Mix

Preparation time: 10 minutes
Cooking time: 0 minutes
Servings: 4

Ingredients:
- 1 whole wheat bread slice, toasted and torn into small pieces
- 6 tablespoons low-fat cheddar, grated
- 3 tablespoons olive oil
- 5 tablespoons lemon juice
- 1 garlic clove, minced
- 7 cups kale, torn
- A pinch of black pepper

Directions:
In a bowl, combine the bread with cheese and kale. In another bowl, combine the oil with the lemon juice, garlic and black pepper, whisk, add to the salad, toss, divide between plates and serve as a side dish.
Enjoy!

Nutrition: calories 200, fat 4, fiber 5, carbs 14, protein 8

Asparagus Salad

Preparation time: 10 minutes
Cooking time: 4 minutes
Servings: 4

Ingredients:

- 4 tablespoons avocado oil
- 2 tablespoons balsamic vinegar
- 1 tablespoon coconut aminos
- 1 garlic clove, minced
- 1 pound asparagus, trimmed
- 6 cups frisee lettuce leaves, torn
- 1 cup edamame, shelled
- 1 cup parsley, chopped

Directions:
Heat up a pan with 1 tablespoon oil over medium-high heat, add asparagus, cook for 4 minutes and transfer to a salad bowl. Add lettuce, edamame and parsley and toss. In another bowl, combine the rest of the oil with the vinegar, aminos and garlic, whisk well, add over the salad, toss, divide between plates and serve as a side dish.
Enjoy!

Nutrition: calories 200, fat 4, fiber 5, carbs 14, protein 6

Green Side Salad

Preparation time: 10 minutes
Cooking time: 0 minutes
Servings: 4

Ingredients:

- 4 cups baby spinach leaves
- 1 cucumber, sliced
- 3 ounces broccoli florets
- 3 ounces green beans, blanched and halved
- ¾ cup edamame, shelled
- 1 and ½ cups green grapes, halved
- 1 cup orange juice
- ¼ cup olive oil
- 1 tablespoon cider vinegar
- 2 tablespoons parsley, chopped
- 2 teaspoons mustard
- A pinch of black pepper

Directions:
In a salad bowl, combine the baby spinach with cucumber, broccoli, green beans, edamame and grapes and toss. Add orange juice, olive oil, vinegar, parsley, mustard and black pepper, toss well, divide between plates and serve as a side dish.
Enjoy!

Nutrition: calories 117, fat 4, fiber 5, carbs 14, protein 4

Baked Zucchini

Preparation time: 10 minutes
Cooking time: 20 minutes
Servings: 4

Ingredients:

- 4 zucchinis, quartered lengthwise
- ½ teaspoon thyme, dried
- ½ teaspoon oregano, dried
- ½ cup low-fat parmesan, grated
- ½ teaspoon basil, dried
- ¼ teaspoon garlic powder
- 2 tablespoons olive oil
- 2 tablespoons parsley, chopped
- A pinch of black pepper

Directions:
Arrange zucchini pieces on a lined baking sheet add thyme, oregano, basil, garlic powder, oil, parsley and black pepper and toss well. Sprinkle parmesan on top, introduce in the oven and bake at 350 degrees F for 20 minutes. Divide between plates and serve as a side dish.
Enjoy!

Nutrition: calories 198, fat 4, fiber 4, carbs 14, protein 5

Baked Mushrooms

Preparation time: 10 minutes
Cooking time: 15 minutes
Servings: 4

Ingredients:

- 1 and ½ pounds white mushrooms, sliced
- ¼ cup lemon juice
- 3 tablespoons olive oil
- Zest of 1 lemon, grated
- 3 garlic cloves, minced
- 2 teaspoons thyme, dried
- ¼ cup low-fat parmesan, grated
- A pinch of salt and black pepper

Directions:
In a bowl, combine the mushrooms with the lemon juice, oil, lemon zest, garlic, thyme, parmesan, salt and pepper, toss, spread on a lined baking sheet, introduce in the oven at 375 degrees F for 15 minutes, divide between plates and serve as a side dish.
Enjoy!

Nutrition: calories 164, fat 12, fiber 3, carbs 10, protein 7

Garlic Potatoes

Preparation time: 10 minutes
Cooking time: 30 minutes
Servings: 6

Ingredients:

- 3 pounds red potatoes, halved
- 4 garlic cloves, minced
- 2 tablespoons olive oil
- 1 teaspoon thyme, dried
- ½ teaspoon basil, dried
- 1/3 cup low-fat parmesan, grated
- 2 tablespoons low-fat butter, melted
- 2 tablespoons parsley, chopped
- Black pepper to the taste

Directions:

In a roasting pan, combine the red potatoes with garlic, oil, thyme, basil, parmesan, butter and black pepper, toss, introduce in the oven and cook at 400 degrees F for 30 minutes. Add parsley, toss, divide between plates and serve as a side dish.
Enjoy!

Nutrition: calories 251, fat 12, fiber 4, carbs 13, protein 6

Corn Pudding

Preparation time: 10 minutes
Cooking time: 15 minutes
Servings: 4

Ingredients:

- 8 ears corn, grated
- 3 bacon slices, chopped
- 1 yellow onion, chopped
- ½ cup coconut milk
-
- ½ cup basil, torn
- A pinch of black pepper
- ½ teaspoon red pepper flakes

Directions:

Heat up a pan over medium-high heat, add bacon, stir and cook for 2 minutes. Add corn, onion, black pepper and pepper flakes, stir and cook for 8 minutes. Add milk and basil, stir and cook for 5 minutes more, divide between plates and serve as a side dish.
Enjoy!

Nutrition: calories 201, fat 3, fiber 5, carbs 14, protein 7

Corn Sauté

Preparation time: 10 minutes
Cooking time: 12 minutes
Servings: 4

Ingredients:

- 4 cups corn
- 4 bacon slices, cut into strips
- A pinch of red pepper flakes
-
- 3 scallions, chopped
- A pinch of black pepper

Directions:
Heat up a pan over medium-high heat, add bacon, toss and cook for 5 minutes. Add corn, pepper flakes, black pepper and scallions, toss, cook for 7 minutes more, divide between plates and serve as a side dish.
Enjoy!

Nutrition: calories 199, fat 3, fiber 6, carbs 13, protein 8

Pineapple Potato Salad

Preparation time: 10 minutes
Cooking time: 40 minutes
Servings: 4

Ingredients:

- 2 cups pineapple, peeled and cubed
- 4 sweet potatoes, cubed
- 1 tablespoon olive oil
- ¼ cup coconut, unsweetened and shredded
- 1/3 cup almonds, chopped
- 1 cup coconut cream

Directions:
Arrange sweet potatoes on a lined baking sheet, add the olive oil, introduce in the oven at 350 degrees F, roast for 40 minutes, put them in a salad bowl, add coconut, pineapple, almonds and cream, toss, divide between plates and serve as a side dish.
Enjoy!

Nutrition: calories 200, fat 4, fiber 3, carbs 7, protein 8

Coconut Sweet Potatoes

Preparation time: 10 minutes
Cooking time: 1 hour
Servings: 4

Ingredients:
- 4 sweet potatoes, sliced
- A drizzle of olive oil
- A pinch of salt and black pepper
- 1 small thyme bunch, chopped
- 1/3 cup coconut cream
- ½ teaspoon parsley, chopped
- 1 tablespoon Dijon mustard
- ½ teaspoon garlic

Directions:
Arrange sweet potato slices on a lined baking sheet, sprinkle thyme, drizzle oil, season with a pinch of salt and black pepper, toss well, introduce in the oven at 400 degrees F and bake for about 1 hour. Meanwhile, in a bowl, mix coconut cream with parsley, garlic and mustard and whisk well. Arrange baked potatoes on plates drizzle the mustard sauce all over and serve as a side dish.
Enjoy!

Nutrition: calories 237, fat 5, fiber 4, carbs 12, protein 9

Cashew and Coconut Sweet Potatoes

Preparation time: 10 minutes
Cooking time: 1 hour
Servings: 4

Ingredients:
- 2 sweet potatoes, peeled and sliced
- ½ cup cashews, soaked for a couple of hours and drained
- 1 cup coconut milk
- ¼ teaspoon cinnamon powder

Directions:
In your food processor, mix cashews, milk and cinnamon and pulse. Spread some of the potato slices in a greased baking pan and drizzle some of the cashews cream. Repeat with the rest of the potatoes and cream, bake in the oven for 1 hour at 350 degrees F, divide between plates and serve as a side dish.
Enjoy!

Nutrition: calories 200, fat 5, fiber 3, carbs 9, protein 8

Sage Celery Mix

Preparation time: 10 minutes
Cooking time: 10 minutes
Servings: 6

Ingredients:
- 2 tablespoons olive oil
- 5 celery ribs, chopped
- 1 yellow onion, chopped
- 1 teaspoon sage, dried
- 8 ounces walnuts, chopped
- A pinch of black pepper
- 3 tablespoons sage, chopped

Directions:
Heat up a pan with the oil over medium heat, add celery and onion, stir and cook for 5 minutes. Add dried sage, pepper, fresh sage and walnuts, stir, cook for 5 minutes more, divide between plates and serve as a side dish.
Enjoy!

Nutrition: calories 250, fat 7, fiber 5, carbs 9, protein 4

Garlic Zucchini Fries

Preparation time: 10 minutes
Cooking time: 20 minutes
Servings: 4

Ingredients:
- 4 zucchinis, cut into medium fries
- A pinch of black pepper
- ½ teaspoon chili powder
- 1 tablespoon olive oil
- ¼ teaspoon garlic powder

Directions:
Spread the zucchini fries on a lined baking sheet, add black pepper, chili powder, garlic powder and oil, toss, introduce in the oven, bake at 400 degrees F for 20 minutes, divide between plates and serve as a side dish.
Enjoy!

Nutrition: calories 185, fat 3, fiber 2, carbs 6, protein 8

Tahini Green Beans

Preparation time: 10 minutes
Cooking time: 10 minutes
Servings: 4

Ingredients:
- 1 and ½ tablespoons tahini paste
- Juice of 1 lemon
- Zest of 1 lemon, grated
- 2 tablespoons olive oil
- 1 garlic clove, minced
- 1 red onion, sliced
- 1 yellow bell pepper, sliced
- 10 ounces green beans, halved
- A pinch of black pepper

Directions:
In a bowl, mix lemon zest, lemon juice, tahini and black pepper and whisk well. Heat up a pan with the oil over medium-high heat, add onion, stir and cook for 5 minutes. Add the bell pepper, garlic and green beans, toss and cook for 10 minutes. Add tahini dressing, toss, cook for 2 minutes more, divide between plates and serve as a side dish.
Enjoy!

Nutrition: calories 180, fat 10, fiber 6, carbs 13, protein 8

Mustard Tarragon Beets

Preparation time: 10 minutes
Cooking time: 0 minutes
Servings: 5

Ingredients:
- 1 tablespoon Dijon mustard
- 1 and ½ tablespoon olive oil
- 8 ounces beets, cooked and sliced
- 2 tablespoons tarragon, chopped
- A pinch of black pepper

Directions:
In a bowl, mix mustard with oil and black pepper and whisk. In a bowl, combine the beets with the tarragon and the mustard mix, toss, divide between plates and serve as a side dish.
Enjoy!

Nutrition: calories 170, fat 5, fiber 7, carbs 8, proteins 10

Almond Green Beans

Preparation time: 10 minutes
Cooking time: 20 minutes
Servings: 6

Ingredients:
- 5 tablespoons olive oil
- 3 pounds green beans, halved
- 8 tablespoons almonds, toasted and sliced
- A pinch of black pepper
- 2 yellow onions, chopped
- 2 and ½ tablespoons parsley, chopped

Directions:
Heat up a pan over medium-high heat, add green beans, cook them for 5 minutes and transfer to a bowl. Heat up the same pan with the olive oil over medium heat, add onions and a pinch of black pepper, stir and cook for 10 minutes. Add beans, almonds and parsley, toss, cook for 5 minutes, divide between plates and serve as a side dish.
    Enjoy!

Nutrition: calories 130, fat 1, fiber 2, carbs 7, protein 6

Tomatoes Side Salad

Preparation time: 10 minutes
Cooking time: 0 minutes
Servings: 4

Ingredients:
- ½ bunch mint, chopped
- 8 plum tomatoes, sliced
- 1 teaspoon mustard
- 1 tablespoon rosemary vinegar
- A pinch of black pepper

Directions:
In a bowl, mix vinegar with mustard and pepper and whisk. In another bowl, combine the tomatoes with the mint and the vinaigrette, toss, divide between plates and serve as a side dish. Enjoy!

Nutrition: calories 70, fat 2, fiber 2, carbs 6, protein 4

Squash Salsa

Preparation time: 10 minutes
Cooking time: 13 minutes
Servings: 6

Ingredients:

- 3 tablespoons olive oil
- 5 medium squash, peeled and sliced
- 1 cup pepitas, toasted
- 7 tomatillos
- A pinch of black pepper
- 1 small onion, chopped
- 2 tablespoons fresh lime juice
- 2 tablespoons cilantro, chopped

Directions:
Heat up a pan over medium heat, add tomatillos, onion and black pepper, stir, cook for 3 minutes, transfer to your food processor and pulse. Add limejuice and cilantro, pulse again and transfer to a bowl. Heat up your kitchen grill over high heat, drizzle the oil over squash slices, grill them for 10 minutes, divide them between plates, add pepitas and tomatillos mix on top and serve as a side dish.
Enjoy!

Nutrition: calories 120, fat 2, fiber 1, carbs 7, protein 1

Apples and Fennel Mix

Preparation time: 10 minutes
Cooking time: 0 minutes
Servings: 3

Ingredients:

- 3 big apples, cored and sliced
- 1 and ½ cup fennel, shredded
- 1/3 cup coconut cream
- 3 tablespoons apple vinegar
- ½ teaspoon caraway seeds
- Black pepper to the taste

Directions:
In a bowl, mix fennel with apples and toss. In another bowl, mix coconut cream with vinegar, black pepper and caraway seeds, whisk well, add over the fennel mix, toss, divide between plates and serve as a side dish.
Enjoy!

Nutrition: calories 130, fat 3, fiber 6, carbs 10, protein 3

Simple Roasted Celery Mix

Preparation time: 10 minutes
Cooking time: 25 minutes
Servings: 3

Ingredients:

- 3 celery roots, cubed
- 2 tablespoons olive oil
- A pinch of black pepper
- 2 cups natural and unsweetened apple juice
- ¼ cup parsley, chopped
- ¼ cup walnuts, chopped

Directions:
In a baking dish, combine the celery with the oil, pepper, parsley, walnuts and apple juice, toss to coat, introduce in the oven at 450 degrees F, bake for 25 minutes, divide between plates and serve as a side dish.
Enjoy!

Nutrition: calories 140, fat 2, fiber 2, carbs 7, protein 7

Thyme Spring Onions

Preparation time: 10 minutes
Cooking time: 40 minutes
Servings: 8

Ingredients:

- 15 spring onions
- A pinch of black pepper
- 1 teaspoon thyme, chopped
- 1 tablespoon olive oil

Directions:
Put onions in a baking dish, add thyme, black pepper and oil, toss, bake in the oven at 350 degrees F for 40 minutes, divide between plates and serve as a side dish.
Enjoy!

Nutrition: calories 120, fat 2, fiber 2, carbs 7, protein 2

Carrot Slaw

Preparation time: 10 minutes
Cooking time: 10 minutes
Servings: 4

Ingredients:

- ¼ yellow onion, chopped
- 5 carrots, cut into thin matchsticks
- 1 tablespoon olive oil
- 1 garlic clove, minced
- 1 tablespoon Dijon mustard
- 1 tablespoon red vinegar
- A pinch of black pepper
- 1 tablespoon lemon juice

Directions:
In a bowl, mix vinegar with black pepper, mustard and lemon juice and whisk. Heat up a pan with the oil over medium heat, add onion, stir and cook for 5 minutes. Add garlic and carrots, stir, cook for 5 minutes more, transfer to a salad bowl, cool down, add the vinaigrette, toss, divide between plates and serve as a side dish.
Enjoy!

Nutrition: calories 120, fat 3, fiber 3, carbs 7, protein 5

Watermelon Tomato Salsa

Preparation time: 10 minutes
Cooking time: 0 minutes
Servings: 16

Ingredients:

- 4 yellow tomatoes, seedless and chopped
- A pinch of black pepper
- 1 cup watermelon, seedless and chopped
- 1/3 cup red onion, chopped
- 2 jalapeno peppers, chopped
- ¼ cup cilantro, chopped
- 3 tablespoons lime juice

Directions:
In a bowl, mix tomatoes with watermelon, onion and jalapeno. Add cilantro, limejuice and pepper, toss, divide between plates and serve as a side dish.
Enjoy!

Nutrition: calories 87, fat 1, fiber 2, carbs 4, protein 7

Sprouts Side Salad

Preparation time: 10 minutes
Cooking time: 0 minutes
Servings: 4

Ingredients:
- 2 zucchinis, cut with a spiralizer
- 2 cups bean sprouts
- 4 green onions, chopped
- 1 red bell pepper, chopped
- Juice of 1 lime
- 1 tablespoon olive oil
- ½ cup cilantro, chopped
- ¾ cup almonds, chopped
- Black pepper to the taste

Directions:
In a salad bowl, mix zucchinis with bean sprouts, onions and bell pepper. Add black pepper, limejuice, almonds, cilantro and olive oil, toss everything, divide between plates and serve as a side dish.
Enjoy!

Nutrition: calories 120, fat 4, fiber 2, carbs 7, protein 12

Cabbage Slaw

Preparation time: 10 minutes
Cooking time: 0 minutes
Servings: 4

Ingredients:
- 1 green cabbage head, shredded
- 1/3 cup coconut, shredded
- ¼ cup olive oil
- 2 tablespoons lemon juice
- ¼ cup coconut aminos
- 3 tablespoons sesame seeds
- ½ teaspoon curry powder
- 1/3 teaspoon turmeric powder
- ½ teaspoon cumin, ground

Directions:
In a bowl, mix cabbage with coconut and lemon juice and stir. Add oil, aminos, sesame seeds, curry powder, turmeric and cumin, toss to coat and serve as a side dish.
Enjoy!

Nutrition: calories 130, fat 4, fiber 5, carbs 8, protein 6

Edamame Side Salad

Preparation time: 10 minutes
Cooking time: 0 minutes
Servings: 4

Ingredients:
- 1 tablespoon ginger, grated
- 2 green onions, chopped
- 3 cups edamame, blanched
- 2 tablespoons rice vinegar
- 1 tablespoon sesame seeds

Directions:
In a bowl, combine the ginger with the onions, edamame, vinegar and sesame seeds, toss, divide between plates and serve as a side dish.
Enjoy!

Nutrition: calories 120, fat 3, fiber 2, carbs 5, protein 9

Flavored Beets Side Salad

Preparation time: 10 minutes
Cooking time: 0 minutes
Servings: 4

Ingredients:
- 4 carrots, sliced
- 12 radishes, sliced
- 1 beet, peeled and grated
- 2 tablespoons raisins
- Juice of 2 lemons
- 1 sugar beet, peeled and chopped
- 1 tablespoon chives, chopped
- 1 tablespoon parsley, chopped
- 1 tablespoon lemon thyme, chopped
- 1 tablespoon white sesame seeds
- 4 handfuls spinach leaves
- 4 tablespoons olive oil
- Black pepper to the taste

Directions:
In a salad bowl, mix carrots, radishes, beets, sugar beet, raisins, chives, parsley, spinach, thyme and sesame seeds. Add lemon juice, oil and black pepper, toss well and serve as a side dish.
Enjoy!

Nutrition: calories 110, fat 2, fiber 2, carbs 4, protein 7

Tomato and Avocado Salad

Preparation time: 10 minutes
Cooking time: 0 minutes
Servings: 4

Ingredients:

- 1 cucumber, chopped
- 1 pound tomatoes, chopped
- 2 avocados, pitted, peeled and chopped
- 1 small red onion, sliced
- 2 tablespoons olive oil
- 2 tablespoons lemon juice
- ¼ cup cilantro, chopped
- Black pepper to the taste

Directions:
In a salad bowl, mix tomatoes with onion, avocado, cucumber and cilantro. In a small bowl, mix oil with lemon juice and black pepper, whisk well, pour this over the salad, toss and serve as a side dish.
Enjoy!

Nutrition: calories 120, fat 2, fiber 2, carbs 3, protein 4

Greek Side Salad

Preparation time: 10 minutes
Cooking time: 0 minutes
Servings: 4

Ingredients:

- 4 pounds heirloom tomatoes, sliced
- 1 yellow bell pepper, thinly sliced
- 1 green bell pepper, thinly sliced
- 1 red onion, thinly sliced
- Black pepper to the taste
- ½ teaspoon oregano, dried
- 2 tablespoons mint leaves, chopped
- A drizzle of olive oil

Directions:
In a salad bowl, mix tomatoes with yellow and green peppers, onion, salt and pepper, toss to coat and leave aside for 10 minutes. Add oregano, mint and olive oil, toss to coat and serve as a side salad.
Enjoy!

Nutrition: calories 100, fat 2, fiber 2, carbs 3, protein 6

Cucumber Salad

Preparation time: 10 minutes
Cooking time: 0 minutes
Servings: 4

Ingredients:
- 2 English cucumbers, chopped
- 8 dates, pitted and sliced
- ¾ cup fennel, sliced
- 2 tablespoons chives, chopped
- ½ cup walnuts, chopped
- 2 tablespoons lemon juice
- 4 tablespoons olive oil
- Black pepper to the taste

Directions:
In a salad bowl, combine the cucumbers with dates, fennel, chives, walnuts, lemon juice, oil and black pepper, toss, divide between plates and serve as a side dish.
Enjoy!

Nutrition: calories 100, fat 1, fiber 1, carbs 7, protein 6

Black Beans and Veggies Side Salad

Preparation time: 10 minutes
Cooking time: 0 minutes
Servings: 4

Ingredients:
- 1 big cucumber, cut into chunks
- 15 ounces canned black beans, no-salt-added, drained and rinsed
- 1 cup corn
- 1 cup cherry tomatoes, halved
- 1 small red onion, chopped
- 3 tablespoons olive oil
- 4 and ½ teaspoons orange marmalade
- Black pepper to the taste
- ½ teaspoon cumin, ground
- 1 tablespoon lemon juice

Directions:
In a bowl, mix beans with cucumber, corn, onion and tomatoes. In another bowl, mix marmalade with oil, lemon juice, black pepper to the taste and cumin, whisk, pour over the salad, toss and serve as a side dish.
Enjoy!

Nutrition: calories 110, fat 0, fiber 3, carbs 6, protein 8

Endives and Escarole Side Salad

Preparation time: 10 minutes
Cooking time: 0 minutes
Servings: 4

Ingredients:
- 1 teaspoon shallot, minced
- ¼ cup apple cider vinegar
- 1 teaspoon Dijon mustard
- 3 Belgian endives, roughly chopped
- ¾ cup olive oil
- 1 cup escarole leaves, torn

Directions:
In a bowl, mix escarole leaves with endives, shallot, vinegar, mustard and oil, toss, divide between plates and serve as a side salad.
Enjoy!

Nutrition: calories 100, fat 1, fiber 3, carbs 6, protein 7

Radicchio and Lettuce Side Salad

Preparation time: 10 minutes
Cooking time: 0 minutes
Servings: 4

Ingredients:
- ½ cup olive oil
- Black pepper to the taste
- 2 tablespoons shallot, chopped
- ¼ cup mustard
- Juice of 2 lemons
- ½ cup basil, chopped
- 5 baby romaine lettuce heads, chopped
- 3 radicchios, sliced
- 3 endives, roughly chopped

Directions:
In a salad bowl, mix romaine lettuce with radicchios and endives. In another bowl, mix oil with the pepper, shallot, mustard, lemon juice and basil, whisk, add to the salad, toss and serve as a side salad.
Enjoy!

Nutrition: calories 120, fat 2, fiber 1, carbs 8, protein 2

Jicama Side Salad

Preparation time: 10 minutes
Cooking time: 0 minutes
Servings: 4

Ingredients:

- 1 romaine lettuce head, leaves torn
- 1 Jicama, peeled and grated
- 1 cup cherry tomatoes, halved
- 1 yellow bell pepper, chopped
- 1 cup carrot, shredded
- 3 ounces low-fat cheese, crumbled
- 3 tablespoons red wine vinegar
- 5 tablespoons non-fat yogurt
- 1 and ½ tablespoons olive oil
- 1 teaspoon parsley, chopped
- 1 teaspoon dill, chopped
- Black pepper to the taste

Directions:
In a salad bowl, mix lettuce leaves with Jicama, tomatoes, bell pepper and carrot and toss. In another bowl, combine the cheese with vinegar, yogurt, oil, pepper, dill and parsley, whisk, add to the salad, toss to coat, divide between plates and serve as a side dish.
Enjoy!

Nutrition: calories 170, fat 4, fiber 8, carbs 14, protein 11

Cauliflower Risotto

Preparation time: 10 minutes
Cooking time: 7 minutes
Servings: 4

Ingredients:

- 2 tablespoons olive oil
- 2 garlic cloves, minced
- 12 ounces cauliflower rice
- 2 tablespoons thyme, chopped
- 1 tablespoon lemon juice
- Zest of ½ lemon, grated
- A pinch of black pepper

Directions:
Heat up a pan with the oil over medium-high heat, add cauliflower rice and garlic, stir and cook for 5 minutes. Add lemon juice, lemon zest, thyme, salt and pepper, stir, cook for 2 minutes more, divide between plates and serve as a side dish.
Enjoy!

Nutrition: calories 130, fat 2, fiber 2, carbs 6, protein 8

Cranberry and Broccoli Mix

Preparation time: 10 minutes
Cooking time: 0 minutes
Servings: 4

Ingredients:
- ½ cup avocado mayonnaise
- 1 tablespoon apple cider vinegar
- 1 tablespoon lemon juice
- 1 tablespoon coconut sugar
- ¼ cup cranberries
- ½ cup almonds, sliced
- 9 ounces broccoli florets, separated

Directions:
In a bowl, mix broccoli with cranberries and almond slices and toss. In another bowl, mix coconut sugar with vinegar, mayo and lemon juice, whisk well, add to the broccoli mix, toss, divide between plates and serve as a side dish.
Enjoy!

Nutrition: calories 120, fat 1, fiber 3, carbs 7, protein 8

Three Beans Mix

Preparation time: 10 minutes
Cooking time: 0 minutes
Servings: 4

Ingredients:
- 15 ounces canned kidney beans, no-salt-added, drained and rinsed
- 15 ounces canned garbanzo beans, no-salt-added and drained
- 15 ounces canned pinto beans, no-salt- added and drained
- 3 tablespoons balsamic vinegar
- 2 tablespoons olive oil
- 2 teaspoon Italian seasoning
- 2 teaspoons garlic powder
- 1 teaspoon onion powder

Directions:
In a large salad bowl, combine the beans with vinegar, oil, seasoning, garlic powder and onion powder, toss, divide between plates and serve as a side dish.
Enjoy!

Nutrition: calories 140, fat 1, fiber 10, carbs 10, protein 7

Creamy Cucumber Mix

Preparation time: 10 minutes
Cooking time: 0 minutes
Servings: 2

Ingredients:
- 1 big cucumber, peeled and chopped
- 1 small red onion, chopped
- 4 tablespoons non-fat yogurt
- 1 teaspoon balsamic vinegar

Directions:
In a bowl, mix onion with cucumber, yogurt and vinegar, toss, divide between plates and serve as a side dish.
Enjoy!

Nutrition: calories 90, fat 1, fiber 3, carbs 7, protein 2

Bell Peppers Mix

Preparation time: 10 minutes
Cooking time: 10 minutes
Servings: 2

Ingredients:
- 1 tablespoon olive oil
- 2 teaspoons garlic powder
- 2 red bell peppers, chopped
- 2 yellow bell peppers, chopped
- 2 orange bell peppers, chopped
- Black pepper to the taste

Directions:
Heat up a pan with the oil over medium-high heat, add all the bell peppers, stir and cook for 5 minutes. Add garlic powder and black pepper, stir, cook for 5 minutes, divide between plates and serve as a side dish.
Enjoy!

Nutrition: calories 145, fat 3, fiber 5, carbs 5, protein 8

Sweet Potato Mash

Preparation time: 10 minutes
Cooking time: 1 hour
Servings: 6

Ingredients:
- ¼ cup olive oil
- 3 pounds sweet potatoes
- Black pepper to the taste

Directions:
Arrange the sweet potatoes on a lined baking sheet, introduce in the oven, bake at 375 degrees F for 1 hour, cool them down, peel, mash them and put them in a bowl. Add black pepper and the oil whisk well, divide between plates and serve as a side dish.
Enjoy!

Nutrition: calories 140, fat 1, fiber 4, carbs 6, protein 4

Bok Choy Mix

Preparation time: 10 minutes
Cooking time: 15 minutes
Servings: 4

Ingredients:
- 2 tablespoons olive oil
- 3 tablespoons coconut aminos
- 1-inch ginger, grated
- A pinch of red pepper flakes
- 4 bok choy heads, cut into quarters
- 2 garlic cloves, minced
- 1 tablespoon sesame seeds, toasted

Directions:
Heat up a pan with the olive oil over medium heat, add coconut aminos, garlic, pepper flakes and ginger, stir and cook for 3-4 minutes. Add the bok choy and the sesame seeds, toss, cook for 5 minutes more, divide between plates and serve as a side dish.
Enjoy!

Nutrition: calories 140, fat 2, fiber 2, carbs 4, protein 6

Flavored Turnips Mix

Preparation time: 10 minutes
Cooking time: 15 minutes
Servings: 4

Ingredients:

- 1 tablespoon lemon juice
- Zest of 2 oranges, grated
- 16 ounces turnips, sliced
- 3 tablespoons olive oil
- 1 tablespoon rosemary, chopped
- Black pepper to the taste

Directions:
Heat up a pan with the oil over medium-high heat, add turnips, stir and cook for 5 minutes. Add lemon juice, black pepper, orange zest and rosemary, stir, cook for 10 minutes more, divide between plates and serve as a side dish.
Enjoy!

Nutrition: calories 130, fat 1, fiber 2, carbs 8, protein 4

Lemony Fennel Mix

Preparation time: 10 minutes
Cooking time: 0 minutes
Servings: 4

Ingredients:

- 3 tablespoons lemon juice
- 1 pound fennel, chopped
- 2 tablespoons olive oil
- A pinch of black pepper

Directions:
In a salad bowl, mix fennel with and black pepper, oil and lemon juice, toss well, divide between plates and serve as a side dish.
Enjoy!

Nutrition: calories 130, fat 1, fiber 1, carbs 7, protein 7

Simple Cauliflower Mix

Preparation time: 10 minutes
Cooking time: 35 minutes
Servings: 4

Ingredients:
- 6 cups cauliflower florets
- 2 teaspoons sweet paprika
- 2 cups chicken stock
- ¼ cup avocado oil
- Black pepper to the taste

Directions:
In a baking dish, combine the cauliflower with stock, oil, black pepper and paprika, toss, introduce in the oven and bake at 375 degrees F for 35 minutes. Divide between plates and serve as a side dish.
Enjoy!

Nutrition: calories 180, fat 3, fiber 2, carbs 46, protein 6

Coconut Butternut Squash Mix

Preparation time: 10 minutes
Cooking time: 40 minutes
Servings: 4

Ingredients:
- 2 tablespoons coconut oil, melted
- 2 pounds butternut squash, peeled, seeded and cubed
- 2 teaspoons cilantro, chopped
- A pinch of black pepper

Directions
In a bowl, mix squash with oil, cilantro and pepper, toss to coat well, spread on a lined baking sheet, bake in the oven at 425 degrees F for 40 minutes, divide between plates and serve as a side dish.

Enjoy!

Nutrition: calories 170, fat 1, fiber 2, carbs 6, protein 6

Cinnamon Butternut Squash Mix

Preparation time: 10 minutes
Cooking time: 30 minutes
Servings: 4

Ingredients:
- ½ teaspoon cinnamon powder
- 2 tablespoons olive oil
- 2 apples, peeled, cored and cubed
- 1 and ½ pounds butternut squash, peeled, seeded and cubed

Directions:
In a baking dish, mix apples with squash, cinnamon and oil, toss to coat, bake in the oven at 350 degrees F for 30 minutes, divide between plates and serve as a side dish.
Enjoy!

Nutrition: calories 150, fat 2, fiber 2, carbs 8, protein 7

Walnuts Zucchini Spaghetti

Preparation time: 10 minutes
Cooking time: 10 minutes
Servings: 4

Ingredients:
- 1/3 cup olive oil
- 4 zucchinis, cut with a spiralizer
- ¼ cup basil, chopped
- Black pepper to the taste
- ½ cup walnuts, chopped
- 2 garlic cloves, minced

Directions:
Heat up a pan with the oil over medium-high heat, add zucchini spaghetti and garlic, stir and cook for 5 minutes. Add basil, walnuts and black pepper, stir, cook for 5 minutes more, divide between plates and serve as a side dish.
Enjoy!

Nutrition: calories 150, fat 2, fiber 4, carbs 7, protein 10

Bacon Cabbage Mix

Preparation time: 10 minutes
Cooking time: 20 minutes
Servings: 4

Ingredients:
- 1 green cabbage head, shredded
- 2 tablespoons water
- 6 ounces bacon, chopped
- A pinch of black pepper
- 1 teaspoon sweet paprika
- 1 tablespoon dill, chopped

Directions:
Heat up a pan over medium-high heat, add bacon and cook for 10 minutes. Add the cabbage, the water, black pepper, paprika and dill, toss, cook for 10 minutes, divide between plates and serve as a side dish.
Enjoy!

Nutrition: calories 140, fat 2, fiber 6, carbs 8, protein 6

Celery and Kale Mix

Preparation time: 10 minutes
Cooking time: 20 minutes
Servings: 4

Ingredients:
- 2 celery stalks, chopped
- 5 cups kale, torn
- 3 tablespoons water
- 1 tablespoon olive oil

Directions:
Heat up a pan with the oil over medium-high heat, add celery, stir and cook for 10 minutes. Add kale and water, toss, cook for 10 minutes more, divide between plates and serve as a side dish.
Enjoy!

Nutrition: calories 140, fat 1, fiber 2, carbs 6, protein 6

Kale and Red Chard Mix

Preparation time: 10 minutes
Cooking time: 10 minutes
Servings: 4

Ingredients:
- 5 cups kale, roughly chopped
- 1 and ½ tablespoons olive oil
- 3 cups red chard, chopped
- 2 tablespoons water
- Black pepper to the taste

Directions:
Heat up a pan with the oil over medium-high heat, add red chard, kale and water, stir and cook for 10 minutes. Add black pepper to the taste, toss, divide between plates and serve as a side dish.
Enjoy!

Nutrition: calories 150, fat 1, fiber 5, carbs 10, protein 7

Coconut Chard

Preparation time: 10 minutes
Cooking time: 10 minutes
Servings: 2

Ingredients:
- Juice of ½ lemon
- 1 tablespoon olive oil
- 12 ounces canned coconut milk
- 1 bunch chard
- Black pepper to the taste

Directions:
Heat up a pan with the oil over medium-high heat, add chard, stir and cook for 5 minutes. Add lemon juice, black pepper and coconut milk, stir, cook for 5 minutes more, divide between plates and serve as a side dish.
Enjoy!

Nutrition: calories 150, fat 3, fiber 4, carbs 6, protein 7

Cauliflower and Eggplant Mix

Preparation time: 10 minutes
Cooking time: 40 minutes
Servings: 4

Ingredients:

- 1 cauliflower head, florets separated
- 1 small eggplant, cubed
- 1 small red bell pepper, cubed
- 5 tablespoons olive oil
- 4 tablespoons lemon juice
- 1 teaspoon garlic powder
- Black pepper to the taste
- ½ teaspoon cumin powder

Directions:
Arrange eggplant, cauliflower and bell pepper pieces on a lined baking sheet, drizzle the oil, add lemon juice, garlic powder, black pepper and cumin, toss, introduce in the oven, bake at 400 degrees F for 40 minutes, divide between plates and serve as a side dish.
Enjoy!

Nutrition: calories 130, fat 1, fiber 3, carbs 7, protein 7

Artichoke Side Salad

Preparation time: 10 minutes
Cooing time: 0 minutes
Servings: 4

Ingredients:

- 4 ounces prosciutto, cut into strips
- 1 big romaine lettuce head, torn
- ½ cup artichoke hearts, roughly chopped
- ½ cup pickled hot peppers, chopped
- ½ cup black olives, pitted and chopped

For the dressing:

- 1 tablespoon parsley, chopped
- 1 garlic clove, minced
- 1 teaspoon oregano, dried
- Black pepper to the taste
- ¾ cup olive oil
- ¼ cup red wine vinegar

Directions:
In a bowl, mix parsley with garlic, oregano, black pepper, oil and vinegar and whisk well. In a salad bowl, mix prosciutto with romaine lettuce, artichoke hearts, hot peppers and olives, add the salad dressing, toss, divide between plates and serve as a side dish..
Enjoy!

Nutrition: calories 130, fat 1, fiber 2, carbs 7, protein 4

Dash Diet Snack Recipes

Chickpeas and Pepper Hummus

Preparation time: 10 minutes
Cooking time: 0 minutes
Servings: 4

Ingredients:

- 14 ounces canned chickpeas, no-salt-added, drained and rinsed
- 1 tablespoon sesame paste
- 2 roasted red peppers, chopped
- Juice of ½ lemon
- 4 walnuts, chopped

Directions:
In your blender, combine the chickpeas with the sesame paste, red peppers, lemon juice and walnuts, pulse well, divide into bowls and serve as a snack.
Enjoy!

Nutrition: calories 231, fat 12, fiber 6, carbs 15, protein 14

Lemony Chickpeas Dip

Preparation time: 10 minutes
Cooking time: 0 minutes
Servings: 4

Ingredients:

- 14 ounces canned chickpeas, drained, no-salt-added, rinsed
- Zest of 1 lemon, grated
- Juice of 1 lemon
- 1 tablespoon olive oil
- 4 tablespoons pine nuts
- ½ cup coriander, chopped

Directions:
In a blender, combine the chickpeas with lemon zest, lemon juice, coriander and oil, pulse well, divide into small bowls, sprinkle pine nuts on top and serve as a party dip.
Enjoy!

Nutrition: calories 200, fat 12, fiber 4, carbs 9, protein 7

Chili Nuts

Preparation time: 10 minutes
Cooking time: 10 minutes
Servings: 4

Ingredients:
- ½ teaspoon chili flakes
- 1 egg white
- ½ teaspoon curry powder
- ½ teaspoon ginger powder
- 4 tablespoons coconut sugar
- A pinch of cayenne pepper
- 14 ounces mixed nuts

Directions:
In a bowl, combine the egg white with the chili flakes, curry powder, curry powder, ginger powder, coconut sugar and cayenne and whisk well. Add the nuts, toss well, spread them on a lined baking sheet, introduce in the oven and bake at 400 degrees F for 10 minutes. Divide the nuts into bowls and serve as a snack.
Enjoy!

Nutrition: calories 234, fat 12, fiber 5, carbs 14, protein 7

Protein Bars

Preparation time: 10 minutes
Cooking time: 0 minutes
Servings: 4

Ingredients:
- 4 ounces apricots, dried
- 2 ounces water
- 2 tablespoons rolled oats
- 1 tablespoon sunflower seeds
- 2 tablespoons coconut, shredded
- 1 tablespoon sesame seeds
- 1 tablespoon cranberries
- 3 tablespoons hemp seeds
- 1 tablespoon chia seeds

Directions:
In your food processor, combine the apricots with the water and the oats, pulse well, transfer to a bowl, add coconut, sunflower seeds, sesame seeds, cranberries, hemp and chia seeds and stir until you obtain a paste. Roll this into a log, wrap, cool in the fridge, slice and serve as a snack.
Enjoy!

Nutrition: calories 100, fat 3, fiber 4, carbs 8, protein 5

Red Pepper Muffins

Preparation time: 10 minutes
Cooking time: 30 minutes
Servings: 12

Ingredients:
- 1 and ¾ cups whole wheat flour
- 2 teaspoons baking powder
- 2 tablespoons coconut sugar
- A pinch of black pepper
- 1 egg
- ¾ cup almond milk
- 2/3 cup roasted red pepper, chopped
- ½ cup low-fat mozzarella, shredded

Directions:
In a bowl, combine the flour with baking powder, coconut sugar, black pepper, egg, milk, red pepper and mozzarella, stir well, divide into a lined muffin tray, introduce in the oven and bake at 400 degrees F for 30 minutes. Serve as a snack.
Enjoy!

Nutrition: calories 149, fat 4, fiber 2, carbs 14, protein 5

Nuts and Seeds Mix

Preparation time: 10 minutes
Cooking time: 0 minutes
Servings: 6

Ingredients:
- 1 cup pecans
- 1 cup hazelnuts
- 1 cup almonds
- ¼ cup coconut, shredded
- 1 cup walnuts
- ½ cup papaya pieces, dried
- ½ cup dates, dried, pitted and chopped
- ½ cup sunflower seeds
- ½ cup pumpkin seeds
- 1 cup raisins

Directions:
In a bowl, combine the pecans with the hazelnuts, almonds, coconut, walnuts, papaya, dates, sunflower seeds, pumpkin seeds and raisins, toss and serve as a snack.
Enjoy!

Nutrition: calories 188, fat 4, fiber 6, carbs 8, protein 6

Tortilla Chips

Preparation time: 10 minutes
Cooking time: 25 minutes
Servings: 6

Ingredients:

- 12 whole wheat tortillas, cut into 6 wedges each
- 2 tablespoons olive oil
- 1 tablespoon chili powder
- A pinch of cayenne pepper

Directions:
Spread the tortillas on a lined baking sheet, add the oil, chili powder and cayenne, toss, introduce in the oven and bake at 350 degrees F for 25 minutes. Divide into bowls and serve as a side dish. Enjoy!

Nutrition: calories 199, fat 3, fiber 4, carbs 12, protein 5

Kale Chips

Preparation time: 10 minutes
Cooking time: 15 minutes
Servings: 8

Ingredients:

- 1 bunch kale leaves
- 1 tablespoon olive oil
- 1 teaspoon smoked paprika
- A pinch of black pepper

Directions:
Spread the kale leaves on a baking sheet, add black pepper, oil and paprika, toss, introduce in the oven and bake at 350 degrees F for 15 minutes. Divide into bowls and serve as a snack. Enjoy!

Nutrition: calories 177, fat 2, fiber 4, carbs 13, protein 6

Potato Chips

Preparation time: 10 minutes
Cooking time: 30 minutes
Servings: 6

Ingredients:
- 2 gold potatoes, cut into thin rounds
- 1 tablespoon olive oil
- 2 teaspoons garlic, minced

Directions:
In a bowl, combine the potato chips with the oil and the garlic, toss, spread on a lined baking sheet, introduce in the oven and bake at 400 degrees F for 30 minutes. Divide into bowls and serve.
Enjoy!

Nutrition: calories 200, fat 3, fiber 5, carbs 13, protein 6

Peach Dip

Preparation time: 10 minutes
Cooking time: 0 minutes
Servings: 2

Ingredients:
- ½ cup nonfat yogurt
- 1 cup peaches, chopped
- A pinch of cinnamon powder
- A pinch of nutmeg, ground

Directions:
In a bowl, combine the yogurt with the peaches, cinnamon and nutmeg, whisk, divide into small bowls and serve as a snack.
Enjoy!

Nutrition: calories 165, fat 2, fiber 3, carbs 14, protein 13

Cereal Mix

Preparation time: 10 minutes
Cooking time: 40 minutes
Servings: 6

Ingredients:
- 3 tablespoons olive oil
- 1 teaspoon hot sauce
- ½ teaspoon garlic powder
- ½ teaspoon onion powder
- ½ teaspoon cumin, ground
- A pinch of cayenne pepper
- 3 cups rice cereal squares
- 1 cup cornflakes
- ½ cup pepitas

Directions:
In a bowl, combine the oil with the hot sauce, garlic powder, onion powder, cumin, cayenne, rice cereal, cornflakes and pepitas, toss, spread on a lined baking sheet, introduce in the oven and bake at 350 degrees F for 40 minutes. Divide into bowls and serve as a snack.
Enjoy!

Nutrition: calories 199, fat 3, fiber 4, carbs 12, protein 5

Goji Berry Mix

Preparation time: 10 minutes
Cooking time: 0 minutes
Servings: 4

Ingredients:
- 1 cup almonds
- 1 cup goji berries
- ½ cup sunflower seeds
- ½ cup pumpkin seeds
- ½ cup walnuts, halved
- 12 apricots, dried and quartered

Directions:
In a bowl, combine the almond with the goji berries, sunflower seeds, pumpkin seeds, walnuts and apricots, toss, divide into bowls and serve.
Enjoy!

Nutrition: calories 187, fat 2, fiber 5, carbs 12, protein 6

Artichoke Spread

Preparation time: 10 minutes
Cooking time: 15 minutes
Servings: 4

Ingredients:

- 10 ounces spinach, chopped
- 12 ounces canned artichoke hearts, no-salt-added, drained and chopped
- 1 cup coconut cream
- 1 cup low-fat cheddar, shredded
- A pinch of black pepper

Directions:
In a bowl, combine the spinach with the artichokes, cream, cheese and black pepper, stir well, transfer to a baking dish, introduce in the oven and bake at 400 degrees F for 15 minutes. Divide into bowls and serve.
Enjoy!

Nutrition: calories 200, fat 4, fiber 6, carbs 14, protein 8

Avocado Salsa

Preparation time: 10 minutes
Cooking time: 0 minutes
Servings: 4

Ingredients:

- 1 small yellow onion, minced
- 1 jalapeno, minced
- ¼ cup cilantro, chopped
- A pinch of black pepper
- 2 avocados, peeled, pitted and cubed
- 2 tablespoons lime juice

Directions:
In a bowl, combine the onion with the jalapeno, cilantro, black pepper, avocado and limejuice, toss and serve.
Enjoy!

Nutrition: calories 198, fat 2, fiber 5, carbs 14, protein 7

Onion Spread

Preparation time: 10 minutes
Cooking time: 35 minutes
Servings: 4

Ingredients:
- 2 tablespoons olive oil
- 2 yellow onions, sliced
- A pinch of black pepper
- 8 ounces low-fat cream cheese
- 1 cup coconut cream
- 2 tablespoons chives, chopped

Directions:
Heat up a pan with the oil over low heat, add the onions and the black pepper, stir and cook for 35 minutes. In a bowl, combine the onions with the cream cheese, coconut cream and chives, stir well and serve as a party spread.
Enjoy!

Nutrition: calories 212, fat 3, fiber 5, carbs 14, protein 8

Simple Salsa

Preparation time: 10 minutes
Cooking time: 0 minutes
Servings: 6

Ingredients:
- 1 yellow bell pepper, cubed
- 2 tomatoes, cubed
- 1 cucumber, cubed
- 1 small red onion, cubed
- 1 tablespoon olive oil
- 1 tablespoon red vinegar

Directions:
In a bowl, combine the bell pepper with the tomatoes, cucumber, onion, oil and vinegar, toss, divide into small cups and serve.
Enjoy!

Nutrition: calories 142, fat 4, fiber 4, carbs 6, protein 7

Spinach Dip

Preparation time: 10 minutes
Cooking time: 0 minutes
Servings: 4

Ingredients:
- 1 tablespoon olive oil
- 10 ounces spinach
- 1 and ½ cups canned chickpeas, no-salt-added, drained and rinsed

Directions:
In your blender, combine the chickpeas with the oil and the spinach, pulse well, divide into bowls and serve.
Enjoy!

Nutrition: calories 200, fat 3, fiber 5, carbs 14, protein 6

Avocado Dip

Preparation time: 10 minutes
Cooking time: 0 minutes
Servings: 8

Ingredients:
- 4 avocados, peeled and pitted
- 1 cup cilantro leaves
- ½ cup coconut cream
- 1 jalapeno, chopped
- ¼ cup lime juice
- A pinch of black pepper

Directions:
In your blender, combine the avocados with the cilantro, coconut cream, jalapeno, limejuice and black pepper, pulse well, divide into bowls and serve.
Enjoy!

Nutrition: calories 187, fat 3, fiber 7, carbs 17, protein 8

Chives Dip

Preparation time: 10 minutes
Cooking time: 0 minutes
Servings: 4

Ingredients:

- 2 tablespoons chives, chopped
- 1 shallot, minced
- 1 tablespoon lemon juice
- A pinch of black pepper
- 2 ounces low-fat cheese, shredded
- 1 cup coconut cream

Directions:
In a bowl, combine the chives with the shallot, lemon juice, black pepper, and cheese and coconut cream, whisk well and serve as a party dip.
Enjoy!

Nutrition: calories 211, fat 3, fiber 5, carbs 15, protein 6

Dill Dip

Preparation time: 10 minutes
Cooking time: 0 minutes
Servings: 6

Ingredients:

- 8 ounces coconut cream
- ¼ cup horseradish
- 2 tablespoons dill
- A pinch of black pepper

Directions:
In a bowl, combine the cream with the horseradish, dill and black pepper, stir really well and serve as a party dip.
Enjoy!

Nutrition: calories 181, fat 3, fiber 7, carbs 16, protein 7

Chickpeas Salsa

Preparation time: 10 minutes
Cooking time: 0 minutes
Servings: 6

Ingredients:

- 15 ounces canned chickpeas, no-salt-added, drained and rinsed
- 4 scallions, chopped
- 2 roasted red peppers, chopped
- 1 cup baby arugula leaves
- 2 tablespoons lemon juice
- 2 tablespoons olive oil
- A pinch of black pepper

Directions:
In a bowl, combine the chickpeas with the scallions, red peppers, arugula, lemon juice, oil and black pepper, toss, divide into small bowls and serve.
Enjoy!

Nutrition: calories 189, fat 3, fiber 6, carbs 14, protein 6

Cilantro Dip

Preparation time: 10 minutes
Cooking time: 0 minutes
Servings: 6

Ingredients:

- 2 bunches cilantro leaves
- ½ cup ginger, sliced
- 3 tablespoons balsamic vinegar
- ½ cup olive oil
- 2 tablespoons coconut aminos
- 2 teaspoons sesame oil

Directions:
In your blender, combine the cilantro with the ginger, vinegar, oil, aminos and sesame oil, pulse well, and divide into small cups and serve.
Enjoy!

Nutrition: calories 188, fat 4, fiber 6, carbs 7, protein 8

Yogurt and Dill Dip

Preparation time: 10 minutes
Cooking time: 0 minutes
Servings: 4

Ingredients:
- 2 cup non-fat yogurt
- 1 garlic clove, minced
- ¼ cup walnuts, chopped
- ¼ cup dill, chopped

Directions:
In a bowl, combine the yogurt with the garlic, walnuts and dill, stir well and serve cold.
Enjoy!

Nutrition: calories 181, fat 2, fiber 6, carbs 11, protein 7

Broccoli Dip

Preparation time: 10 minutes
Cooking time: 0 minutes
Servings: 4

Ingredients:
- 14 ounces broccoli florets
- 1 cup low-fat cottage cheese
- A pinch of black pepper

Directions:
In your food processor, combine the broccoli with the cheese and black pepper, pulse well, divide into small cups and serve.
Enjoy!

Nutrition: calories 189, fat 4, fiber 6, carbs 15, protein 7

Easy Salmon Spread

Preparation time: 10 minutes
Cooking time: 0 minutes
Servings: 4

Ingredients:
- 2 tablespoons horseradish
- 8 ounces low-fat cream cheese
- 2 tablespoons dill, chopped
- ¼ pound smoked salmon, chopped
- A pinch of black pepper

Directions:
In a bowl, combine the horseradish with the cream cheese, dill, salmon and black pepper, stir well and serve as a party spread.
Enjoy!

Nutrition: calories 212, fat 3, fiber 6, carbs 14, protein 7

Turkey Wraps

Preparation time: 10 minutes
Cooking time: 0 minutes
Servings: 2

Ingredients:
- 1 peach, cut into 8 wedges
- 3 ounces turkey breast, cooked and cut into 8 pieces

Directions:
Roll 2 peach wedges in 2 slices of turkey, wrap, secure with a toothpick, repeat with the rest of the peach wedges and turkey and serve as a snack.
Enjoy!

Nutrition: calories 200, fat 2, fiber 5, carbs 13, protein 9

Plantain Chips

Preparation time: 10 minutes
Cooking time: 10 minutes
Servings: 4

Ingredients:

- 4 green plantains, peeled and thinly sliced
- 4 cups coconut oil, melted
- A pinch of red pepper flakes

Directions:
Heat up a pan with the coconut oil over medium-high heat, add plantain chips, sprinkle pepper flakes, fry them for 5 minutes on each side, transfer to paper towels, drain grease, divide into bowls and serve as a snack.
    Enjoy!

Nutrition: calories 180, fat 3, fiber 3, carbs 8, protein 12

Green Beans Snack

Preparation time: 10 minutes
Cooking time: 16 minutes
Servings: 8

Ingredients:

- 1/3 cup coconut oil, melted
- 5 pounds green beans
- 1 teaspoon garlic powder
- 1 teaspoon onion powder

Directions:
In a bowl, mix green beans with coconut oil, garlic and onion powder, toss to coat very well, spread on a lined baking sheet, introduce in the oven and bake at 425 degrees F for 16 minutes. Serve cold as a snack.
Enjoy!

Nutrition: calories 120, fat 3, fiber 4, carbs 7, protein 7

Dates Snack

Preparation time: 10 minutes
Cooking time: 0 minutes
Servings: 2

Ingredients:
- 4 medjol dates, cut on one side
- 6 pistachios, raw and chopped
- 1 teaspoon coconut, shredded

Directions:
In a bowl, mix chopped pistachios with coconut, stir, stuff the dates with this, divide into bowls and serve.
Enjoy!

Nutrition: calories 100, fat 1, fiber 2, carbs 2, protein 6

Baby Spinach Snack

Preparation time: 10 minutes
Cooking time: 10 minutes
Servings: 3

Ingredients:
- 2 cups baby spinach, washed
- A pinch of black pepper
- ½ tablespoon olive oil
- ½ teaspoon garlic powder

Directions:
Spread the baby spinach on a lined baking sheet, add oil, black pepper and garlic powder, toss a bit, introduce in the oven, bake at 350 degrees F for 10 minutes, divide into bowls and serve as a snack.
Enjoy!

Nutrition: calories 125, fat 4, fiber 1, carbs 4, protein 2

Potato Bites

Preparation time: 10 minutes
Cooking time: 20 minutes
Servings: 3

Ingredients:
- 1 potato, sliced
- 2 bacon slices, already cooked and crumbled
- 1 small avocado, pitted and cubed
-
- Cooking spray

Directions:
Spread potato slices on a lined baking sheet, spray with cooking oil, introduce in the oven at 350 degrees F, bake for 20 minutes, arrange on a platter, top each slice with avocado and crumbled bacon and serve as a snack.
Enjoy!

Nutrition: calories 180, fat 4, fiber 1, carbs 8, protein 6

Sesame Dip

Preparation time: 10 minutes
Cooking time: 0 minutes
Servings: 6

Ingredients:
- 1 cup sesame seed paste, pure
- Black pepper to the taste
- 1 cup veggie stock
- ½ cup lemon juice
- ½ teaspoon cumin, ground
- 3 garlic cloves, chopped

Directions:
In your food processor, mix the sesame paste with black pepper, stock, lemon juice, cumin and garlic, pulse very well, divide into bowls and serve as a party dip.
Enjoy!

Nutrition: calories 120, fat 12, fiber 2, carbs 7, protein 4

Rosemary Squash Dip

Preparation time: 10 minutes
Cooking time: 40 minutes
Servings: 4

Ingredients:
- 1 cup butternut squash, peeled and cubed
- 1 tablespoon water
- Cooking spray
- 2 tablespoons coconut milk
- 2 teaspoons rosemary, dried
- Black pepper to the taste

Directions:
Spread squash cubes on a lined baking sheet, spray some cooking oil, introduce in the oven, bake at 365 degrees F for 40 minutes, transfer to your blender, add water, milk, rosemary and black pepper, pulse well, divide into small bowls and serve
Enjoy!

Nutrition: calories 182, fat 5, fiber 7, carbs 12, protein 5

Bean Spread

Preparation time: 10 minutes
Cooking time: 7 hours
Servings: 4

Ingredients:
- 1 cup white beans, dried
- 1 teaspoon apple cider vinegar
- 1 cup veggie stock
- 1 tablespoon water

Directions:
In your slow cooker, mix beans with stock, stir, cover, cook on Low for 6 hours, drain, transfer to your food processor, add vinegar and water, pulse well, divide into bowls and serve.
Enjoy!

Nutrition: calories 181, fat 6, fiber 5, carbs 9, protein 7

Eggplant Salsa

Preparation time: 10 minutes
Cooking time: 10 minutes
Servings: 4

Ingredients:

- 1 and ½ cups tomatoes, chopped
- 3 cups eggplant, cubed
- A drizzle of olive oil
- 2 teaspoons capers
- 6 ounces green olives, pitted and sliced
- 4 garlic cloves, minced
- 2 teaspoons balsamic vinegar
- 1 tablespoon basil, chopped
- Black pepper to the taste

Directions:
Heat up a pan with the oil over medium-high heat, add eggplant, stir and cook for 5 minutes. Add tomatoes, capers, olives, garlic, vinegar, basil and black pepper, toss, cook for 5 minutes more, divide into small cups and serve cold.
Enjoy!

Nutrition: calories 120, fat 6, fiber 5, carbs 9, protein 7

Carrots and Cauliflower Spread

Preparation time: 10 minutes
Cooking time: 40 minutes
Servings: 4

Ingredients:

- 1 cup carrots, sliced
- 2 cups cauliflower florets
- ½ cup cashews
- 2 and ½ cups water
- 1 cup almond milk
- 1 teaspoon garlic powder
- ¼ teaspoon smoked paprika

Directions:
In a small pot, mix the carrots with cauliflower, cashews and water, stir, cover, bring to a boil over medium heat, cook for 40 minutes, drain and transfer to a blender. Add almond milk, garlic powder and paprika, pulse well, divide into small bowls and serve
Enjoy!

Nutrition: calories 201, fat 7, fiber 4, carbs 7, protein 7

Italian Veggie Salsa

Preparation time: 10 minutes
Cooking time: 10 minutes
Servings: 4

Ingredients:

- 2 red bell peppers, cut into medium wedges
- 3 zucchinis, sliced
- ½ cup garlic, minced
- 2 tablespoons olive oil
- A pinch of black pepper
- 1 teaspoon Italian seasoning

Directions:
Heat up a pan with the oil over medium-high heat, add bell peppers and zucchini, toss and cook for 5 minutes. Add garlic, black pepper and Italian seasoning, toss, cook for 5 minutes more, divide into small cups and serve as a snack.
Enjoy!

Nutrition: calories 132, fat 3, fiber 3, carbs 7, protein 4

Black Bean Salsa

Preparation time: 10 minutes
Cooking time: 0 minutes
Servings: 6

Ingredients:

- 1 tablespoon coconut aminos
- ½ teaspoon cumin, ground
- 1 cup canned black beans, no-salt-added, drained and rinsed
- 1 cup salsa
- 6 cups romaine lettuce leaves, torn
- ½ cup avocado, peeled, pitted and cubed

Directions:
In a bowl, combine the beans with the aminos, cumin, salsa, lettuce and avocado, toss, divide into small bowls and serve as a snack.
Enjoy!

Nutrition: calories 181, fat 4, fiber 7, carbs 14, protein 7

Corn Spread

Preparation time: 10 minutes
Cooking time: 10 minutes
Servings: 6

Ingredients:
- 30 ounces canned corn, drained
- 2 green onions, chopped
- ½ cup coconut cream
- 1 jalapeno, chopped
- ½ teaspoon chili powder

Directions:
In a small pan, combine the corn with green onions, jalapeno and chili powder, stir, bring to a simmer, cook over medium heat for 10 minutes, leave aside to cool down, add coconut cream, stir well, divide into small bowls and serve as a spread.
Enjoy!

Nutrition: calories 192, fat 5, fiber 10, carbs 11, protein 8

Mushroom Dip

Preparation time: 10 minutes
Cooking time: 20 minutes
Servings: 6

Ingredients:
- 1 cup yellow onion, chopped
- 3 garlic cloves, minced
- 1 pound mushrooms, chopped
-
- 28 ounces tomato sauce, no-salt-added
- Black pepper to the taste

Directions:
Put the onion in a pot, add garlic, mushrooms, black pepper and tomato sauce, stir, cook over medium heat for 20 minutes, leave aside to cool down, divide into small bowls and serve.
Enjoy!

Nutrition: calories 215, fat 4, fiber 7, carbs 3, protein 7

Salsa Bean Dip

Preparation time: 10 minutes
Cooking time: 20 minutes
Servings: 6

Ingredients:
- ½ cup salsa
- 2 cups canned white beans, no-salt-added, drained and rinsed
- 1 cup low-fat cheddar, shredded
- 2 tablespoons green onions, chopped

Directions:
In a small pot, combine the beans with the green onions and salsa, stir, bring to a simmer over medium heat, cook for 20 minutes, add cheese, stir until it melts, take off heat, leave aside to cool down, divide into bowls and serve.
Enjoy!

Nutrition: calories 212, fat 5, fiber 6, carbs 10, protein 8

Mung Sprouts Salsa

Preparation time: 10 minutes
Cooking time: 0 minutes
Servings: 2

Ingredients:
- 1 red onion, chopped
- 2 cups mung beans, sprouted
- A pinch of red chili powder
- 1 green chili pepper, chopped
- 1 tomato, chopped
- 1 teaspoon chaat masala
- 1 teaspoon lemon juice
- 1 tablespoon coriander, chopped
- Black pepper to the taste

Directions:
In a salad bowl, mix onion with mung sprouts, chili pepper, tomato, chili powder, chaat masala, lemon juice, coriander and pepper, toss well, divide into small cups and serve.
Enjoy!

Nutrition: calories 100, fat 2, fiber 1, carbs 3, protein 6

Mung Beans Snack Salad

Preparation time: 10 minutes
Cooking time: 0 minutes
Servings: 6

Ingredients:

- 2 cups tomatoes, chopped
- 2 cups cucumber, chopped
- 3 cups mixed greens
- 2 cups mung beans, sprouted
- 2 cups clover sprouts

For the salad dressing:

- 1 tablespoon cumin, ground

- 1 cup dill, chopped
- 4 tablespoons lemon juice
- 1 avocado, pitted, peeled and roughly chopped
- 1 cucumber, roughly chopped

Directions:

In a salad bowl, mix tomatoes with 2 cups cucumber, greens, clover and mung sprouts. In your blender, mix cumin with dill, lemon juice, 1 cucumber and avocado, blend really well, add this to your salad, toss well and serve as a snack
Enjoy!

Nutrition: calories 120, fat 0, fiber 2, carbs 1, protein 6

Sprouts and Apples Snack Salad

Preparation time: 10 minutes
Cooking time: 0 minutes
Servings: 4

Ingredients:

- 1 pound Brussels sprouts, shredded
- 1 cup walnuts, chopped
- 1 apple, cored and cubed
- 1 red onion, chopped

For the salad dressing:

- 3 tablespoons red vinegar

- 1 tablespoon mustard
- ½ cup olive oil
- 1 garlic clove, minced
- Black pepper to the taste

Directions:

In a salad bowl, mix sprouts with apple, onion and walnuts. In another bowl, mix vinegar with mustard, oil, garlic and pepper, whisk really well, add this to your salad, toss well and serve as a snack.
Enjoy!

Nutrition: calories 120, fat 2, fiber 2, carbs 8, protein 6

Moroccan Leeks Snack Salad

Preparation time: 10 minutes
Cooking time: 0 minutes
Servings: 4

Ingredients:

- 1 bunch radishes, sliced
- 3 cups leeks, chopped
- 1 and ½ cups olives, pitted and sliced
- A pinch of turmeric powder
- Black pepper to the taste
- 2 tablespoons olive oil
- 1 cup cilantro, chopped

Directions:
In a bowl, mix radishes with leeks, olives and cilantro. Add black pepper, oil and turmeric, toss to coat and serve as a snack.
Enjoy!

Nutrition: calories 120, fat 1, fiber 1, carbs 8, protein 6

Celery and Raisins Snack Salad

Preparation time: 10 minutes
Cooking time: 0 minutes
Servings: 4

Ingredients:

- ½ cup raisins
- 4 cups celery, sliced
- ¼ cup parsley, chopped
- ½ cup walnuts, chopped
- Juice of ½ lemon
- 2 tablespoons olive oil
- Salt and black pepper to the taste

Directions:
In a salad bowl, mix celery with raisins, walnuts, parsley, lemon juice, oil and black pepper, toss, divide into small cups and serve as a snack.
Enjoy!

Nutrition: calories 120, fat 1, fiber 2, carbs 6, protein 5

Dijon Celery Salad

Preparation time: 10 minutes
Cooking time: 0 minutes
Servings: 4

Ingredients:
- 5 teaspoons stevia
- ½ cup lemon juice
- 1/3 cup Dijon mustard
- 2/3 cup olive oil
- Black pepper to the taste
- 2 apples, cored, peeled and cubed
- 1 bunch celery and leaves, roughly chopped
- ¾ cup walnuts, chopped

Directions:
In a salad bowl, mix celery and its leaves with apple pieces and walnuts. Add black pepper, lemon juice, mustard, stevia and olive oil, whisk well, add to your salad, toss, divide into small cups and serve as a snack.
Enjoy!

Nutrition: calories 125, fat 2, fiber 2, carbs 7, protein 7

Napa Cabbage Slaw

Preparation time: 10 minutes
Cooking time: 0 minutes
Servings: 4

Ingredients:
- ½ cup red bell pepper, cut into thin strips
- 1 carrot, grated
- 4 cups napa cabbage, shredded
- 3 green onions, chopped
- 1 tablespoon olive oil
- 2 teaspoons ginger, grated
- ½ teaspoon red pepper flakes, crushed
- 3 tablespoons balsamic vinegar
- 1 tablespoon coconut aminos
- 3 tablespoons low-fat peanut butter

Directions:
In a salad bowl, mix bell pepper with carrot, cabbage and onions and toss. Add oil, ginger, pepper flakes, vinegar, aminos and peanut butter, toss, divide into small cups and serve.
Enjoy!

Nutrition: calories 160, fat 10, fiber 3, carbs 10, protein 5

Dill Bell Pepper Snack Bowls

Preparation time: 10 minutes
Cooking time: 0 minutes
Servings: 4

Ingredients:

- 2 tablespoons dill, chopped
- 1 yellow onion, chopped
- 1 pound multi colored bell peppers, cut into halves, seeded and cut into thin strips
- 3 tablespoons olive oil
- 2 and ½ tablespoons white vinegar
- Black pepper to the taste

Directions:
In a salad bowl, mix bell peppers with onion, dill, pepper, oil and vinegar, toss to coat, divide into small bowls and serve as a snack.
Enjoy!

Nutrition: calories 120, fat 3, fiber 4, carbs 2, protein 3

Bulgur Appetizer Salad

Preparation time: 30 minutes
Cooking time: 0 minutes
Servings: 4

Ingredients:

- 1 cup bulgur
- 2 cups hot water
- Black pepper to the taste
- 2 cups corn
- 1 cucumber, chopped
- 2 tablespoons lemon juice
- 2 tablespoons balsamic vinegar
- ¼ cup olive oil

Directions:
In a bowl, mix bulgur with the water, cover, leave aside for 30 minutes, fluff with a fork and transfer to a salad bowl. Add corn, cucumber, oil with lemon juice, vinegar and pepper, toss, divide into small cups and serve.
Enjoy!

Nutrition: calories 130, fat 2, fiber 2, carbs 7, protein 6

Cocoa Bars

Preparation time: 2 hours
Cooking time: 0 minutes
Servings: 12

Ingredients:
- 1 cup unsweetened cocoa chips
- 2 cups rolled oats
- 1 cup low-fat peanut butter
- ½ cup chia seeds
- ½ cup raisins
- ¼ cup coconut sugar
- ½ cup coconut milk

Directions:
Put 1 and ½ cups oats in your blender, pulse well, transfer this to a bowl, add the rest of the oats, cocoa chips, chia seeds, raisins, sugar and milk, stir really well, spread this into a square pan, press well, keep in the fridge for 2 hours, slice into 12 bars and serve.
Enjoy!

Nutrition: calories 198, fat 5, fiber 4, carbs 10, protein 89

Cinnamon Apple Chips

Preparation time: 10 minutes
Cooking time: 2 hours
Servings: 4

Ingredients:
- Cooking spray
- 2 teaspoons cinnamon powder
- 2 apples, cored and thinly sliced

Directions:
Arrange apple slice on a lined baking sheet, spray them with cooking oil, sprinkle cinnamon, introduce in the oven and bake at 300 degrees F for 2 hours. Divide into bowls and serve as a snack.
Enjoy!

Nutrition: calories 80, fat 0, fiber 3, carbs 7, protein 4

Greek Party Dip

Preparation time: 10 minutes
Cooking time: 0 minutes
Servings: 4

Ingredients:

- ½ cup coconut cream
- 1 cup fat-free Greek yogurt
- 2 teaspoons dill, dried
- 2 teaspoons thyme, dried
- 1 teaspoon sweet paprika
- 2 teaspoons no-salt-added sun-dried tomatoes, chopped
- 2 teaspoons parsley, chopped
- 2 teaspoons chives, chopped
- Black pepper to the taste

Directions:
In a bowl, mix cream with yogurt, dill with thyme, paprika, tomatoes, parsley, chives and pepper, stir well, divide into smaller bowls and serve as a dip.
Enjoy!

Nutrition: calories 100, fat 1, fiber 4, carbs 8, protein 3

Spicy Pumpkin Seeds Bowls

Preparation time: 10 minutes
Cooking time: 20 minutes
Servings: 6

Ingredients:

- ½ tablespoon chili powder
- ½ teaspoon cayenne pepper
- 2 cups pumpkin seeds
- 2 teaspoons lime juice

Directions:
Spread pumpkin seeds on a lined baking sheet, add limejuice, cayenne and chili powder, toss well, introduce in the oven, roast at 275 degrees F for 20 minutes, divide into small bowls and serve as a snack.
Enjoy!

Nutrition: calories 170, fat 2, fiber 7, carbs 12, protein 6

Apple and Pecans Bowls

Preparation time: 10 minutes
Cooking time: 0 minutes
Servings: 4

Ingredients:
- 4 big apples, cored, peeled and cubed
- 2 teaspoons lemon juice
- ¼ cup pecans, chopped

Directions:
In a bowl, mix apples with lemon juice and pecans, toss, divide into small bowls and serve as a snack.
Enjoy!

Nutrition: calories 120, fat 4, fiber 3, carbs 12, protein 3

Shrimp Muffins

Preparation time: 10 minutes
Cooking time: 45 minutes
Servings: 6

Ingredients:
- 1 spaghetti squash, peeled and halved
- 2 tablespoons avocado mayonnaise
- 1 cup low-fat mozzarella cheese, shredded
- 8 ounces shrimp, peeled, cooked and chopped
- 1 and ½ cups almond flour
- 1 teaspoon parsley, dried
- 1 garlic clove, minced
- Black pepper to the taste
- Cooking spray

Directions:
Arrange the squash on a lined baking sheet, introduce in the oven at 375 degrees F, bake for 30 minutes, scrape flesh into a bowl, add pepper, parsley flakes, flour, shrimp, mayo and mozzarella and stir well, divide this mix into a muffin tray greased with cooking spray, bake in the oven at 375 degrees F for 15 minutes and serve them cold as a snack.
Enjoy!

Nutrition: calories 140, fat 2, fiber 4, carbs 14, protein 12

Zucchini Bowls

Preparation time: 10 minutes
Cooking time: 20 minutes
Servings: 12

Ingredients:

- Cooking spray
- ½ cup dill, chopped
- 1 egg
- ½ cup whole wheat flour
- Black pepper to the taste
- 1 yellow onion, chopped
- 2 garlic cloves, minced
- 3 zucchinis, grated

Directions:
In a bowl, mix zucchinis with garlic, onion, flour, pepper, egg and dill, stir well, shape small bowls out of this mix, arrange them on a lined baking sheet, grease them with some cooking spray, bake at 400 degrees F for 20 minutes, flipping them halfway, divide them into bowls and serve as a snack.
Enjoy!

Nutrition: calories 120, fat 1, fiber 4, carbs 12, protein 6

Cheesy Mushrooms Caps

Preparation time: 10 minutes
Cooking time: 30 minutes
Servings: 20

Ingredients:

- 20 white mushroom caps
- 1 garlic clove, minced
- 3 tablespoons parsley, chopped
- 2 yellow onions, chopped
- Black pepper to the taste
- ½ cup low-fat parmesan, grated
- ¼ cup low-fat mozzarella, grated
- A drizzle of olive oil
- 2 tablespoons non-fat yogurt

Directions:
Heat up a pan with some oil over medium heat, add garlic and onion, stir, cook for 10 minutes and transfer to a bowl. Add black pepper, garlic, parsley, mozzarella, parmesan and yogurt, stir well, stuff the mushroom caps with this mix, arrange them on a lined baking sheet, bake in the oven at 400 degrees F for 20 minutes and serve them as an appetizer.
Enjoy!

Nutrition: calories 120, fat 1, fiber 3, carbs 11, protein 7

Mozzarella Cauliflower Bars

Preparation time: 10 minutes
Cooking time: 40 minutes
Servings: 12

Ingredients:

- 1 big cauliflower head, riced
- ½ cup low-fat mozzarella cheese, shredded
- ¼ cup egg whites
- 1 teaspoon Italian seasoning
- Black pepper to the taste

Directions:
Spread the cauliflower rice on a lined baking sheet, cook in the oven at 375 degrees F for 20 minutes, transfer to a bowl, add black pepper, cheese, seasoning and egg whites, stir well, spread into a rectangle pan and press well on the bottom. Introduce in the oven at 375 degrees F, bake for 20 minutes, cut into 12 bars and serve as a snack.
Enjoy!

Nutrition: calories 140, fat 1, fiber 3, carbs 6, protein 6

Shrimp and Pineapple Salsa

Preparation time: 10 minutes
Cooking time: 40 minutes
Servings: 4

Ingredients:

- 1 pound large shrimp, peeled and deveined
- 20 ounces canned pineapple chunks
- 1 tablespoon garlic powder
- 1 cup red bell peppers, chopped
- Black pepper to the taste

Directions:
Place shrimp in a baking dish, add pineapple, garlic, bell peppers and black pepper, toss a bit, introduce in the oven, bake at 375 degrees F for 40 minutes, divide into small bowls and serve cold.
Enjoy!

Nutrition: calories 170, fat 5, fiber 4, carbs 14, protein 12

Dash Diet Poultry Recipes

Easy Chicken Skillet

Preparation time: 10 minutes
Cooking time: 20 minutes
Servings: 4

Ingredients:

- 2 tablespoons olive oil
- 4 chicken breasts, skinless and boneless
- A pinch of black pepper
- 2 tablespoons low-fat butter
- ½ teaspoon oregano, dried
- 3 garlic cloves, minced
- 2 cups baby spinach
- 14 ounces canned artichokes, no-salt-added, chopped
- ½ cup roasted red peppers, chopped
- 1 cup coconut cream
- ¾ cup low-fat mozzarella, shredded
- ¼ cup low-fat parmesan, grated

Directions:

Heat up a pan with the oil over medium-high heat, add chicken, season with black pepper and oregano, and cook for 6 minutes on each side and transfer to a bowl. Heat up the same pan with the butter over medium-high heat, add garlic, spinach, artichokes and red peppers, stir and cook for 3 minutes more. Return chicken breasts, also add mozzarella, parmesan and coconut cream, and toss, bring to a simmer, cook for 5 minutes more, divide into bowls and serve.
Enjoy!

Nutrition: calories 211, fat 4, fiber 5, carbs 14, protein 11

Chicken and Onion Mix

Preparation time: 10 minutes
Cooking time: 45 minutes
Servings: 4

Ingredients:

- 3 tablespoons olive oil
- 1 yellow onion, roughly chopped
- 2 teaspoons thyme, chopped
- 2 garlic cloves, minced
- A pinch of black pepper
- 4 chicken breasts, skinless, boneless and cubed
- ½ teaspoon oregano, dried
- 1 and ½ cup low-sodium beef stock
- 1 tablespoon parsley, chopped

Directions:

Heat up a pan with 2 tablespoons olive oil over medium-low heat, add the onion, black pepper and thyme, toss and cook for 24 minutes. Add garlic, cook for 1 more minute and transfer to a bowl. Clean the pan, heat it up with the rest of the oil over medium-high heat, add chicken, black pepper, and oregano, stir and cook for 8 minutes more. Add beef, add the onion mix and the parsley, toss, cook for 10 minutes, divide into bowls and serve.
Enjoy!

Nutrition: calories 231, fat 4, fiber 7, carbs 14, protein 15

Balsamic Chicken Mix

Preparation time: 10 minutes
Cooking time: 35 minutes
Servings: 4

Ingredients:

- 1 tablespoon olive oil
- 1 pound chicken thighs, bone-in, skin-on
- ½ cup cranberries
- 2 garlic cloves, minced
- 1/3 cup balsamic vinegar
- 2 teaspoons thyme, chopped
- 1 teaspoon rosemary, chopped
- Zest of 1 orange, grated

Directions:

Heat up a pan with the oil over medium-high heat, add chicken thighs skin side down, cook for 5 minutes and transfer to a plate. Heat up the same pan over medium heat, add cranberries, garlic, vinegar, thyme, rosemary and orange zest, toss and bring to a simmer. Return chicken to the pan as well, cook everything for 10 minutes, introduce the pan in the oven and bake at 325 degrees F for 25 minutes. Divide between plates and serve.
Enjoy!

Nutrition: calories 235, fat 5, fiber 6, carbs 14, protein 15

Asian Glazed Chicken

Preparation time: 10 minutes
Cooking time: 30 minutes
Servings: 4

Ingredients:

- 8 chicken thighs, boneless and skinless
- 1/3 cup coconut aminos
- ½ cup balsamic vinegar
- 3 tablespoon garlic, minced
- ¼ cup olive oil
- A pinch of black pepper
- 1 tablespoon green onion, chopped
- 3 tablespoons garlic chili sauce

Directions:

Put the oil in a baking dish, add chicken, aminos, vinegar, garlic, black pepper, onion and chili sauce, toss well, introduce in the oven and bake at 425 degrees F for 30 minutes. Divide the chicken and the sauce between plates and serve.
Enjoy!

Nutrition: calories 254, fat 12, fiber 6, carbs 15, protein 20

Easy Greek Chicken

Preparation time: 10 minutes
Cooking time: 15 minutes
Servings: 4

Ingredients:

- 1 pound chicken breasts, skinless and boneless
- A pinch of black pepper
- 1 tablespoon olive oil
- 2 garlic cloves, minced
- 1 teaspoon oregano, dried
- 1 cup coconut milk
- 1 tablespoon lemon juice
- 1 teaspoon lemon zest, grated
- 1 and ½ cups cherry tomatoes, halved
- ½ cup kalamata olives, pitted and sliced
- ¼ cup dill, chopped
- 1 cucumber, sliced

Directions:
Heat up a pan with the oil over medium-high heat, add chicken and cook for 4 minutes on each side. Add black pepper, garlic, oregano, milk, lemon juice, lemon zest, tomatoes, olives, dill and cucumber, toss, cook for 10 minutes more, divide between plates and serve.
Enjoy!

Nutrition: calories 241, fat 4, fiber 8, carbs 15, protein 16

Summer Chicken Mix

Preparation time: 10 minutes
Cooking time: 27 minutes
Servings: 4

Ingredients:

- 1 tablespoon olive oil
- 4 chicken breasts, skinless and boneless
- A pinch of black pepper
- 1 shallot, chopped
- 2 garlic cloves, minced
- 4 peaches, sliced
- ¼ cup balsamic vinegar
- ¼ cup basil, chopped

Directions:
Heat up a pan with the oil over medium-high heat, add chicken, season with black pepper, and cook for 8 minutes on each side and transfer to a plate. Heat up the same pan over medium-high heat, add shallot and garlic, stir and cook for 2 minutes. Add peaches, stir and cook for 5 minutes more. Add the vinegar, return the chicken, also add the basil, toss, cook for 3-4 minutes more, divide everything between plates and serve.
Enjoy!

Nutrition: calories 241, fat 4, fiber 7, carbs 15, protein 15

Cajun Chicken

Preparation time: 10 minutes
Cooking time: 20 minutes
Servings: 4

Ingredients:

- 1 tablespoon olive oil
- 1 pound chicken breast, skinless and boneless
- ½ teaspoon oregano, dried
- A pinch of black pepper
- ¼ cup low-sodium veggie stock
- 2 cups cherry tomatoes, halved
- 4 green onions, chopped
- 1 tablespoon Cajun seasoning
- 3 garlic cloves, minced
- ½ teaspoon sweet paprika
- 2/3 cup coconut cream
- 2 tablespoons lemon juice

Directions:

Heat up a pan with the oil over medium-high heat, add chicken and a pinch of black pepper and cook for 5 minutes on each side. Add oregano, stock, green onions, Cajun seasoning, garlic, paprika, cream and lemon juice, toss, cook for 10 minutes, divide into bowls and serve. Enjoy!

Nutrition: calories 233, fat 4, fiber 6, carbs 15, protein 20

Chicken and Veggies

Preparation time: 10 minutes
Cooking time: 25 minutes
Servings: 4

Ingredients:

- 4 chicken breasts, skinless, boneless and cubed
- 2 tablespoons olive oil
- ½ teaspoon Italian seasoning
- A pinch of black pepper
- ½ cup yellow onion, chopped
- 14 ounces canned tomatoes, no-salt-added, drained and chopped
- 16 ounces cauliflower florets

Directions:

Heat up a pan with the oil over medium-high heat, add chicken, black pepper, onion and Italian seasoning, toss and cook for 5 minutes. Add tomatoes and cauliflower, toss, cover the pan and cook over medium heat for 20 minutes. Toss again, divide everything between plates and serve. Enjoy!

Nutrition: calories 310, fat 6, fiber 4, carbs 14, protein 20

Chicken and Broccoli

Preparation time: 10 minutes
Cooking time: 25 minutes
Servings: 4

Ingredients:
- 1 tablespoon olive oil
- 4 chicken breasts, skinless and boneless
- 1 cup red onions, chopped
- 2 garlic cloves, minced
- 1 tablespoon oregano, chopped
- 2 cups broccoli florets
- ½ cup coconut cream

Directions:
Heat up a pan with the oil over medium-high heat, add chicken breasts and cook for 5 minutes on each side. Add onions and garlic, stir and cook for 5 minutes more. Add oregano, broccoli and cream, toss everything, cook for 10 minutes more, divide between plates and serve.
Enjoy!

Nutrition: calories 287, fat 10, fiber 2, carbs 14, protein 19

Artichoke and Spinach Chicken

Preparation time: 10 minutes
Cooking time: 20 minutes
Servings: 4

Ingredients:
- 2 tablespoons olive oil
- 10 ounces baby spinach
- 14 ounces artichoke hearts, chopped
- 4 chicken breasts, boneless and skinless
- 28 ounces tomato sauce, no-salt-added
- ½ teaspoon red pepper flakes, crushed

Directions:
Heat up a pan with the oil over medium-high heat, add chicken and red pepper flakes and cook for 5 minutes on each side. Add spinach, artichokes and tomato sauce, toss, cook for 10 minutes more, divide between plates and serve.
Enjoy!

Nutrition: calories 212, fat 3, fiber 7, carbs 16, protein 20

Pumpkin and Black Beans Chicken

Preparation time: 10 minutes
Cooking time: 25 minutes
Servings: 4

Ingredients:

- 1 pound chicken breasts, skinless and boneless
- 2 cups water
- 1 tablespoon olive oil
- 1 cup coconut milk
- ½ cup pumpkin flesh
- 15 ounces canned black beans, no-salt-added, drained and rinsed
- 1 tablespoon cilantro, chopped

Directions:

Heat up a pan with the oil over medium-high heat, add the chicken and cook for 5 minutes. Add the water, milk, pumpkin and black beans, toss, cover the pan, reduce heat to medium and cook for 20 minutes. Add cilantro, toss, divide between plates and serve.
Enjoy!

Nutrition: calories 254, fat 6, fiber 4, carbs 16, protein 22

Chutney Chicken Mix

Preparation time: 10 minutes
Cooking time: 10 minutes
Servings: 4

Ingredients:

- 4 chicken breast halves, skinless and boneless
- 2 tablespoons lime juice
- 2 tablespoons olive oil
- 4 tablespoons mango chutney
- ½ teaspoon ginger, grated
- 1 avocado, peeled, pitted and chopped
- 8 cups micro greens
- A pinch of black pepper

Directions:

In a bowl, mix chicken breasts with oil with chutney, limejuice and ginger and toss to coat. Heat up your kitchen grill over medium-high heat, add chicken, cook for 5 minutes on each side, cut into thin strips and put in a salad bowl. Add avocado, black pepper and greens, drizzle the chutney dressing, toss to coat and serve.
Enjoy!

Nutrition: calories 210, fat 3, fiber 4, carbs 12, protein 9

Chicken and Sweet Potato Soup

Preparation time: 10 minutes
Cooking time: 20 minutes
Servings: 6

Ingredients:

- 2 chicken breasts, skinless, boneless and cubed
- 1 yellow onion, chopped
- 2 tablespoons olive oil
- 1 garlic clove, minced
- 4 sweet potatoes, cubed
- 2 carrots, chopped
- ½ teaspoon ginger, grated
- ½ teaspoon cumin, ground
- A pinch of black pepper
- 20 ounces low-sodium veggie stock

Directions:
Heat up a pot with the oil over medium-high heat, add onion and garlic, stir and cook for 5 minutes. Add carrots and potatoes, stir and cook for 5 minutes. Add ginger, cumin, stock, pepper and chicken, stir, bring to a boil, reduce heat to medium, simmer for 10 minutes, ladle into soup bowls and serve.
Enjoy!
Nutrition: calories 209, fat 5, fiber 5, carbs 13, protein 9

Chicken and Dill Soup

Preparation time: 10 minutes
Cooking time: 1 hour and 20 minutes
Servings: 6

Ingredients:

- 1 whole chicken
- 1 pound carrots, sliced
- 6 cups low-sodium veggie stock
- 1 cup yellow onion, chopped
- A pinch of salt and black pepper
- 2 teaspoons dill, chopped
- ½ cup red onion, chopped

Directions:
Put chicken in a pot, add water to cover, bring to a boil over medium heat, cook for 1 hour, transfer to a cutting board, discard bones, shred the meat, strain the soup, return it to the pot, heat it up over medium heat and add the chicken. Also, add the carrots, yellow onion, red onion, a pinch of salt, black pepper and the dill, cook for 15 minutes, ladle into bowls and serve.
Enjoy!

Nutrition: calories 202, fat 6, fiber 4, carbs 8, protein 12

Cilantro Serrano Chicken Soup

Preparation time: 10 minutes
Cooking time: 1 hour
Servings: 4

Ingredients:

- 4 chicken thighs, skin and bone in
- 1 cup cilantro, chopped
- 2 small Serrano peppers, chopped
- 4 and ¼ cups low-sodium veggie stock
- 2 whole garlic cloves+ 2 garlic cloves, minced
- 2 tablespoons olive oil
- ½ red bell pepper chopped
- ½ yellow onion, chopped
- A pinch of salt and black pepper

Directions:
Put cilantro in your food processor, add Serrano peppers, 2 whole garlic cloves and ¼-cup stock, blend very well and transfer to a bowl. Heat up a pot with the olive oil over medium-high heat, add chicken thighs, and cook for 5 minutes on each side and transfer to a bowl. Return pot to medium heat, add onion, stir and cook for 5 minutes. Add bell pepper, salt, pepper, minced garlic, cilantro paste, chicken and the rest of the stock, toss, bring to a simmer over medium heat, cook for 40 minutes, ladle into bowls and serve
Enjoy!

Nutrition: calories 291, fat 5, fiber 8, carbs 10, protein 12

Leek and Chicken Soup

Preparation time: 15 minutes
Cooking time: 1 hour and 20 minutes
Yield: 4

Ingredients:

- 1 whole chicken, cut into medium pieces
- A pinch of salt and black pepper
- 12 cups low-sodium veggie stock
- 3 leek, roughly chopped
- 3 tablespoons olive oil
- 2 cups yellow onion, chopped
- ½ cup lemon juice

Directions:
Put chicken in a pot, add the stock, a pinch of salt and black pepper, stir, bring to a boil over medium heat and skim foam. Add leeks, toss and simmer for 1 hour. Heat up a pan with the oil over medium heat, add onion, stir and cook for 5 minutes. Add this to the pot, also add the lemon juice, toss, cook for 20 minutes more, ladle into bowls and serve.
Enjoy!

Nutrition: calories 199, fat 3, fiber 5, carbs 6, protein 11

Collard Greens and Chicken Soup

Preparation time: 10 minutes
Cooking time: 30 minutes
Servings: 4

Ingredients:

- 4 cups low-sodium chicken stock
- 1 garlic clove, minced
- 1 yellow onion, chopped
- 8 ounces chicken breast skinless, boneless and chopped
- 2 cups collard greens, chopped
- A pinch of salt and black pepper
- 2 tablespoons ginger, grated

Directions:
Put the stock in a pot, add garlic, chicken and onion, stir, bring to a boil over medium heat and simmer for 20 minutes. Add collard greens, salt, pepper and ginger, stir and cook for 10 more minutes, ladle into bowls and serve.
Enjoy!

Nutrition: calories 199, fat 5, fiber 5, carbs 8, protein 12

Chicken, Scallions and Avocado Soup

Preparation time: 10 minutes
Cooking time: 25 minutes
Servings: 4

Ingredients:

- 2 cups chicken breast, skinless, boneless, cooked and shredded
- 2 avocados, peeled, pitted and chopped
- 5 cups low-sodium veggie stock
- 1 and ½ cups scallions, chopped
- 2 garlic cloves, minced
- ½ cup cilantro, chopped
- A pinch of salt and black pepper
- 2 teaspoons olive oil

Directions:
Heat up a pot with the oil over medium heat, add 1-cup scallions and garlic, stir and cook for 5 minutes. Add stock, salt and pepper, bring to a boil, reduce heat to low, cover and simmer for 20 minutes. Divide chicken, the rest of the scallions and avocado in bowls, add soup, top with chopped cilantro and serve.
Enjoy!

Nutrition: calories 205, fat 5, fiber 6, carbs 14, protein 8

Coconut Chicken and Mushrooms

Preparation time: 10 minutes
Cooking time: 52 minutes
Servings: 8

Ingredients:

- 3 tablespoons olive oil
- 8 chicken thighs
- A pinch of salt and black pepper
- 3 garlic cloves, minced
- 8 ounces mushrooms, halved
- 1 cup coconut cream
- ½ teaspoon basil, dried
- ½ teaspoon oregano, dried
- 1 tablespoon mustard

Directions:
Heat up a pot with 2 tablespoons oil over medium-high heat, add chicken, salt and pepper, brown for 3 minutes on each side and transfer to a plate. Heat up the same pot with the rest of the oil over medium heat, add mushroom and garlic, stir and cook for 6 minutes. Add salt, pepper, oregano, basil and chicken, stir and bake in the oven at 400 degrees F for 30 minutes. Add cream and mustard, stir, simmer for 10 minutes more, divide everything between plates and serve.
Enjoy!

Nutrition: calories 269, fat 5, fiber 6, carbs 13, protein 12

Chicken Chili

Preparation time: 10 minutes
Cooking time: 1 hour and 10 minutes
Servings: 6

Ingredients:

- 1 cup coconut flour
- 8 lemon tea bags
- A pinch of salt and black pepper
- 4 pounds chicken breast, skinless, boneless and cubed
- 4 ounces olive oil
- 4 ounces celery, chopped
- 3 garlic cloves, minced
- 2 yellow onion, chopped
- 2 red bell pepper, chopped
- 7 ounces poblano pepper, chopped
- 1-quart low-sodium stock veggie stock
- 1 teaspoon chili powder
- ¼ cup cilantro, chopped

Directions:
Dredge the chicken pieces in coconut flour. Heat up a pot with the oil over medium-high heat, add chicken, cook for 5 minutes on each side and transfer to a bowl. Heat up the pot again over medium-high heat, add onion, celery, garlic, bell pepper and poblano pepper, stir and cook for 2 minutes. Add stock, chili powder, salt, pepper, chicken and tea bags, stir, bring to a simmer, reduce heat to medium-low, cover and cook for 1 hour. Discard tea bags, add cilantro, stir, ladle into bowls and serve.
Enjoy!

Nutrition: calories 205, fat 8, fiber 3, carbs 12, protein 6

Chicken, Spinach and Asparagus Soup

Preparation time: 10 minutes
Cooking time: 30 minutes
Servings: 6

Ingredients:
- 2 chicken breasts, cooked, skinless, boneless and shredded
- 1 tablespoon olive oil
- A pinch of salt and black pepper
- 1 yellow onion, finely chopped
- 2 carrots, chopped
- 3 garlic cloves, minced
- 4 cups spinach
- 12 asparagus spears, chopped
- 6 cups low-sodium veggie stock
- Zest of ½ lime, grated
- 1 handful cilantro, chopped

Directions:
Heat up a pot with the oil over medium heat, add onions, stir and cook for 5 minutes. Add carrots, garlic and asparagus, stir and cook for 5 minutes. Add spinach, salt, pepper, stock and chicken, stir and cook for 20 minutes. Add lime zest and cilantro, stir soup again, ladle into bowls and serve.
Enjoy!

Nutrition: calories 245, fat 2, fiber 3, carbs 5, protein 6

Chicken and Broccoli Salad

Preparation time: 10 minutes
Cooking time: 10 minutes
Servings: 4

Ingredients:
- 3 medium chicken breasts, skinless, boneless and cut into thin strips
- 12 ounces broccoli florets, roughly chopped
- 5 tablespoon olive oil
- A pinch of salt and black pepper
-
- 2 tablespoon vinegar
- 1 and ½ cups peaches, pitted and sliced
- 1 tablespoon chives, chopped
- 2 bacon slices, cooked and crumbled

Directions:
In a salad bowl, mix 4-tablespoon oil with vinegar, salt, pepper, broccoli and peaches and toss. Heat up a pan with the rest of the oil over medium-high heat, add chicken, season with salt and pepper, cook for 5 minutes on each side, transfer to the salad bowl, add bacon and chives, toss and serve.
Enjoy!

Nutrition: calories 210, fat 12, fiber 3, carbs 10, protein 23

Pineapple Chicken Stew

Preparation time: 10 minutes
Cooking time: 1 hour and 5 minutes
Servings: 6
Ingredients:

- 1 and ½ pounds chicken thighs, boneless and skinless
- ¼ cup olive oil
- 1 yellow onion, chopped
- A pinch of salt and black pepper
- 1 red bell pepper, chopped
- 1 carrot, chopped
- 1 teaspoon thyme, dried
- 1 cup pineapple, peeled and chopped
- 6 garlic cloves, minced
- 1 jalapeno pepper, chopped
- 4 cups veggie stock
- 3 tablespoons capers
- 1 tablespoon cilantro, chopped
- 14 ounces canned tomatoes in juice, low-sodium and chopped
- Juice of 1 lime

Directions:

Heat up a pot with the oil over medium-high heat, add chicken, salt and pepper, stir, cook for 15 minutes, shred, transfer to a plate and leave aside. Heat up the same pot over medium heat, add carrot, bell pepper and onion, stir and cook for 8 minutes. Add thyme, pineapple, garlic, jalapeno, return chicken, capers, also add stock, tomatoes, lime juice and tomatoes, stir, cook for 35 minutes more, divide into bowls and serve.
Enjoy!

Nutrition: calories 190, fat 3, fiber 4, carbs 7, protein 10

Tomato and Chicken Soup

Preparation time: 10 minutes
Cooking time: 1 hour and 10 minutes
Servings: 6
Ingredients:

- 1 medium chicken, cut into medium pieces
- 3 and ½ pounds small tomatoes, halved
- 2 tablespoons olive oil
- 2 yellow onions, roughly chopped
- 3 garlic cloves, minced
- 3 red chili peppers, chopped
- 1 tablespoon coriander seeds, ground
- 4 tablespoons chipotle chili peppers paste
- Zest of 1 lime, grated
- Juice of 1 lime
- A pinch of salt and black pepper
- A handful coriander leaves, chopped

Directions:

Put all tomatoes in a baking dish, add onions and chicken, 1-tablespoon oil, salt and pepper, toss to coat, bake in the oven at 350 degrees F for 50 minutes, transfer to a blender and pulse. Heat up a pot with the rest of the oil over medium heat, add chilies, garlic and coriander, stir and cook for 3 minutes. Discard bones and skin from chicken pieces, shred, add to the pot, and add lime zest, chipotle paste, blended tomatoes mix, cook for 10 minutes more, and ladle into bowls, drizzle limejuice, sprinkle coriander and serve.
Enjoy!

Nutrition: calories 250, fat 5, fiber 3, carbs 7, protein 12

Simple Herbed Chicken Mix

Preparation time: 10 minutes
Cooking time: 1 hour
Servings: 4

Ingredients:
- 3 and ½ pounds chicken, cut into medium pieces
- 2 yellow onions, chopped
- 2 tablespoons olive oil
- 1 garlic clove, minced
- ¼ quart low-sodium chicken stock
- 1 tablespoon coconut flour
- 2 tablespoons mixed parsley and basil, chopped
- 14 ounces canned tomatoes, chopped
- Salt and black pepper to the taste

Directions:
Heat up a pot with the oil over medium heat, add chicken, brown for 5 minutes and transfer to a plate. Heat up the pot again over medium heat, add garlic and onion, stir and cook for 3 minutes. Add flour, herbs, tomatoes, stock, salt, pepper and chicken stir, bring to a boil, cook for 50 minutes, divide into bowls and serve.
Enjoy!

Nutrition: calories 230, fat 5, fiber 5, carbs 12, protein 9

Chicken Thighs and Apples Mix

Preparation time: 10 minutes
Cooking time: 1 hour
Servings: 4

Ingredients:
- 8 chicken thighs, bone in and skin on
- A pinch of salt and black pepper
- 1 tablespoon apple cider vinegar
- 3 tablespoons onion, chopped
- 1 tablespoon ginger, grated
- 3 apples, cored and cut into wedges
- ¾ cup natural apple juice

Directions:
In a bowl, mix chicken with salt, pepper, vinegar, onion, ginger and apple juice, toss well, cover, keep in the fridge for 10 minutes, transfer to a baking dish, also add apples, introduce in the oven at 400 degrees F for 1 hour, divide between plates and serve.
Enjoy!

Nutrition: calories 214, fat 3, fiber 3, carbs 14, protein 15

Thai Chicken Thighs

Preparation time: 10 minutes
Cooking time: 1 hour and 10 minutes
Servings: 6

Ingredients:
- 4 pounds chicken thighs, skin on and bone in
- 1 bunch green onions, chopped
- ½ cup Thai chili sauce

Directions:
Heat up a pan over medium-high heat, add chicken thighs, brown them for 5 minutes on each side, transfer to a baking dish, add chili sauce and green onions, toss, introduce in the oven and bake at 400 degrees F for 1 hour. Divide everything between plates and serve.
Enjoy!

Nutrition: calories 220, fat 4, fiber 2, carbs 12, protein 10

Chicken Quinoa Soup

Preparation time: 10 minutes
Cooking time: 1 hour
Servings: 6

Ingredients:
- 2 pounds chicken breast, skinless and boneless and cubed
- 2 red bell peppers, chopped
- 1 tablespoon olive oil
- 2 cups quinoa, already cooked
- ¼ cup cilantro, chopped
- Juice of ½ lime
- A pinch of salt and black pepper
- 1 small ginger piece, grated
- 1 tablespoon red curry paste
- 2 cups water
- 2 cups zucchinis, cubed
- 14 ounces coconut milk

Directions:
Heat up a pot with the oil over medium-high heat, add chicken and brown for 5 minutes on each side. Add bell peppers, limejuice, salt, pepper, ginger, curry paste, water, zucchini and coconut milk, toss, bring to a simmer and cook for 50 minutes. Add quinoa and cilantro, stir, ladle everything into bowls and serve.
Enjoy!

Nutrition: calories 260, fat 5, fiber 11, carbs 30, protein 24

Oregano Chicken Thighs

Preparation time: 30 minutes
Cooking time: 40 minutes
Servings: 6

Ingredients:
- 1 cup oregano, chopped
- 1 teaspoon parsley, dried
- ½ cup olive oil
- ¼ cup low-sodium veggie stock
- 4 garlic cloves, minced
- A pinch of salt and black pepper
- 12 chicken thighs

Directions:
In your food processor, mix parsley with oregano, garlic, salt, pepper and stock and pulse. Put chicken thighs in a bowl, add oregano paste, toss, cover and leave aside in the fridge for 10 minutes. Heat up your kitchen grill over medium heat, add chicken pieces, close the lid and cook for 20 minutes on each side. Divide between plates and serve with a side salad.
Enjoy!

Nutrition: calories 254, fat 3, fiber 3, carbs 7, protein 17

Baked Chicken and Lentils

Preparation time: 10 minutes
Cooking time: 1 hour and 10 minutes
Servings: 8

Ingredients:
- 1 and ½ cups green lentils
- 3 cups low-sodium chicken stock
- 2 pound chicken breasts, skinless, boneless and chopped
- A pinch of salt and black pepper
- 3 teaspoons cumin, ground
- 1 tablespoons olive oil
- 5 garlic cloves, minced
- 1 yellow onion, chopped
- 2 red bell peppers, chopped
- 14 ounces canned tomatoes, no-salt-added and chopped
- 2 cups corn
- 2 cups low-fat cheddar cheese, shredded
- 1 cup cilantro, chopped

Directions:
Put the stock in a pot, add a pinch of salt and black pepper and the lentils, stir, bring to a boil over medium heat, cover, simmer for 35 minutes and drain. Heat up a pan with the oil over medium-high heat, add chicken, cook for 5 minutes on each side and transfer to a bowl. Heat up the same pan over medium heat, add bell peppers, garlic and onion, stir and cook for 10 minutes. Add lentils, tomatoes, cumin, and corn, return chicken, sprinkle the cheese on top, introduce in the oven and bake at 350 degrees F for 50 minutes. Sprinkle cilantro, divide everything between plates and serve.
Enjoy!

Nutrition: calories 304, fat 11, fiber 4, carbs 12, protein 17

Chicken and Bell Peppers

Preparation time: 10 minutes
Cooking time: 30 minutes
Servings: 5

Ingredients:

- 3 pounds chicken breasts, skinless and boneless
- 1 yellow onion, chopped
- 1 garlic clove, minced
- A pinch of salt and black pepper
- 1 tablespoon coconut oil
- 4 red bell peppers, chopped
- 1 cup low-fat mozzarella cheese, shredded

COTIJA SHREDDED

Directions:
Put chicken in a baking dish greased with the oil, add garlic, bell peppers, salt and black pepper, cover with tin foil, introduce in the oven and bake at 425 degrees F for 20 minutes. Sprinkle the cheese, bake for 10 minutes more, divide between plates and serve.
Enjoy!

Nutrition: calories 225, fat 12, fiber 5, carbs 12, protein 27

Chicken, Beans and Quinoa Mix

Preparation time: 10 minutes
Cooking time: 30 minutes
Servings: 6

Ingredients:

- 1 cup quinoa, already cooked
- 3 cups chicken breast, cooked and shredded
- 14 ounces canned black beans, no-salt-added, drained and rinsed
- ½ cup cilantro, chopped
- ½ cup green onions, chopped
- 1 cup clean tomato sauce, no-salt-added
- 1 cup chunky salsa
- 2 teaspoons chili powder
- 1 tablespoon olive oil
- 3 cups low-fat cheddar cheese, shredded

Directions:
Grease a baking dish with the oil, spread salsa on the bottom, add chicken, quinoa, beans, cilantro, onions, chili powder, tomato sauce and sprinkle cheese at the end, introduce in the oven and bake at 350 degrees F for 30 minutes. Slice, divide between plates and serve.
Enjoy!

Nutrition: calories 275, fat 12, fiber 6, carbs 12, protein 26

Easy and Fast Chicken

Preparation time: 10 minutes
Cooking time: 35 minutes
Servings: 6

Ingredients:
- 1 tablespoon olive oil
- 2 pounds chicken breasts, skinless, boneless and cubed
- ½ teaspoon allspice
- 1 teaspoon cumin, ground
- A pinch of salt and black pepper
- 2 yellow onions, chopped
- 3 garlic clove, minced
- 1 teaspoon olive oil
- 3 tablespoons low-sodium tomato sauce
- 2 quinoa, already cooked

Directions:
Heat up a pot with the oil over medium-high heat, add chicken, cumin, allspice, salt and pepper, stir, cook for 10 minutes and transfer to a bowl. Heat up the pot again over medium heat, add carrot, onion and garlic, stir and cook for 5 minutes. Add quinoa, return chicken, also add tomato sauce, stir, and cover, bring to a simmer, reduce heat to low, cook for 20 minutes divide into bowls and serve.
Enjoy!

Nutrition: calories 308, fat 7, fiber 4, carbs 20, protein 40

Chicken, Carrots and Celery

Preparation time: 10 minutes
Cooking time: 1 hour
Servings: 8

Ingredients:
- 2 yellow onions, chopped
- 2 pounds chicken thighs, skinless, boneless and chopped
- 5 garlic cloves, minced
- 2 tablespoons olive oil
- 16 ounces mixed carrots and celery, cubed
- 2 cups low-sodium chicken stock
- Black pepper to the taste
- 2 tablespoons cilantro, chopped

Directions:
Heat up a pot with half of the oil over medium heat, add chicken, cook for 4 minutes on each side and transfer to a bowl. Heat up the pot again with the rest of the oil over medium-high heat, add garlic and onion, stir and cook for 1 minute. Add stock, celery, carrots, black pepper and return the chicken, toss, cook over medium-low heat for 45 minutes, sprinkle parsley, divide into bowls and serve.
Enjoy!

Nutrition: calories 210, fat 4, fiber 4, carbs 10, protein 14

Chicken, Tomato and Green Beans

Preparation time: 10 minutes
Cooking time: 30 minutes
Servings: 4

Ingredients:
- 1 and ½ pounds chicken breasts, skinless, boneless and cubed
- 2 tablespoons olive oil
- 2 pounds green beans, trimmed
- 25 ounces canned tomato sauce, no-salt-added
- 2 tablespoons parsley, chopped
- 6 ounces canned tomato paste, low-sodium
- A pinch of black pepper to the taste

Directions:
Heat up a pan with half of the oil over medium heat, add chicken, stir, cover, and cook for 5 minutes on each side and transfer to a bowl. Heat up the same pan with the rest of the oil over medium heat, add green beans, stir and cook for 10 minutes. Return chicken to the pan, add black pepper, tomato sauce, tomato paste and parsley, stir, cover, cook for 10 minutes more, divide between plates and serve.
Enjoy!

Nutrition: calories 190, fat 4, fiber 2, carbs 12, protein 9

Chicken Curry

Preparation time: 10 minutes
Cooking time: 30 minutes
Servings: 6

Ingredients:
- 1 yellow onion, chopped
- 3 garlic cloves, minced
- 1 tablespoon olive oil
- 2 red bell peppers, chopped
- 14 ounces coconut milk
- 2 tablespoons yellow curry powder
- 2 teaspoons turmeric powder
- A pinch of salt and black pepper
- 4 cups cauliflower, florets separated and chopped
- 1/3 cup cilantro, chopped
- 1 and ½ pounds chicken breasts, skinless, boneless and cubed
- 1/3 cup green onions, chopped

Directions:
Heat up a pot with the oil over medium heat, add garlic, onion and bell peppers, stir and cook for 7 minutes. Add curry powder, coconut milk, turmeric, chicken, cauliflower, salt and pepper, stir, bring to a boil, cover and simmer for 20 minutes. Add green onions and cilantro, stir, divide between plates and serve.
Enjoy!

Nutrition: calories 220, fat 6, fiber 3, carbs 8, protein 27

Chicken and Cabbage Soup

Preparation time: 10 minutes
Cooking time: 30 minutes
Servings: 6

Ingredients:

- 1 big chicken breast, skinless, boneless and cubed
- 10 cups chicken stock
- 2 carrots, chopped
- 1 tablespoon olive oil
- 1 pound cabbage, shredded
- 3 tomatoes, chopped
- A pinch of salt and black pepper
- 1/3 cup parsley, chopped
- 2 garlic cloves, minced

Directions:
Put the stock in a pot, bring to a simmer over medium heat, add cabbage and chicken, stir and cook for 15 minutes. Add oil, tomatoes, carrots, salt and pepper, stir, cover again and cook for 15 minutes. Add parsley and garlic, stir, ladle into bowls and serve.
Enjoy!

Nutrition: calories 224, fat 3, fiber 5, carbs 10, protein 22

Chicken, Mango and Arugula Salad

Preparation time: 10 minutes
Cooking time: 10 minutes
Servings: 4

Ingredients:

- 4 chicken breast halves, skinless and boneless
- 2 tablespoons lime juice
- 2 tablespoons olive oil
- ¾ teaspoon ginger, grated
- A drizzle of olive oil
- 1 cup mango, peeled and chopped
- 3 cups baby arugula
- A pinch of salt and black pepper

Directions:
In a bowl, mix the chicken with limejuice, ginger, oil, salt and pepper, toss well and keep in the fridge for 10 minutes. Heat up a pan over medium-high heat, add chicken, reserve the marinade, cook for 5 minutes on each side, transfer to a cutting board, cut into cubes and put in a salad bowl. Add mango, arugula, salt, pepper and the lime marinade, toss and serve.
Enjoy!

Nutrition: calories 300, fat 6, fiber 3, carbs 13, protein 15

Chicken and Kale

Preparation time: 10 minutes
Cooking time: 35 minutes
Servings: 4

Ingredients:

- ½ tablespoon ginger, grated
- 3 garlic cloves, minced
- 1 tablespoon coconut aminos
- 1 teaspoon black peppercorns
- 8 chicken legs
- 2 cups kale, torn
- A pinch of salt and black pepper
- 2 tablespoons spring onions, chopped

Directions:

In a pot, mix the ginger with garlic, aminos, peppercorns, salt, pepper and the chicken and rub. Add water to cover, bring to a boil over medium, and cook for 30 minutes, drain, discard bones and shred meat. Heat up a pan with the oil over medium-high heat, add onions, stir and cook for 1 minute. Add shredded meat and kale, toss, cook for 5 minutes more, divide between plates and serve.
Enjoy!

Rosemary Roasted Chicken

Preparation time: 10 minutes
Cooking time: 1 hour and 20 minutes
Servings: 8

Ingredients:

- 1 chicken
- 1 garlic clove, minced
- 1 tablespoon rosemary, chopped
- 1 tablespoon olive oil
- Black pepper to the taste
- 8 rosemary springs

Directions:

In a bowl, mix garlic with rosemary, rub the chicken with black pepper, the oil and rosemary mix, place it in a roasting pan, introduce in the oven at 350 degrees F and roast for 1 hour and 20 minutes. Carve chicken, divide between plates and serve with a side dish.
Enjoy!

Nutrition: calories 325, fat 5, fiber 1, carbs 15, protein 14

Chicken, Scallions and Carrot Mix

Preparation time: 10 minutes
Cooking time: 0 minutes
Servings: 6

Ingredients:

- 4 cups chicken, cooked, boneless, skinless and shredded
- ¼ cup olive oil
- 1/3 cup balsamic vinegar
- 1 small red cabbage head, shredded
- 1 cup carrot, grated
- 6 scallions, sliced
- Black pepper to the taste

Directions:
In a bowl, mix olive oil with vinegar and whisk. In a salad bowl, mix chicken with scallions, cabbage, black pepper and carrot. Add the vinegar and oil mix, toss and serve.
Enjoy!

Nutrition: calories 170, fat 2, fiber 2, carbs 12, protein 6

Chicken Sandwich

Preparation time: 10 minutes
Cooking time: 16 minutes
Servings: 4

Ingredients:

- 4 chicken breasts
- ½ teaspoon Italian seasoning
- 1 eggplant, thinly sliced
- Black pepper to the taste
- A drizzle of olive oil
- ½ cup low sodium tomato sauce
- 16 basil leaves, torn
- 8 ounces low-fat mozzarella cheese, shredded
- 8 whole wheat bread slices

Directions:
Grease the chicken with a drizzle of oil, season with black pepper to the taste and sprinkle Italian seasoning. Heat up a grill over medium-high heat, add chicken, cook for 5 minutes on each side, take off heat and leave aside for now. Season eggplant slices with black pepper to the taste, arrange them on heated grill and cook them for 3 minutes on each side. Arrange 2 bread slices on a working surface, place 1-ounce mozzarella cheese on each bread slice, add 2 eggplant slices on one slice, 1 grilled chicken piece, 2 tablespoons tomato sauce, 4 basil leaves and top with the other bread slice. Repeat this with the rest of the bread slices and the rest of the ingredients, divide them between plates and serve.
Enjoy!

Nutrition: calories 200, fat 2, fiber 6, carbs 14, protein 12

Chicken Tortillas

Preparation time: 10 minutes
Cooking time: 0 minutes
Servings: 4

Ingredients:
- 4 whole wheat tortillas, heated up
- 1/3 cup fat-free yogurt
- 6 ounces chicken breasts, skinless, boneless, cooked and cut into strips
- 2 tomatoes, chopped
- Black pepper to the taste

Directions:
Heat up a pan over medium heat, add one tortilla at the time, heat up and arrange them on a working surface. Spread yogurt on each tortilla, add chicken and tomatoes, roll, divide between plates and serve.
Enjoy!

Nutrition: calories 190, fat 2, fiber 2, carbs 12, protein 6

Chicken Cream

Preparation time: 10 minutes
Cooking time: 20 minutes
Servings: 4

Ingredients:
- 2 chicken breasts, skinless, boneless and cut into strips
- 1 yellow onion, chopped
- 2 tablespoons olive oil
- 1 garlic clove, chopped
- 12 ounces zucchini, cubed
- 2 carrots, chopped
- Black pepper to the taste
- 14 ounces coconut milk
- 17 ounces low sodium chicken stock

Directions:
Heat up a pot with the oil over medium-high heat, add garlic and onion, stir and cook for 5 minutes. Add carrots, chicken, zucchini, black pepper and chicken stock, stir, bring to a boil, reduce heat to medium and simmer for 15 minutes. Add the milk, transfer soup to your blender, pulse, ladle into soup bowls and serve.
Enjoy!

Nutrition: calories 210, fat 7, fiber 4, carbs 15, protein 12

Italian Chicken Wings

Preparation time: 10 minutes
Cooking time: 1 hour and 15 minutes
Servings: 4

Ingredients:
- 2 pounds chicken wings
- 1 tablespoon Italian seasoning
- Black pepper to the taste
- 2 tablespoons olive oil
- 1 and ¼ cups balsamic vinegar
- 3 garlic cloves, minced

Directions:
In a baking dish, mix chicken wings with Italian seasoning, garlic, vinegar, salt, pepper and the olive oil, toss to coat, introduce in the oven at 425 degrees F and bake for 1 hour and 15 minutes. Divide everything between plates and serve.
Enjoy!

Nutrition: calories 280, fat 7, fiber 3, carbs 12, protein 14

Salsa Chicken

Preparation time: 10 minutes
Cooking time: 1 hour
Servings: 4

Ingredients:
- 1 pound chicken breast, boneless and skinless
- 16 ounces canned Salsa Verde
- Black pepper to the taste
- 1 tablespoon olive oil
- 1 and ½ cups fat-free cheddar cheese, shredded
- ¼ cup parsley, chopped
- Juice of 1 lime

Directions:
Spread salsa in a baking dish, add chicken on top, add oil, black pepper, lime juice, sprinkle cheese on top, introduce in the oven at 400 degrees F and bake for 1 hour. Sprinkle cilantro on top, divide everything between plates and serve.
Enjoy!

Nutrition: calories 250, fat 1, fiber 4, carbs 14, protein 12

Hot Chicken Mix

Preparation time: 10 minutes
Cooking time: 10 minutes
Servings: 4

Ingredients:

- 1 and ½ cups chicken breasts, skinless, boneless and cut into strips
- A drizzle of olive oil
- ½ cup hot sauce
- 2 green onions, chopped
- 1 teaspoon garlic powder
- 1 cup coconut milk
- Black pepper to the taste

Directions:

Heat up a pan with the oil over medium-high heat, add chicken, cook for 4 minutes on each side, add hot sauce, green onions, garlic powder, coconut milk and black pepper, toss, cook for 2 minutes more, divide into bowls and serve.
Enjoy!

Nutrition: calories 200, fat 11, fiber 6, carbs 14, protein 11

Chicken and Shrimp Soup

Preparation time: 10 minutes
Cooking time: 25 minutes
Servings: 4

Ingredients:

- 5 tablespoons curry paste
- 1 tablespoon olive oil
- 1 big chicken breast, skinless, boneless and cut into thin strips
- 4 tablespoons coconut aminos
- 4 cups chicken stock
- Juice of 1 lime
- 1 pound shrimp, peeled and deveined
- ½ cup coconut cream
- 1 zucchini, chopped
- 1 carrot, chopped
- 1 tablespoon cilantro, chopped

Directions:

Heat up a pot with the oil over medium heat, add curry paste and the chicken, stir and cook for 5 minutes. Add stock, aminos, limejuice, cream, zucchini and carrot, stir and cook for 10 minutes. Add shrimp and cilantro, toss, cook for 5 minutes more, ladle into bowls and serve.
Enjoy!

Nutrition: calories 170, fat 3, fiber 2, carbs 12, protein 8

Chicken and Olives Stew

Preparation time: 10 minutes
Cooking time: 2 hours
Servings: 4

Ingredients:

- 2 pounds chicken pieces
- 30 ounces canned tomatoes, no-salt-added, chopped
- 30 black olives, pitted and chopped
- 2 cups chicken stock
- 2 tablespoons parsley, chopped
- 2 tablespoons basil, chopped
- 2 tablespoons olive oil
- A pinch of sea salt and black pepper

Directions:

Heat up a pot with the oil over medium-high heat, add chicken pieces, season with a pinch of salt and black pepper and brown them for 2 minutes on each side. Add stock, tomatoes, olives, basil and parsley, stir, cover, introduce in the oven at 325 degrees F, bake for 2 hours, divide into bowls and serve.
Enjoy!

Nutrition: calories 260, fat 10, fiber 4, carbs 12, protein 24

Cashew Chicken Stew

Preparation time: 10 minutes
Cooking time: 40 minutes
Servings: 4

Ingredients:

- 4 chicken thighs
- 1 yellow onion, chopped
- ½ tablespoon olive oil
- Black pepper to the taste
- 1 tablespoon ginger, grated
- 1 tablespoon garlic, minced
- ½ teaspoon sweet paprika
- ½ teaspoon chili powder
- 1 and ½ cups tomatoes, chopped
- 2 and ½ tablespoons cashew butter
- ¼ cup water
- 1 tablespoon parsley, chopped

Directions:

Heat up a pan with the oil over medium-high heat, add chicken pieces, season with black pepper to the taste, stir, brown for 4 minutes on each side and transfer them to a bowl. Heat up the same pan over medium heat, add ginger and onion, stir and cook for 6 minutes. Add garlic, paprika, chili powder, water, tomatoes and return the chicken pieces, stir, and cover, bring to a boil and simmer for 30 minutes. Add cashew butter and parsley, stir, cook for 2 minutes more, divide into bowls and serve.
Enjoy!

Nutrition: calories 252, fat 4, fiber 2, carbs 12, protein 8

Apple Chicken Stew

Preparation time: 10 minutes
Cooking time: 1 hour and 5 minutes
Servings: 6

Ingredients:
- 1 lemongrass stalk, chopped
- 2 pounds chicken breasts, skinless, boneless and cubed
- 1 and ½ teaspoons curry powder
- 2 and ½ tablespoons ginger, grated
- 2 tablespoons unsweetened apple juice
- 1 tablespoon olive oil
- 1 yellow onion, chopped
- 2 cups tomatoes, chopped
- 3 cups water
- 1 pound carrots, chopped
- ¼ cup cilantro, chopped
- Black pepper to the taste

Directions:
In a bowl, mix apple juice with lemongrass, curry powder, ginger and chicken and toss to coat. Heat up a pot with the oil over medium-high heat, add chicken stir, brown for 4 minutes on each side and transfer to a bowl. Heat up the same pot over medium heat, add onion, stir and cook for 1 minute. Return the chicken, also add the apple juice marinade, tomatoes, water, carrots and black pepper, toss, bring to a simmer and cook for 50 minutes. Add cilantro, stir, divide into bowls and serve.
Enjoy!

Nutrition: calories 320, fat 4, fiber 3, carbs 12, protein 15

Chicken Breasts and Tomato Mix

Preparation time: 10 minutes
Cooking time: 30 minutes
Servings: 4

Ingredients:
- 2 teaspoons chili powder
- 1 cup tomatoes, crushed
- 4 chicken breast halves, skinless and boneless
- 2 teaspoons onion powder
- 2 tablespoons coconut aminos
- 1 jalapeno pepper, chopped
- Black pepper to the taste
- 1 tablespoons hot pepper
- 2 tablespoons lime juice

Directions:
In a bowl, mix tomatoes with hot pepper, aminos, chili powder, onion powder, black pepper, jalapeno, limejuice and the chicken and toss well. Transfer this to a baking dish, introduce in the oven and bake at 400 degrees F for 30 minutes. Divide everything between plates and serve. Enjoy!

Nutrition: calories 230, fat 8, fiber 7, carbs 13, protein 14

Chicken and Brussels Sprouts

Preparation time: 10 minutes
Cooking time: 15 minutes
Servings: 4

Ingredients:
- 1 pound chicken meat, ground
- 1 apple, cored, peeled and chopped
- 1 yellow onion, chopped
- 3 cups Brussels sprouts, shredded
- Black pepper to the taste
- 1 tablespoon olive oil

Directions:
Heat up a pan with the oil over medium-high heat, add chicken, stir and brown for 5 minutes. Add Brussels sprouts, onion, black pepper and apple, stir, cook for 10 minutes, divide into bowls and serve.
Enjoy!

Nutrition: calories 200, fat 8, fiber 8, carbs 13, protein 9

Almond Chicken Mix

Preparation time: 10 minutes
Cooking time: 15 minutes
Servings: 2

Ingredients:
- 2 mushrooms, chopped
- 2 tablespoons almonds, chopped
- 2 tablespoons olive oil
- 4 ounces chicken meat, ground
- ½ teaspoon chili flakes
- Black pepper to the taste
- 1 tablespoon capers
- ¼ cup kalamata olives, pitted
- 1 tablespoon almond butter

Directions:
Heat up a pan with the oil over medium-high heat, add mushrooms, stir and cook for 3 minutes. Add almonds, chicken, chili flakes, black pepper, capers, olives and almond butter, stir and cook for 12 minutes, divide into bowls and serve.
Enjoy!

Nutrition: calories 220, fat 2, fiber 5, carbs 13, protein 15

Chili Chicken and Basil

Preparation time: 10 minutes
Cooking time: 15 minutes
Servings: 4

Ingredients:

- 6 garlic cloves, minced
- 2 red chilies, chopped
- 1 tablespoon olive oil
- 1 yellow onion, chopped
- 1 pound chicken breasts, skinless, boneless and cut into strips
- Black pepper to the taste
- 3 cups basil, chopped
- ½ cup low-sodium chicken stock
- 2 cups carrot, grated
- 4 tablespoons lime juice

Directions:

Heat up a pan with the oil over medium heat, add onions, stir and cook for 4 minutes. Add garlic, black pepper, chili peppers and chicken, stir and cook for 7 minutes more. Add stock, limejuice and basil, stir, cook for 4 more minutes, divide into bowls and serve.
Enjoy!

Nutrition: calories 240, fat 3, fiber 5, carbs 12, protein 17

Smoked Chicken and Apple Mix

Preparation time: 10 minutes
Cooking time: 0 minutes
Servings: 6

Ingredients:

- 1 celery rib, chopped
- 1 carrot, shredded
- ½ small green cabbage head, shredded
- ½ cup avocado mayonnaise
- 1 red apple, cored and chopped
- ½ cup smoked chicken breast, skinless, boneless, cooked and shredded
- 1 teaspoon parsley, chopped

Directions:

In a bowl, mix chicken with celery, carrot, cabbage, apple, mayo and parsley, toss and serve cold.
Enjoy!

Nutrition: calories 280, fat 7, fiber 2, carbs 10, protein 13

Chicken and Grapes Salad

Preparation time: 10 minutes
Cooking time: 0 minutes
Servings: 6

Ingredients:

- 20 ounces chicken meat, already cooked and chopped
- ½ cup pecans, chopped
- 1 cup green grapes, seedless and cut into halves
- 1 cup celery, chopped
- A drizzle of olive oil
- 1 teaspoon lemon juice
- 1 cup fat-free yogurt

Directions:
In a bowl, combine the chicken with the pecans, grapes, celery, oil, lemon juice and yogurt, toss well and serve cold.
Enjoy!

Nutrition: calories 250, fat 3, fiber 6, carbs 2, protein 9, protein 12

French Lentils and Chicken Soup

Preparation time: 10 minutes
Cooking time: 1 hour and 10 minutes
Servings: 8

Ingredients:

- 2 tablespoons olive oil
- 2 celery stalks, chopped
- 2 carrots, chopped
- 1 yellow onion, chopped
- 2 tablespoons no-salt-added tomato paste
-
- 2 garlic cloves, chopped
- 4 cups chicken stock
- 2 cups French lentils
- 1 pound chicken thighs, skinless and boneless
- Black pepper to the taste

Directions:
Heat up a pot with the oil over medium-high heat; add onion, celery, carrots and the garlic, stir and sauté for 10 minutes. Add tomato paste, the chicken, lentils, stock and black pepper, toss, bring to a simmer, reduce heat to medium and cook for 1 hour. Ladle into bowls and serve.
Enjoy!

Nutrition: calories 261, fat 7, fiber 2, carbs 14, protein 17

Chicken and Barley Soup

Preparation time: 10 minutes
Cooking time: 1 hour
Servings: 6

Ingredients:

- 4 chicken things, bone-in and skin-on
- 1 tablespoon olive oil
- Black pepper to the taste
- 2 celery stalks, chopped
- 2 carrots, chopped
- 1 yellow onion, chopped
- 4 cups chicken stock
- ½ cup parsley, chopped
- ½ cup barley
- 1 teaspoon lemon zest, grated

Directions:
Heat up a pot with the oil over medium-high heat, add chicken, season with black pepper, brown for 8 minutes and transfer to a plate. Return pot to medium heat, add onion, celery, carrots, stock, barley and return the chicken, stir, bring to a boil, cover, reduce heat to medium, simmer for 50 minutes, add parsley and lemon zest, toss, ladle into bowls and serve.
Enjoy!

Nutrition: calories 213, fat 2, fiber 2, carbs 7, protein 14

Chicken and Radish Mix

Preparation time: 10 minutes
Cooking time: 30 minutes
Servings: 4

Ingredients:

- 4 chicken things, bone-in
- Black pepper to the taste
- 1 tablespoon olive oil
- 1 cup low-sodium chicken stock
- 10 radishes, halved
- 2 tablespoon chives, chopped

Directions:
Heat up a pan with the oil over medium-high heat, add chicken, season with black pepper and brown for 6 minutes on each side. Add stock and radishes, reduce heat to medium and simmer for 20 minutes. Add the chives, toss, divide between plates and serve.
Enjoy!

Nutrition: calories 247, fat 10, fiber 3, carbs 12, protein 22

Dash Diet Meat Recipes

Caraway Pork Mix

Preparation time: 10 minutes
Cooking time: 40 minutes
Servings: 6

Ingredients:

- 2 pounds pork meat, boneless and cubed
- 2 yellow onions, chopped
- 1 tablespoon olive oil
- 1 garlic clove, minced
- 3 cups low-sodium chicken stock
- 2 tablespoons sweet paprika
- 1 teaspoon caraway seeds
- Black pepper to the taste
- 2 tablespoons parsley, chopped

Directions:

Heat up a pot with the oil over medium heat, add pork and brown it for 10 minutes. Add onions, garlic, stock, caraway seeds, paprika and pepper, bring to a boil, reduce temperature, cover and cook for 30 minutes. Add parsley, toss, divide into bowls and serve.
Enjoy!

Nutrition: calories 310, fat 4, fiber 4, carbs 13, protein 15

Mustard Pork Chops

Preparation time: 10 minutes
Cooking time: 20 minutes
Servings: 6

Ingredients:

- 2 pork chops
- ¼ cup olive oil
- 2 yellow onions, sliced
- 2 garlic cloves, minced
- 2 teaspoons mustard
- 1 teaspoon sweet paprika
- Black pepper to the taste
- ½ teaspoon oregano, dried

Directions:

In a small bowl, mix oil with garlic, mustard, paprika, black pepper, and oregano and whisk well. Add the pork chops, toss well and leave aside to 10 minutes. Place the meat on the preheated grill over medium-high heat and cook for 10 minutes on each side. Divide pork chops between plates and serve with a side salad.
Enjoy!

Nutrition: calories 314, fat 4, fiber 4, carbs 7, protein 17

Pork and Lentils Soup

Preparation time: 10 minutes
Cooking time: 1 hour and 5 minutes
Servings: 6

Ingredients:

- 1 small yellow onion, chopped
- 1 tablespoon olive oil
- 1 and ½ teaspoons basil, chopped
- 1 and ½ teaspoons ginger, grated
- 3 garlic cloves, chopped
- Black pepper to the taste
- 1 carrot, chopped
- 1 pound pork chops, boneless and cubed
- 3 ounces brown lentils, rinsed
- 3 cups low sodium chicken stock
- 2 tablespoons tomato paste
- 2 tablespoons lime juice

Directions:

Heat up a pot with the oil over medium heat, add garlic, onion, basil, ginger, carrots and black pepper, stir and cook for 10 minutes. Add the pork and brown for 5 minutes more. Add lentils, tomato paste and stock, bring to a boil, cover pot and simmer for 50 minutes. Add limejuice, toss, ladle into bowls and serve.
Enjoy!

Nutrition: calories 273, fat 4, fiber 6, carbs 12, protein 16

Pork and Veggies Stew

Preparation time: 10 minutes
Cooking time: 1 hour and 10 minutes
Servings: 4

Ingredients:

- ½ cup low-sodium chicken stock
- 1 tablespoon ginger, grated
- 1 teaspoon coriander, ground
- 2 teaspoons cumin, ground
- Black pepper to the taste
- 2 and ½ pounds pork butt, cubed
- 28 ounces canned tomatoes, no-salt-added, drained and chopped
-
- 4 ounces carrots, chopped
- 1 red onion, cut into wedges
- 4 garlic cloves, minced
- 15 ounces canned chickpeas, no-salt-added, drained and rinsed
- 1 tablespoon cilantro, chopped

Directions:

Heat up a pot over medium heat, add pork cubes and brown them to 5 minutes. Add ginger, coriander, cumin, black pepper, onion, carrots and garlic, stir and cook for 5 minutes more. Add the stock, the tomatoes and the chickpeas, toss, bring to a simmer, cover the pot and cook for 1 hour. Add cilantro, stir, divide into bowls and serve.
Enjoy!

Nutrition: calories 256, fat 6, fiber 8, carbs 12, protein 24

Pork and Snow Peas Salad

Preparation time: 10 minutes
Cooking time: 0 minutes
Servings: 4

Ingredients:
- 1 red chili, chopped
- 2 tablespoons balsamic vinegar
- 1/3 cup coconut aminos
- 1 tablespoon lime juice
- 1 teaspoon olive oil
- 4 ounces mixed salad greens
- 4 ounces snow peas, blanched
- 1 red bell pepper, sliced
- 4 ounces pork, cooked and cut into thin strips

Directions:
In a salad bowl, mix greens with peas, bell pepper and pork. Add the chili, vinegar, aminos, limejuice and oil, toss well and serve.
Enjoy!

Nutrition: calories 235, fat 4, fiber 4, carbs 12, protein 17

Pork and Beans Stew

Preparation time: 20 minutes
Cooking time: 1 hour and 10 minutes
Servings: 4

Ingredients:
- 2 pounds pork butt, trimmed and cubed
- 1 and ½ tablespoons olive oil
- 2 eggplants, chopped
- 1 yellow onion, chopped
- 1 red bell pepper, chopped
- 3 garlic cloves, minced
- 1 tablespoon thyme, dried
- 2 teaspoons sage, dried
- 4 ounces canned white beans, no-salt-added, drained and rinsed
- 1 cup low-sodium chicken stock
- 12 ounces zucchinis, chopped
- 2 tablespoons tomato paste

Directions:
Heat up a pot with the oil over medium-high heat, add pork and brown for 5 minutes. Add the onion, garlic, thyme, sage, bell pepper and eggplants, toss and cook for 5 minutes more. Add beans, stock and tomato paste, and toss, bring to a simmer, cover the pot and cook for 50 minutes. Add the zucchinis, toss, cook for 10 minutes more, divide into bowls and serve.
Enjoy!

Nutrition: calories 310, fat 3, fiber 5, carbs 12, protein 22

Herbed Pork

Preparation time: 10 minutes
Cooking time: 1 hour and 10 minutes
Servings: 6

Ingredients:

- 2 and ½ pounds pork loin boneless, trimmed and cubed
- ¾ cup low-sodium chicken stock
- 2 tablespoons olive oil
- ½ tablespoon sweet paprika
- 2 and ¼ teaspoon sage, dried
- ½ tablespoon garlic powder
- ¼ teaspoon rosemary, dried
- ¼ teaspoon marjoram, dried
- 1 teaspoon basil, dried
- 1 teaspoon oregano, dried
- Black pepper to the taste

Directions:
In a bowl, mix oil with stock, paprika, garlic powder, sage, rosemary, thyme, marjoram, oregano, pepper to the taste, and whisk well. Heat up a pan over medium-high heat, add the pork and brown it for 5 minutes on each side. Add the herbed mix, toss well, cook over medium heat for 1 hour, divide between plates and serve with a side salad.
Enjoy!

Nutrition: calories 310, fat 4, fiber 6, carbs 12, protein 14

Garlic Pork Shoulder

Preparation time: 10 minutes
Cooking time: 4 hours and 30 minutes
Servings: 6

Ingredients:

- 3 tablespoons garlic, minced
- 3 tablespoons olive oil
- 4 pounds pork shoulder
- 2 teaspoons sweet paprika
- Black pepper to the taste

Directions:
In a bowl, mix olive oil with paprika, black pepper and oil and whisk well. Brush pork shoulder with this mix, arrange in a baking dish and introduce in the oven at 425 degrees for 20 minutes. Reduce heat to 325 degrees F and bake for 4 hours. Slice the meat, divide it between plates and serve with a side salad.
Enjoy!

Nutrition: calories 321, fat 6, fiber 4, carbs 12, protein 18

Pork and Creamy Veggie Sauce

Preparation time: 10 minutes
Cooking time: 1 hour and 20 minutes
Servings: 4

Ingredients:
- 2 pounds pork roast
- 1 cup low-sodium veggie stock
- 2 carrots, chopped
- 1 leek, chopped
- 1 celery stalk, chopped
- 1 teaspoon black peppercorns
- 2 yellow onions, cut into quarters
- 1 tablespoon chives, chopped
- 1 tablespoon parsley, chopped
- 2 cups nonfat yogurt
- 1 cup coconut cream
- 1 teaspoon mustard
- Black pepper to the taste

Directions:
Put the roast in a baking dish, add carrots, leek, celery, peppercorns, onions, stock and black pepper, cover, introduce in the oven and bake at 400 degrees F for 1 hour and 10 minutes Transfer the roast to a platter and all the veggies mix to a pan. Heat this mix over medium heat, add yogurt, cream and mustard, toss, cook for 10 minutes, drizzle over the roast and serve. Enjoy!

Nutrition: calories 263, fat 4, fiber 2, carbs 12, protein 22

Ground Pork Pan

Preparation time: 10 minutes
Cooking time: 20 minutes
Servings: 4

Ingredients:
- Zest of 1 lemon, grated
- Juice of 1 lemon
- 2 garlic cloves, minced
- 1 tablespoon olive oil
- 1 pound pork meat, ground
- Black pepper to the taste
- 1-pint cherry tomatoes, chopped
- 1 small red onion, chopped
- ½ cup low-sodium veggie stock,
- 2 tablespoons low-sodium tomato paste
- 1 tablespoon basil, chopped

Directions:
Heat up a pan with the oil over medium heat, add garlic and onion, stir and cook for 5 minutes. Add pork, black pepper, tomatoes, stock, lemon juice, lemon zest and tomato paste, toss and cook for 15 minutes. Add basil, toss, divide between plates and serve. Enjoy!

Nutrition: calories 286, fat 8, fiber 7, carbs 14, protein 17

Tarragon Pork Steak

Preparation time: 10 minutes
Cooking time: 22 minutes
Servings: 4

Ingredients:
- 4 medium pork steaks
- Black pepper to the taste
- 1 tablespoon olive oil
- 8 cherry tomatoes, halved
- A handful tarragon, chopped

Directions:
Heat up a pan with the oil over medium-high heat, add steaks, season with black pepper, cook them for 6 minutes on each side and divide between plates. Heat up the same pan over medium heat, add the tomatoes and the tarragon, cook for 10 minutes, divide next to the pork and serve. Enjoy!

Nutrition: calories 263, fat 4, fiber 6, carbs 12, protein 16

Pork Meatballs

Preparation time: 10 minutes
Cooking time: 10 minutes
Servings: 4

Ingredients:
- 1 pound pork, ground
- 1/3 cup cilantro, chopped
- 1 cup red onion, chopped
- 4 garlic cloves, minced
- 1 tablespoon ginger, grated
- 1 Thai chili, chopped
- 2 tablespoons olive oil

Directions:
In a bowl, combine the meat with cilantro, onion, garlic, ginger and chili, stir well and shape medium meatballs out of this mix. Heat up a pan with the oil over medium-high heat, add the meatballs, cook them for 5 minutes on each side, divide them between plates and serve with a side salad.
Enjoy!

Nutrition: calories 220, fat 4, fiber 2, carbs 8, protein 14

Pork with Peanuts and Scallions

Preparation time: 10 minutes
Cooking time: 16 minutes
Servings: 4

Ingredients:
- 2 tablespoons lime juice
- 2 tablespoons coconut aminos
- 1 and ½ tablespoons brown sugar
- 5 garlic cloves, minced
- 3 tablespoons olive oil
- Black pepper to the taste
-
- 1 yellow onion, cut into wedges
- 1 and ½ pound pork tenderloin, cubed
- 3 tablespoons peanuts, chopped
- 2 scallions, chopped

Directions:
In a bowl, mix limejuice with aminos and sugar and stir very well. In another bowl, mix garlic with 1 and ½-teaspoon oil and some black pepper and stir. Heat up a pan with the rest of the oil over medium-high heat, add meat, and cook for 3 minutes on each side and transfer to a bowl. Heat up the same pan over medium-high heat, add onion, stir and cook for 3 minutes. Add the garlic mix, return the pork, also add the aminos mix, toss, cook for 6 minutes, divide between plates, sprinkle scallions and peanuts on top and serve.
Enjoy!

Nutrition: calories 273, fat 4, fiber 5, carbs 12, protein 18

Mediterranean Lamb Mix

Preparation time: 10 minutes
Cooking time: 10 minutes
Servings: 4

Ingredients:
- 1 garlic clove, minced
- 2 red chilies, chopped
- 1 cucumber, sliced
- 2 tablespoons balsamic vinegar
- 1 carrot, sliced
- 1 radish, sliced
-
- ½ cup mint leaves, chopped
- ½ cup coriander leaves, chopped
- Black pepper to the taste
- 2 tablespoons olive oil
- 3 ounces bean sprouts
- 2 lamb fillets

Directions:
Put the chilies in a pan, add garlic and vinegar, bring to a boil, stir well and take off heat. In a bowl, mix cucumber with radish, carrot, coriander, mint and sprouts. Heat up your kitchen grill over medium-high heat, brush lamb fillets with the oil, season them with pepper, cook for 3 minutes on each side, slice the meat, add over the veggies, also add the vinegar mix, toss and serve.
Enjoy!

Nutrition: calories 231, fat 3, fiber 5, carbs 7, protein 17

Pork and Eggplant Mix

Preparation time: 15 minutes
Cooking time: 1 hour
Servings: 6

Ingredients:
- 4 eggplants, cut into halves lengthwise
- 4 ounces olive oil
- 2 yellow onions, chopped
- 4 ounces pork meat, ground
- 2 green bell peppers, chopped
- 1 pound tomatoes, chopped
- 4 tomato slices
- 2 tablespoons low-sodium tomato paste
- ½ cup parsley, chopped
- 4 garlic cloves, minced
- ½ cup hot water
- Black pepper to the taste

Directions:
Heat up a pan with the olive oil over medium-high heat, add eggplant halves, cook for 5 minutes and transfer to a plate. Heat up the same pan over medium-high heat, add onion, stir and cook for 3 minutes. Add bell peppers, pork, tomato paste, pepper, parsley and chopped tomatoes, stir and cook for 7 minutes. Arrange the eggplant halves in a baking tray, divide garlic in each, spoon meat filling and top with a tomato slice. Pour the water over them, cover tray with foil, bake in the oven at 350 degrees F for 40 minutes, divide between plates and serve.
Enjoy!

Nutrition: calories 253, fat 3, fiber 2, carbs 12, protein 14

Pork Chili

Preparation time: 10 minutes
Cooking time: 1 hour and 10 minutes
Servings: 6

Ingredients:
- 1 green bell pepper, chopped
- 1 pound pork, cubed
- 1 yellow onion, chopped
- 4 carrots, chopped
- Black pepper to the taste
- 26 ounces canned tomatoes, no-salt-added and chopped
- 1 teaspoon onion powder
- 1 tablespoon parsley, chopped
- 4 teaspoons chili powder
- 1 teaspoon garlic powder
- 1 teaspoon sweet paprika

Directions:
Heat up a pot over medium-high heat, add the meat and brown for 5 minutes. Add bell pepper, carrots, onions, tomatoes, black pepper, onion powder, chili powder, paprika and garlic powder, and toss, bring to a simmer, reduce heat to medium, cover the pot and cook for 1 hour and 5 minutes. Add parsley, toss, divide into bowls and serve.
Enjoy!

Nutrition: calories 284, fat 6, fiber 6, carbs 12, protein 24

Pork and Sweet Potatoes Chili

Preparation time: 10 minutes
Cooking time: 1 hour and 20 minutes
Servings: 8

Ingredients:

- 2 pounds sweet potatoes, chopped
- A drizzle of olive oil
- 1 yellow onion, chopped
- 2 pounds pork meat, ground
- 1 tablespoon chili powder
- Black pepper to the taste
- 1 teaspoon cumin, ground
- ½ teaspoon garlic powder
- ½ teaspoon oregano, chopped
- ½ teaspoon cinnamon powder
- 1 cup low-sodium veggie stock
- ½ cup cilantro, chopped

Directions:
Heat up the a pan with the oil over medium-high heat, add sweet potatoes and onion, stir, cook for 15 minutes and transfer to a bowl. Heat up the pan again over medium-high heat, add pork, stir and brown for 5 minutes. Add black pepper, cumin, garlic powder, oregano, chili powder, and cinnamon, stock, return potatoes and onion, stir and cook for 1 hour over medium heat. Add the cilantro, toss, divide into bowls and serve.
Enjoy!

Nutrition: calories 320, fat 7, fiber 6, carbs 12, protein 22

Pork and Pumpkin Chili

Preparation time: 10 minutes
Cooking time: 1 hour and 30 minutes
Servings: 6

Ingredients:

- 1 green bell pepper, chopped
- 2 cups yellow onion, chopped
- 1 tablespoon olive oil
- 6 garlic cloves, minced
- 28 ounces canned tomatoes, no-salt-added and chopped
- 1 and ½ pounds pork, ground
- 6 ounces low-sodium tomato paste
- 14 ounces pumpkin puree
- 1 cup low-sodium chicken stock
- 2 and ½ teaspoons oregano, dried
- 1 and ½ teaspoon cinnamon, ground
- 1 and ½ tablespoon chili powder
- Black pepper to the taste

Directions:
Heat up a pot with the oil over medium-high heat, add bell peppers and onion, stir and cook for 7 minutes. Add garlic and the pork, toss and cook for 10 minutes. Add tomatoes, tomato paste, pumpkin puree, stock, oregano, cinnamon, chili powder and pepper, stir, cover, cook over medium heat for 1 hour and 10 minutes, divide into bowls and serve.
Enjoy!

Nutrition: calories 289, fat 12, fiber 8, carbs 12, protein 20

Chinese Pork Soup

Preparation time: 10 minutes
Cooking time: 1 hour and 30 minutes
Servings: 6

Ingredients:
- 3 carrots, chopped
- 1 pound pork meat, cubed
- 1 tomato, chopped
- 3 mushrooms, sliced
- 6 star anise
- 4 bay leaves
- 5 ginger slices
- 2 tablespoons Sichuan peppercorns
- 1 an ½ tablespoons fennel powder
- 1 teaspoon coriander, ground
- 1 tablespoon cumin powder
- ¼ teaspoon five spice powder
- Black pepper to the taste
- A bunch of scallions, chopped
- 8 cups water
- 1/3 cup coconut aminos

Directions:
Put the water in a pot and heat up over medium heat. Add carrots, pork, tomato, mushrooms, star anise, bay leaves, ginger, peppercorns, fennel, coriander, cumin, five spice, black pepper, aminos and scallions, stir, bring to a boil and cook for 1 hour and 30 minutes. Discard star anise, ginger, bay leaves and peppercorns, ladle the soup into bowls and serve.
Enjoy!

Nutrition: calories 250, fat 2, fiber 7, carbs 14, protein 14

Ground Pork and Kale Soup

Preparation time: 10 minutes
Cooking time: 30 minutes
Servings: 4

Ingredients:
- 1 pound pork, ground
- 3 carrots, chopped
- 4 potatoes, chopped
- 1 yellow onion, chopped
- ½ bunch kale, chopped
- 4 garlic cloves, minced
- 2 cups squash, cooked and pureed
- 2 quarts low-sodium veggie stock
- Black pepper to the taste
- 3 teaspoons Italian seasoning

Directions:
Heat up a pot over medium-high heat; add pork, stir, and brown for 5 minutes and transfer to a bowl. Heat up the pot again over medium heat, add potatoes, onion, carrots, kale, garlic and pepper, stir and cook for 10 minutes. Return beef, also add stock, squash puree and Italian seasoning, stir, simmer over medium heat for 15 minutes, ladle into bowls and serve.
Enjoy!

Nutrition: calories 270, fat 12, fiber 6, carbs 12, protein 23

Steak Salad with Peaches and Kale

Preparation time: 10 minutes
Cooking time: 12 minutes
Servings: 2

Ingredients:
- 2 peaches, chopped
- 3 handfuls kale, chopped
- 8 ounces pork steak, cut into strips
- 1 tablespoon avocado oil
- A drizzle of olive oil
- 1 tablespoon balsamic vinegar

Directions:
Heat up a pan with the avocado oil over medium-high heat, add steak strips, cook them for 6 minutes on each side and transfer to a salad bowl. Add peaches, kale, olive oil and vinegar, toss and serve.
Enjoy!

Nutrition: calories 240, fat 5, fiber 4, carbs 8, protein 15

Balsamic Chili Roast

Preparation time: 10 minutes
Cooking time: 4 hours
Servings: 6

Ingredients:
- 4 pound pork roast
- 6 garlic cloves, minced
- 1 yellow onion, chopped
- ½ cup balsamic vinegar
- 1 cup low-sodium chicken stock
- 2 tablespoons coconut aminos
- Black pepper to the taste
- A pinch of red chili pepper flakes

Directions:
Put the roast in a baking dish, add garlic, onion, vinegar, stock, aminos, black pepper and chili flakes, and cover, introduce in the oven and cook at 325 degrees F for 4 hours. Slice, divide between plates and serve with a side salad.
Enjoy!

Nutrition: calories 265, fat 7, fiber 6, carbs 15, protein 32

Winter Pork Roast

Preparation time: 10 minutes
Cooking time: 3 hours and 20 minutes
Servings: 6

Ingredients:
- 2 and ½ pounds pork roast
- Black pepper to the taste
- 1 teaspoon chili powder
- ½ teaspoon onion powder
- ¼ teaspoon cumin, ground
- 1 teaspoon cocoa powder

Directions:
In a roasting pan, combine the roast with black pepper, chili powder, onion powder, cumin and cocoa, rub, cover the pan, introduce in the oven and bake at 325 degrees F for 3 hours and 20 minutes. Slice, divide between plates and serve with a side salad.
Enjoy!

Nutrition: calories 288, fat 5, fiber 6, carbs 12, protein 23

Creamy Smoky Pork Chops

Preparation time: 10 minutes
Cooking time: 20 minutes
Servings: 4

Ingredients:
- 2 tablespoons olive oil
- 4 pork chops
- 1 tablespoon chili powder
- Black pepper to the taste
- 1 teaspoon sweet paprika
- 1 garlic clove, minced
- 1 cup coconut milk
- 1 teaspoon liquid smoke
- ¼ cup cilantro, chopped
- Juice of 1 lemon

Directions:
In a bowl, mix pork chops with pepper, chili powder, paprika and garlic and rub well. Heat up a pan with the oil over medium-high heat, add pork chops and cook for 5 minutes on each side. In a blender, mix coconut milk with liquid smoke, lemon juice and cilantro, blend well, pour over the chops, cook for 10 minutes more, divide everything between plates and serve.
Enjoy!

Nutrition: calories 240, fat 8, fiber 6, carbs 10, protein 22

Pork and Dates Sauce

Preparation time: 10 minutes
Cooking time: 40 minutes
Servings: 6

Ingredients:

- 1 and ½ pounds pork tenderloin
- 2 tablespoons water
- 1/3 cup dates, pitted
- ¼ teaspoon onion powder
- ¼ teaspoon smoked paprika
- 2 tablespoons mustard
- ¼ cup coconut aminos
- Black pepper to the taste

Directions:

In your food processor, mix dates with water, coconut aminos, mustard, paprika, pepper and onion powder and blend well. Put pork tenderloin in a roasting pan, add the dates sauce, toss to coat very well, introduce everything in the oven at 400 degrees F, bake for 40 minutes, slice the meat, divide it and the sauce between plates and serve.
Enjoy!

Nutrition: calories 240, fat 8, fiber 4, carbs 13, protein 24

Pork Chops and Apples

Preparation time: 10 minutes
Cooking time: 1 hour
Servings: 4

Ingredients:

- 1 and ½ cups low-sodium chicken stock
- Black pepper to the taste
- 4 pork chops
- 1 yellow onion, chopped
- 1 tablespoon olive oil
- 2 garlic cloves, minced
- 3 apples, cored and sliced
- 1 tablespoon thyme, chopped

Directions:

Heat up a pan with the oil over medium-high heat, add pork chops, season with black pepper and cook for 5 minutes on each side. Add onion, garlic, apples, thyme and stock, toss, introduce in the oven and bake at 350 degrees F for 50 minutes. Divide everything between plates and serve.
Enjoy!

Nutrition: calories 340, fat 12, fiber 9, carbs 14, protein 27

Pork Bowls

Preparation time: 10 minutes
Cooking time: 23 minutes
Servings: 6

Ingredients:

- Juice of 1 lime
- 1 and ½ pounds pork steak, cut into strips
- ½ teaspoon chili powder
- Black pepper to the taste
- 1 teaspoon sweet paprika
- ½ teaspoon oregano, dried
- 2 tablespoons olive oil
- 2 red bell peppers, chopped
- 1 yellow onion, sliced
- 5 ounces mushrooms, chopped
- 1 garlic clove, minced
- 2 green onions, chopped
- 1 jalapeno, chopped
- 1 cup low-sodium veggie stock
- ¼ cup parsley, chopped

Directions:

In a bowl, mix limejuice with black pepper, chili powder, paprika, oregano and meat strips and toss well. Heat up a pan with the oil over medium-high heat, add the meat, and cook for 4 minutes on each side and transfer to a plate. Heat up the same pan over medium heat, add bell peppers, mushrooms, garlic and onions, stir and cook for 5 minutes. Add stock, green onion, limejuice, and jalapeno, return the meat, stir and cook for 10 minutes more. Divide everything between plates and serve with parsley on top.
Enjoy!

Nutrition: calories 250, fat 12, fiber 3, carbs 7, protein 14

Pork and Salsa

Preparation time: 10 minutes
Cooking time: 15 minutes
Servings: 4

Ingredients:

- 8 ounces canned pineapple, crushed
- 1 tablespoon olive oil
- 1 pound pork, ground
- 1 teaspoon chili powder
- 1 teaspoon garlic powder
- 1 teaspoon cumin, ground
- Black pepper to the taste
- 1 mango, chopped
- Juice of 1 lime
- 2 avocados, pitted, peeled and chopped
- ¼ cup cilantro, chopped

Directions:

Heat up a pan with the oil over medium heat, add pork meat stir and brown for 5 minutes. Add garlic, cumin, chili powder, pineapple and pepper, stir and cook for 10 minutes. In a bowl, mix mango with avocados, limejuice, cilantro and pepper and stir. Divide the pork and pineapple mix between plates, top with the mango salsa and serve.
Enjoy!

Nutrition: calories 270, fat 6, fiber 7, carbs 12, protein 22

Hungarian Pork Stew

Preparation time: 10 minutes
Cooking time: 15 minutes
Servings: 4

Ingredients:

- 2 shallots, chopped
- 2 tablespoons olive oil
- 4 garlic cloves, minced
- 1 pound pork, ground
- 1 eggplant, cubed
- 14 ounces canned tomatoes, no-salt-added and chopped
- Black pepper to the taste
- ½ cup basil, chopped
- 2 tablespoons low-sodium tomato paste
- ¾ cup coconut cream

Directions:
Heat up a pan with half of the oil over medium heat, add garlic and shallots, stir and cook for 5 minutes. Add pork, stir and brown for 4 minutes. Heat up another pan with the rest of the oil over medium heat, add eggplant, stir, cook for 5 minutes and add over the meat. Also, add tomatoes, pepper, basil, tomato paste and coconut cream, stir, cook for 1 minute, divide into bowls and serve.
Enjoy!

Nutrition: calories 261, fat 11, fiber 1, carbs 8, protein 22

Pork Loin Chops With Apples and Thyme

Preparation time: 10 minutes
Cooking time: 35 minutes
Servings: 4

Ingredients:

- 1 and ½ cups red onion, cut into wedges
- 2 and ½ teaspoons olive oil
- 2 cups apple, cored and cut into wedges
- Black pepper to the taste
- 2 teaspoons thyme, chopped
- 4 medium pork loin chops, bone-in
- 1 teaspoon cider vinegar
- ½ cup low-sodium chicken stock

Directions:
Heat up a pan with 1-teaspoon oil over medium-high heat, add the onions, stir and cook them for 2 minutes. Add apples, stock, vinegar, black pepper and the thyme, toss introduce the pan in the oven at 400 degrees F and bake for 15 minutes. Heat up another pan with the rest of the oil over medium-high heat, add pork, season with pepper and cook for 5 minutes on each side. Add the apples and thyme mix, toss everything, cook for 5 minutes more, divide between plates and serve.

Nutrition: calories 240, fat 7, fiber 2, carbs 10, protein 17

Pork and Roasted Tomatoes Mix

Preparation time: 10 minutes
Cooking time: 15 minutes
Servings: 6

Ingredients:

- 1 pound pork meat, ground
- 2 cups zucchinis, chopped
- ½ cup yellow onion, chopped
- Black pepper to the taste
- 15 ounces canned roasted tomatoes, no-salt-added and chopped
- ¾ cup low- fat cheddar cheese, shredded

Directions:
Heat up a pan over medium-high heat, add pork, onion, black pepper and zucchini, stir and cook for 7 minutes. Add roasted tomatoes, stir, bring to a boil, cook over medium heat for 8 minutes, divide into bowls, sprinkle cheddar on top and serve.
Enjoy!

Nutrition: calories 270, fat 5, fiber 3, carbs 10, protein 12

Pork and Cabbage Salad

Preparation time: 10 minutes
Cooking time: 0 minutes
Servings: 10

Ingredients:

- 1 green cabbage head, shredded
- 1 and ½ cups brown rice, already cooked
- 2 cups pork roast, already cooked and shredded
- 10 ounces peas
-
- 8 ounces water chestnuts, drained and sliced
- ½ cup low-fat sour cream
- ½ cup avocado mayonnaise
- A pinch of black pepper

Directions:
In a bowl, combine the cabbage with the rice, shredded meat, peas, chestnuts, sour cream, mayo and black pepper, toss and serve cold.
Enjoy!

Nutrition: calories 310, fat 5, fiber 4, carbs 11, protein 17

Pork and Zucchini Stew

Preparation time: 10 minutes
Cooking time: 1 hour
Servings: 4

Ingredients:

- 1 pound ground pork, cubed
- Black pepper to the taste
- ¼ teaspoon sweet paprika
- 1 tablespoon olive oil
- 1 and ½ cups low-sodium veggie stock
- 3 cups zucchinis, cubed
- 1 yellow onion, chopped
- ½ cup low-sodium tomato sauce
- 1 tablespoon parsley, chopped

Directions:

Heat up a pot with the oil over medium-high heat, add the pork, black pepper and paprika, stir and brown for 5 minutes. Add stock, onion and tomato sauce, toss, bring to a simmer, reduce heat to medium and cook for 40 minutes. Add the zucchinis and the parsley, toss, cook for 15 minutes more, divide into bowls and serve.
Enjoy!

Nutrition: calories 270, fat 7, fiber 9, carbs 12, protein 17

Pork Roast, Carrots and Leeks Mix

Preparation time: 10 minutes
Cooking time: 1 hour and 10 minutes
Servings: 4

Ingredients:

- 2 pounds pork roast, trimmed
- 4 carrots, chopped
- 4 leeks, chopped
- 1 teaspoon black peppercorns
- 2 yellow onions, cut into wedges
- 1 tablespoon parsley, chopped
- 1 cup low-sodium veggie stock
- 1 teaspoon mustard
- Black pepper to the taste

Directions:

Put the pork in a roasting pan, add carrots, leeks, peppercorns, onions, stock, mustard and black pepper, toss, cover the pan and bake in the oven at 375 degrees F for 1 hour and 10 minutes. Slice the meat; divide it between plates, sprinkle parsley on top and serve with the carrots and leeks mix on the side.
Enjoy!

Nutrition: calories 260, fat 5, fiber 7, carbs 12, protein 20

Simple Veal Chops

Preparation time: 10 minutes
Cooking time: 20 minutes
Servings: 4

Ingredients:

- 3 tablespoons whole wheat flour
- Black pepper to the taste
- 2 eggs
- 1 tablespoon milk
- 1 and ½ cups whole wheat breadcrumbs
- Zest of 1 lemon, grated
- 4 veal rib chops
- 3 tablespoons olive oil

Directions:
Put whole-wheat flour in a bowl. In another bowl, mix eggs with milk and whisk in a third bowl, mix the breadcrumbs with lemon zest. Season veal chops with black pepper, dredge them in flour, dip in the egg mix and then in breadcrumbs. Heat up a pan with the oil over medium-high heat, add veal chops, cook for 2 minutes on each side and transfer to a baking sheet, introduce them in the oven at 350 degrees F, bake for 15 minutes, divide between plates and serve with a side salad.
Enjoy!

Nutrition: calories 270, fat 6, fiber 7, carbs 10, protein 16

Pork Belly and Apple Sauce

Preparation time: 10 minutes
Cooking time: 1 hour and 30 minutes
Servings: 6

Ingredients:

- 1 tablespoon lemon juice
- 2 cups low-sodium veggie stock
- 17 ounces apples, cored and cut into wedges
- 2 pounds pork belly, trimmed and scored
- 1 teaspoons sweet paprika
- Black pepper to the taste
- A drizzle of olive oil

Directions:
In your blender, mix the stock with apples and lemon juice and pulse very well. Put pork belly in a roasting pan, add applesauce, also add the oil, paprika and black pepper, toss well, introduce in the oven and bake at 380 degrees F for 1 hour and 30 minutes. Slice the pork belly, divide it between plates, drizzle the sauce all over and serve.
Enjoy!

Nutrition: calories 356, fat 14, fiber 4, carbs 10, protein 27

Citrus Pork

Preparation time: 10 minutes
Cooking time: 30 minutes
Servings: 4

Ingredients:

- Zest of 2 limes, grated
- Zest of 1 orange, grated
- Juice of 1 orange
- Juice of 2 limes
- 4 teaspoons garlic, minced
- ¾ cup olive oil
- 1 cup cilantro, chopped
- 1 cup mint, chopped
- Black pepper to the taste
- 4 pork loin steaks

Directions:

In your food processor, mix lime zest and juice with orange zest and juice, garlic, oil, cilantro, mint and pepper and blend well. Put the steaks in a bowl, add the citrus mix and toss really well. Heat up a pan over medium-high heat, add pork steaks and the marinade, cook for 4 minutes on each side, introduce the pan in the oven and bake at 350 degrees F for 20 minutes. Divide the steaks between plates, drizzle some of the cooking juices all over and serve with a side salad. Enjoy!

Nutrition: calories 270, fat 7, fiber 2, carbs 8, protein 20

Nutmeg Pork Chops

Preparation time: 10 minutes
Cooking time: 40 minutes
Servings: 3

Ingredients:

- 8 ounces mushrooms, sliced
- ¼ cup coconut milk
- 1 teaspoon garlic powder
- 1 yellow onion, chopped
- 3 pork chops, boneless
- 2 teaspoons nutmeg, ground
- 1 tablespoon balsamic vinegar
- ½ cup olive oil

Directions:

Heat up a pan with the oil over medium heat, add mushrooms and onions, stir and cook for 5 minutes. Add pork chops, nutmeg and garlic powder and cook for 5 minutes more. Add vinegar and coconut milk, toss, introduce in the oven and bake at 350 degrees F and bake for 30 minutes. Divide between plates and serve.
Enjoy!

Nutrition: calories 260, fat 10, fiber 6, carbs 8, protein 22

Italian Parmesan Pork

Preparation time: 10 minutes
Cooking time: 30 minutes
Servings: 6

Ingredients:

- 2 tablespoons parsley, chopped
- 1 pound pork cutlets, thinly sliced
- 1 tablespoon olive oil
- ¼ cup yellow onion, chopped
- 3 garlic cloves, minced
- 2 tablespoons parmesan, grated
- 15 ounces canned tomatoes, no-salt-added and chopped
- 1/3 cup low sodium chicken stock
- Black pepper to the taste
- 1 teaspoon Italian seasoning

Directions:
Heat up a pan with the oil over medium-high heat, add pork cutlets, season with Italian seasoning and black pepper and cook for 4 minutes on each side. Add onion, garlic, tomatoes, stock and top with parmesan, introduce the pan in the oven and bake at 350 degrees F for 20 minutes. Sprinkle parsley on top, divide everything between plates and serve.
Enjoy!

Nutrition: calories 280, fat 17, fiber 5, carbs 12, protein 34

Pork Roast and Cranberry Roast

Preparation time: 10 minutes
Cooking time: 1 hour and 30 minutes
Servings: 4

Ingredients:

- 1 tablespoon coconut flour
- Black pepper to the taste
- 1 and ½ pounds pork loin roast
- ½ teaspoon ginger, grated
- ½ cup cranberries
- 2 garlic cloves, minced
- Juice of ½ lemon
- ½ cup low-sodium veggie stock

Directions:
Put the stock in a small pan, heat it up over medium-high heat, add black pepper, ginger, garlic, cranberries, lemon juice and the flour, whisk well and cook for 10 minutes. Put the roast in a pan, add the cranberry sauce on top, introduce in the oven and bake at 375 degrees F for 1 hour and 20 minutes. Slice the roast, divide it and the sauce between plates and serve.
Enjoy!

Nutrition: calories 330, fat 13, fiber 2, carbs 13, protein 25

Pork Patties

Preparation time: 10 minutes
Cooking time: 35 minutes
Servings: 6

Ingredients:

- ½ cup coconut flour
- 2 tablespoons olive oil
- 2 egg, whisked
- Black pepper to the taste
- 1 and ½ pounds pork, ground
- 10 ounces low sodium veggie stock
- ¼ cup tomato sauce, no-salt-added
- ½ teaspoon mustard powder

Directions:
Put the flour in a bowl and the egg in another one. Mix the pork with black pepper and a pinch of paprika, shape medium patties out of this mix, dip them in the egg and then dredge in flour. Heat up a pan with the oil over medium-high heat, add the patties and cook them for 5 minutes on each side. In a bowl, combine the stock with tomato sauce and mustard powder and whisk. Add this over the patties, cook for 10 minutes over medium heat, divide everything between plates and serve.
Enjoy!

Nutrition: calories 332, fat 18, fiber 4, carbs 11, protein 25

Roast and Mushrooms

Preparation time: 10 minutes
Cooking time: 1 hour and 20 minutes
Servings: 4

Ingredients:

- 3 and ½ pounds pork roast
- 4 ounces mushrooms, sliced
-
- 12 ounces low-sodium beef stock
- 1 teaspoon Italian seasoning

Directions:
In a roasting pan, combine the roast with mushrooms, stock and Italian seasoning, and toss, introduce in the oven and bake at 350 degrees F for 1 hour and 20 minutes. Slice the roast, divide it and the mushroom mix between plates and serve.
Enjoy!

Nutrition: calories 310, fat 16, fiber 2, carbs 10, protein 22

Pork Meatloaf

Preparation time: 10 minutes
Cooking time: 50 minutes
Servings: 6

Ingredients:

- 1 cup white mushrooms, chopped
- 3 pounds pork, ground
- 2 tablespoons parsley, chopped
- 2 garlic cloves, minced
- ½ cup yellow onion, chopped
- 1 teaspoon balsamic vinegar
- ¼ cup red bell pepper, chopped
- ½ cup almond flour
- 1/3 cup low-fat parmesan, grated
- 3 eggs
- Black pepper to the taste

Directions:

In a bowl, mix the pork with the black pepper, bell pepper, mushrooms, garlic, onion, parsley, almond flour, parmesan, vinegar and eggs, stir very well, transfer this into a loaf pan and bake in the oven at 375 degrees F for 50 minutes. Leave meatloaf to cool down, slice and serve it.
Enjoy!

Nutrition: calories 274, fat 14, fiber 3, carbs 8, protein 24

Meatballs Salad

Preparation time: 10 minutes
Cooking time: 15 minutes
Servings: 6

Ingredients:

- 17 ounces pork ground
- 1 yellow onion, grated
- 1 egg, whisked
- ¼ cup parsley, chopped
- Black pepper to the taste
- 2 garlic cloves, minced
- ¼ cup mint, chopped
- 2 and ½ teaspoons oregano, dried
- ¼ cup olive oil
- 7 ounces cherry tomatoes, halved
- 1 cucumber, thinly sliced
- 1 cup baby spinach
- 1 and ½ tablespoons lemon juice
- A drizzle of avocado oil

Directions:

In a bowl, combine the pork with the onion, egg, parsley, black pepper, mint, garlic and oregano, stir well and shape medium meatballs out of this mix. Heat up a pan with the olive oil over medium-high heat, add the meatballs and cook them for 5 minutes on each side. In a salad bowl, combine the meatballs with the tomatoes, cucumber, spinach, lemon juice and avocado oil, toss and serve.
Enjoy!

Nutrition: calories 220, fat 4, fiber 6, carbs 8, protein 12

Meatballs and Sauce

Preparation time: 10 minutes
Cooking time: 32 minutes
Servings: 6

Ingredients:

- 2 pounds pork, ground
- Black pepper to the taste
- ½ teaspoon garlic powder
- 1 tablespoon coconut aminos
- ¼ cup low sodium veggie
- ¾ cup almond flour
- 1 tablespoon parsley, chopped

For the sauce:

- 1 cup yellow onion, chopped
- 2 cups mushrooms, sliced
- 2 tablespoons olive oil
- 1 teaspoon coconut aminos
- ½ cup coconut cream
- Black pepper to the taste

Directions:

In a bowl, mix the pork with black pepper, garlic powder, 1 tablespoons coconut aminos, stock, almond flour and parsley, stir well, shape medium meatballs out of this mix, arrange them on a baking sheet, introduce in the oven at 375 degrees F and bake for 20 minutes. Meanwhile, heat up a pan with the oil over medium heat, add mushrooms, stir and cook for 4 minutes. Add onions, 1 teaspoon coconut aminos, cream and black pepper, stir and cook for 5 minutes more. Add the meatballs, toss gently, cook for 1-2 minutes more, divide everything into bowls and serve. Enjoy!

Nutrition: calories 435, fat 23, fiber 4, carbs 6, protein 32

Ground Pork Stir Fry

Preparation time: 10 minutes
Cooking time: 25 minutes
Servings: 10

Ingredients:

- 3 garlic cloves, minced
- 1 pound pork, ground
- ½ cup tomato sauce, no-salt-added
- 1 yellow onion, chopped
- 2 habanero peppers, chopped
- 1 teaspoon curry powder
- 1 teaspoon thyme, dried

- 2 teaspoons coriander, ground
- ½ teaspoon allspice, ground
- 2 teaspoons cumin, ground
- ½ teaspoon turmeric powder
- Black pepper to the taste
- 1 teaspoon garlic powder
- 2 tablespoons olive oil

Directions:

Heat up a pan with the oil over medium-high heat, add the onion and the garlic, stir and cook for 5 minutes. Add habanero peppers, curry powder, thyme, coriander, allspice, cumin, turmeric, black pepper and garlic powder, stir and cook for 5 minutes more. Add the pork and the tomato sauce, toss, cook for 15 minutes more, divide everything into bowls and serve.
Enjoy!

Nutrition: calories 267, fat 23, fiber 6, carbs 12, protein 22

Pork and Fennel Mix

Preparation time: 10 minutes
Cooking time: 30 minutes
Servings: 4

Ingredients:

- 12 ounces pork meat, cubed
- 2 fennel bulbs, sliced
- Black pepper to the taste
- 2 tablespoons olive oil
- 4 figs, cut halved
- 1/8 cup apple cider vinegar

Directions:
Heat up a pan with the oil over medium-high heat, add the pork and brown for 5 minutes on each side. Add fennel, black pepper, figs and cider vinegar, toss, reduce heat to medium, cook for 20 minutes more, divide everything between plates and serve.
Enjoy!

Nutrition: calories 260, fat 3, fiber 3, carbs 8, protein 16

Pork and Cabbage Casserole

Preparation time: 10 minutes
Cooking time: 40 minutes
Servings: 4

Ingredients:

- 17 ounces pork meat, cubed
- 1 green cabbage, shredded
- Salt and black pepper to the taste
- 1 small yellow onion, chopped
- 2 garlic cloves, minced
- 1 tablespoon olive oil
- ½ cup low-fat parmesan, grated
- ½ cup coconut cream.

Directions:
Heat up a pot with the oil over medium-high heat, add onion, stir and cook for 2 minutes. Add garlic and the meat and brown for 5 minutes. Add the cabbage, toss and cook everything for 10 minutes more. Add black pepper and coconut cream and toss. Sprinkle parmesan on top, introduce the pan in the oven and bake at 350 degrees F for 20 minutes.
Enjoy!

Nutrition: calories 260, fat 7, fiber 4, carbs 12, protein 17

French Pork Mix

Preparation time: 1 hour
Cooking time: 5 hours and 10 minutes
Servings: 8

Ingredients:

- 3 tablespoons olive oil+ a drizzle
- 2 tablespoons onion, chopped
- 1 tablespoon parsley flakes
- 1 and ½ cups red grapes juice, unsweetened
- 1 teaspoon thyme, dried
- Black pepper to the taste
- 1/3 cup almond flour
- 4 pounds pork meat, cubed
- 24 small white onions
- 2 garlic cloves, minced
- 1 pound mushrooms, roughly chopped

Directions:

In a bowl, mix the grape juice with olive oil, minced onion, thyme, parsley, pepper and pork, toss and keep in the fridge for 1 hour. Drain meat, dredge it in flour and reserve 1 cup of marinade. Heat up a pan with a drizzle of oil over medium-high heat, add the onions and cook them for 5 minutes. Add the garlic, the mushrooms and the meat, cook everything for 5 minutes and transfer to a slow cooker. Add black pepper and reserved marinade cover the pot and cook on High for 5 hours. Divide everything between plates and serve.
Enjoy!

Nutrition: calories 325, fat 11, fiber 1, carbs 7, protein 16

Pork and Okra Stew

Preparation time: 10 minutes
Cooking time: 30 minutes
Servings: 9

Ingredients:

- 1 pound pork meat, cubed
- 1 green bell pepper, chopped
- 2 yellow onions, chopped
- Black pepper to the taste
- 1 cup parsley, chopped
- 8 green onions, chopped
- ¼ cup olive oil
- 1 cup low-sodium veggie stock
- 6 garlic cloves
- 20 ounces canned tomatoes, no-salt-added and chopped
- 20 ounces okra, chopped

Directions:

Heat up a pot with the oil over medium-high heat, add the meat and brown it for 5 minutes. Add yellow onions, bell pepper, green onions, parsley and black pepper, stir and cook for 4 minutes more. Add stock, garlic, tomatoes and okra, stir, bring to a simmer, cook for 20 minutes over medium heat, divide into bowls and serve.
Enjoy!

Nutrition: calories 314, fat 12, fiber 4, carbs 13, protein 17

Burgundy Stew

Preparation time: 10 minutes
Cooking time: 3 hours and 5 minutes
Servings: 6

Ingredients:

- 2 pounds pork roast, cubed
- A drizzle of olive oil
- 15 ounces canned tomatoes, no-salt-added and chopped
- 4 carrots, chopped
- Black pepper to the taste
- ½ pounds mushrooms, sliced
- 2 celery ribs, chopped
- 2 yellow onions, chopped
- 1 cup low-sodium veggie stock
- 1 tablespoon thyme, chopped
- ½ teaspoon mustard powder

Directions:
Heat up a Dutch oven with the oil over medium-high heat, add the meat and brown it for 5 minutes. Add tomatoes, carrot, black pepper, mushrooms, celery, onions, stock, thyme and mustard powder, toss, introduce in the oven and bake at 325 degrees F for 3 hours. Divide everything between plates and serve.
Enjoy!

Nutrition: calories 265, fat 13, fiber 4, carbs 7, protein 18

Simple Pork and Capers

Preparation time: 10 minutes
Cooking time: 15 minutes
Servings: 2

Ingredients:

- 2 tablespoons olive oil
- 1 cup low-sodium chicken stock
- 2 tablespoons capers
- 1 garlic clove, minced
- 8 ounces pork, cubed
- Black pepper to the taste

Directions:
Heat up a pan with the oil over medium-high heat, add the pork season with black pepper and cook for 4 minutes on each side. Add garlic, capers and stock, stir and cook for 7 minutes more. Divide everything between plates and serve.
Enjoy!

Nutrition: calories 224, fat 12, fiber 6, carbs 12, protein 10

Pork and Red Peppers Mix

Preparation time: 10 minutes
Cooking time: 1 hour
Servings: 4

Ingredients:

- 3 red bell peppers, chopped
- 1 and ½ pounds pork meat, cubed
- ¼ cup low-sodium tomato sauce
- Black pepper to the taste
- 2 pounds Portobello mushrooms, sliced
- 2 yellow onions, chopped
- 1 tablespoon olive oil

Directions:
Heat up a pan with the oil over medium-high heat, add the pork and brown it for 5 minutes. Add bell peppers, mushrooms and onions, stir and cook for 5 minutes more. Add tomato sauce and black pepper, toss, introduce in the oven and bake at 350 degrees F for 50 minutes. Divide everything between plates and serve.
Enjoy!

Nutrition: calories 130, fat 12, fiber 1, carbs 3, protein 9

Easy Pork and Kale

Preparation time: 10 minutes
Cooking time: 20 minutes
Servings: 4

Ingredients:

- 1 cup yellow onion, chopped
- 1 and ½ pound pork meat, cut into strips
- ½ cup red bell pepper, chopped
- Black pepper to the taste
- 1 tablespoon olive oil
- 4 pounds kale, chopped
- 1 teaspoon garlic, minced
- ¼ cup red hot chili pepper, chopped
- 1 cup low-sodium veggie stock

Directions:
Heat up a pan with the oil over medium-high heat, add pork strips and cook them for 6 minutes Add onions, bell pepper, black pepper and garlic, stir and cook for 4 minutes more. Add kale, stock and chili pepper, toss, cook for 10 minutes, divide between plates and serve.
Enjoy!

Nutrition: calories 350, fat 4, fiber 7, carbs 8, protein 16

Italian Pork Soup

Preparation time: 10 minutes
Cooking time: 30 minutes
Servings: 10

Ingredients:

- 64 ounces low-sodium veggie stock
- 1 tablespoon olive oil
- 1 cup coconut cream
- 10 ounces spinach
- 1 and ½ pounds pork meat, cubed
- 1 pound radishes, chopped
- 2 garlic cloves, minced
- Black pepper to the taste
- A pinch of red pepper flakes, crushed
- 1 yellow onion, chopped

Directions:

Heat up a pot with the oil over medium-high heat, add the meat, onion and garlic, stir and brown for 5 minutes. Add stock, spinach, radishes, black pepper, pepper flakes and cream, stir, bring to a simmer, reduce heat to medium and cook for 25 minutes. Ladle into bowls and serve.
Enjoy!

Nutrition: calories 301, fat 16, fiber 2, carbs 8, protein 17

Pork and Watercress Soup

Preparation time: 10 minutes
Cooking time: 30 minutes
Servings: 4

Ingredients:

- 6 cups low-sodium chicken stock
- 2 teaspoons coconut aminos
- 6 and ½ cups watercress
- Black pepper to the taste
-
- 1 pound pork meat, cubed
- 1 tablespoon olive oil
- 3 shallots, chopped
- 3 egg whites, whisked

Directions:

Heat up a pot with the oil over medium-high heat, add the meat and some black pepper and brown it for 5 minutes. Add shallots and aminos, toss and cook for 3 minutes more. Add the stock, stir, bring to a simmer and cook over medium heat for 15 minutes more. Add egg whites and the watercress, toss, cook for 6 minutes more, ladle into bowls and serve.
Enjoy!

Nutrition: calories 260, fat 5, fiber 5, carbs 8, protein 16

Pork and Bok Choy Soup

Preparation time: 10 minutes
Cooking time: 30 minutes
Servings: 4

Ingredients:

- 6 cups low-sodium veggie stock
- A drizzle of olive oil
- 1 pound pork meat, cubed
- 1 yellow onion, chopped
- 1 bunch bok choy, chopped
- 1 and ½ cups mushrooms, chopped
- Black pepper to the taste
- ½ tablespoon red pepper flakes
- 3 tablespoons coconut aminos
- 3 tablespoons low-fat parmesan, grated

Directions:
Heat up a pot with the oil over medium-high heat, add the meat and brown it for 5 minutes. Add onion, mushrooms, black pepper and pepper flakes, stir and cook for 5 minutes more. Add the stock, bok choy and the coconut aminos, toss, bring to a simmer and cook over medium heat for 20 minutes. Ladle the soup into bowls, sprinkle the parmesan on top and serve.
Enjoy!

Nutrition: calories 310, fat 6, fiber 6, carbs 12, protein 16

Pork and Celery Mix

Preparation time: 10 minutes
Cooking time: 25 minutes
Servings: 8

Ingredients:

- 26 ounces celery leaves and stalks, chopped
- 1 tablespoon olive oil
- 1 tablespoon onion, chopped
- 1 pound pork meat, cubed
- Black pepper to the taste
- 3 teaspoons fenugreek powder
- 1 and ½ cups coconut cream

Directions:
Heat up a pan with the oil over medium-high heat, add the pork and the onion, black pepper and fenugreek, toss and brown for 5 minutes. Add the celery and the coconut cream, toss, cook over medium heat for 20 minutes, divide everything into bowls and serve.
Enjoy!

Nutrition: calories 340, fat 5, fiber 5, carbs 8, protein 14

Persian Pork Stew

Preparation time: 10 minutes
Cooking time: 40 minutes
Servings: 5

Ingredients:

- 1 celery bunch, roughly chopped
- 1 pound pork meat, cubed
- 1 tablespoon olive oil
- 1 yellow onion, chopped
- 1 bunch green onion, chopped
- 4 garlic cloves, minced
- Black pepper to the taste
- 1 parsley bunch, chopped
- 2 mint bunches, chopped
- 2 cups low-sodium veggie stock

Directions:

Heat up a pot with the oil over medium-high heat, add onion, green onions and garlic, stir and cook for 6 minutes. Add the pork, stir and cook for 5 minutes more. Add celery, black pepper, mint, parsley and stock, toss and cook over medium heat for 30 minutes more. Divide into bowls and serve.
Enjoy!

Nutrition: calories 310, fat 7, fiber 4, carbs 7, protein 17

Pork and Spinach Soup

Preparation time: 10 minutes
Cooking time: 40 minutes
Servings: 6

Ingredients:

- 2 tablespoons olive oil
- 20 ounces spinach, chopped
- 1 pound pork meat, cubed
- 1 yellow onion, chopped
- 1 teaspoon garlic, minced
- Black pepper to the taste
- 45 ounces chicken stock
- ½ teaspoon nutmeg, ground
- 1 cup coconut cream

Directions:

Heat up a pot with the oil over medium heat, add onion and garlic, stir and cook for 4 minutes. Add pork, stir and brown for 6 minutes more. Add black pepper, nutmeg and stock, stir, and bring to a simmer and boil for 20 minutes more. Add spinach and cream, stir, cook for 10 more minutes, ladle into bowls and serve.
Enjoy!

Nutrition: calories 245, fat 14, fiber 3, carbs 13, protein 14

Dash Diet Fish and Seafood Recipes

Salmon and Quinoa Salad

Preparation time: 10 minutes
Cooking time: 10 minutes
Servings: 1

Ingredients:

- 1 medium salmon fillet, boneless
- 1 teaspoon olive oil
- A pinch of black pepper
- Cooking spray
- 1 and ½ cups kale, chopped
- ½ cup quinoa, already cooked
- 1 tablespoon lemon juice
- 5 red grapes, halved

Directions:
Put the salmon in a baking dish greased with cooking spray, drizzle the oil over the fish, season with black pepper and bake in the oven at 425 degrees F for 10 minutes. Meanwhile, in a bowl, combine the quinoa with the grapes, kale and lemon juice and toss well. Arrange the salmon on a plate add the quinoa salad next to it and serve.
Enjoy!

Nutrition: calories 261, fat 5, fiber 7, carbs 10, protein 15

Salmon and Horseradish Sauce

Preparation time: 10 minutes
Cooking time: 10 minutes
Servings: 4

Ingredients:

- 1 and ½ tablespoons olive oil
- 4 medium salmon fillets, boneless and skin-on
- ½ cup coconut cream
- A pinch of black pepper
- 2 tablespoons dill, chopped
- 1 tablespoon prepared horseradish

Directions:
Heat up a pan with the oil over medium-high heat, add salmon fillets, season with black pepper and cook for 5 minutes one each side. In a bowl, combine the cream with the dill and horseradish and whisk well. Divide the salmon between plates and serve with the horseradish cream on top.
Enjoy!

Nutrition: calories 275, fat 12, fiber 4, carbs 14, protein 27

Tuna Salad

Preparation time: 10 minutes
Cooking time: 0 minutes
Servings: 2

Ingredients:

- 2 teaspoons olive oil
- 1 teaspoon red vinegar
- ½ teaspoon lemon juice
- ½ teaspoon mustard
- A pinch of black pepper
- ½ cup already cooked quinoa
- ¼ cup canned chickpeas, no-salt-added, drained and rinsed
- ¼ cup cucumber, chopped
- 5 cherry tomatoes, halved
- 5 ounces white tuna canned in water, drained
- 1 tablespoon low-fat cheese, crumbled

Directions:

In a salad bowl, combine the quinoa with chickpeas, cucumber, tomatoes, tuna and cheese and toss. Add black pepper, oil, vinegar, lemon juice and mustard, toss well and serve.
Enjoy!

Nutrition: calories 241, fat 4, fiber 5, carbs 12, protein 14

Cod and Tasty Relish

Preparation time: 10 minutes
Cooking time: 10 minutes
Servings: 4

Ingredients:

- 1 and ½ tablespoons oregano, chopped
- 1 cup peas
- 2 tablespoons shallots, chopped
- 2 tablespoons lime juice
- 2 tablespoons capers
- 3 tablespoons olive oil
- A pinch of black pepper
- 4 medium cod fillets, boneless

Directions:

Heat up a pan with 1-tablespoon oil over medium-high heat, add the cod fillets, cook for 5 minutes on each side and divide between plates. In a bowl, combine the oregano with the peas, shallots, limejuice, capers, black pepper and 2 tablespoons oil and toss well. Divide this next to the cod and serve.
Enjoy!

Nutrition: calories 221, fat 11, fiber 3, carbs 8, protein 20

Smoked Salmon Mix

Preparation time: 10 minutes
Cooking time: 0 minutes
Servings: 4

Ingredients:

- 2 tablespoons dill, chopped
- 1 teaspoons lemon zest, grated
- 8 ounces low-fat cream cheese
- A pinch of black pepper
- 1 pound smoked salmon, flaked
- 7 ounces cucumber, sliced
- ¼ cup shallot, chopped
- 2 tablespoons mint, chopped

Directions:
In a bowl, combine the dill with lemon zest, cream cheese, black pepper, salmon, cucumber, shallot and mint and toss well. Serve cold with whole wheat bread slices.
Enjoy!

Nutrition: calories 277, fat 4, fiber 6, carbs 15, protein 15

Halibut and Kale Pesto

Preparation time: 10 minutes
Cooking time: 6 minutes
Servings: 4

Ingredients:

- 2 tablespoons almonds, chopped
- 2 garlic cloves
- 4 cups kale, torn
- ½ cup olive oil+1 tablespoon
- ¼ cup low-fat parmesan, grated
- 2 tablespoons lemon juice
- A pinch of black pepper
- 4 halibut fillets
- 1 pound cherry tomatoes, halved

Directions:
In a blender, combine the almonds with the garlic, kale, ½-cup oil, lemon juice and parmesan and pulse well. Heat up a pan with 1 tablespoon oil over medium-high heat, add the fish, season with black pepper, cook for 3 minutes on each side and divide between plates Serve with the cherry tomatoes on the side and with the kale pesto on top.
Enjoy!

Nutrition: calories 261, fat 4, fiber 7, carbs 14, protein 14

Simple Grilled Tilapia

Preparation time: 10 minutes
Cooking time: 8 minutes
Servings: 4

Ingredients:

- 1 and ½ tablespoons olive oil
- 1 teaspoon smoked paprika
- ½ teaspoon garlic powder
- A pinch of black pepper
- 4 medium tilapia fillets

Directions:
Heat up a pan with the oil over medium-high heat, season the fish with paprika, garlic powder and black pepper, add it to the pan, cook for 4 minutes on each side, divide between plates and serve with a side salad.
Enjoy!

Nutrition: calories 222, fat 4, fiber 4, carbs 14, protein 25

Delicious Arctic Char

Preparation time: 10 minutes
Cooking time: 8 minutes
Servings: 4

Ingredients:

- 1 cup orange segments
- 1 tablespoon parsley, chopped
- 2 tablespoons red onions, chopped
- 1 tablespoon capers, chopped
- 1 teaspoon orange zest, grated
- 1 tablespoon orange juice
- 1 tablespoon olive oil
- 1 teaspoon balsamic vinegar
- A pinch of black pepper
- Cooking spray
- 4 arctic char fillets

Directions:
Grease a pan with cooking spray, add fish fillets, season with black pepper, cook for 4 minutes on each side and divide between plates. In a bowl, combine the orange with parsley, onions, capers, orange zest, orange juice, oil and vinegar and toss well. Divide this on top of the fish fillets and serve.
Enjoy!

Nutrition: calories 231, fat 12, fiber 3, carbs 8, protein 14

Tasty Halibut and Cherry Tomatoes

Preparation time: 10 minutes
Cooking time: 13 minutes
Servings: 4

Ingredients:

- 1 and ½ tablespoon olive oil
- 4 halibut fillets, skinless
- 2 cups cherry tomatoes
- A pinch of black pepper
- 3 garlic cloves, minced
- 2 tablespoons balsamic vinegar
- 2 tablespoons basil, chopped

Directions:
Heat up a pan with 1-tablespoon olive oil, add halibut fillets, cook them for 5 minutes on each side and divide between plates. Heat up another pan with the rest of the oil over medium-high heat, add the tomatoes, garlic, vinegar and basil, toss, cook for 3 minutes, add next to the fish and serve.
Enjoy!

Nutrition: calories 221, fat 4 fiber 1, carbs 6, protein 21

Salmon and Sauce

Preparation time: 10 minutes
Cooking time: 10 minutes
Servings: 4

Ingredients:

- 1 and ½ tablespoons avocado mayonnaise
- 3 tablespoons non-fat yogurt
- 1 and ½ tablespoons mustard
- 2 tablespoons dill, chopped
- 2 tablespoons lemon juice
- A pinch of black pepper
- 1 garlic clove minced
- 4 salmon fillets, boneless
- Cooking spray

Directions:
Grease a baking dish with cooking spray, arrange the salmon fillets in the dish and season them with black pepper. In a bowl, combine the mayo with the yogurt, mustard, dill, lemon juice, black pepper, whisk, and pour over the fish, introduce in the oven and cook at 425 degrees F for 10 minutes. Divide everything between plates and serve.
Enjoy!

Nutrition: calories 261, fat 12, fiber 3, carbs 8, protein 16

Arctic Char and Cucumber Relish

Preparation time: 10 minutes
Cooking time: 6 minutes
Servings: 2

Ingredients:

- ¾ cup cucumber, chopped
- ¼ cup shallots, chopped
- 1 tablespoon cilantro, chopped
- 2 teaspoons mint, chopped
- 2 teaspoons lemon juice
- ½ teaspoon mustard
- A pinch of black pepper
- 1 tablespoon olive oil
- 2 arctic char fillets

Directions:

Season the fish with black pepper, drizzle the oil, arrange them in a baking dish, introduce in the oven and bake at 425 degrees F for 6 minutes. In a bowl, combine the cucumber with the shallots, cilantro, mint, lemon juice and mustard, toss well, add next to the fish and serve.
Enjoy!

Nutrition: calories 231, fat 3, fiber 6, carbs 9, protein 22

Soft Parsley Salmon

Preparation time: 10 minutes
Cooking time: 15 minutes
Servings: 6

Ingredients:

- 3 tablespoons olive oil
- 3 tablespoons mustard
- 5 teaspoons stevia
- ½ cup whole wheat breadcrumbs
=
- ½ cup pecans, chopped
- 6 salmon fillets, boneless
- 2 tablespoons parsley, chopped
- Black pepper to the taste

Directions:

In a bowl, mix mustard with oil and stevia and whisk. In another bowl, mix pecans with parsley and breadcrumbs. Season salmon fillets with black pepper to the taste, put in a baking dish brush with mustard mixture, top with breadcrumbs mix, introduce in the oven and bake at 400 degrees F for 15 minutes. Divide between plates and serve with a side salad.
Enjoy!

Nutrition: calories 230, fat 4, fiber 2, carbs 14, protein 12

Salmon and Cauliflower Mix

Preparation time: 10 minutes
Cooking time: 20 minutes
Servings: 4

Ingredients:

- ¼ cup coconut sugar
- 2 tablespoons coconut aminos
- 1 cauliflower head, florets separated
- 4 salmon fillets, boneless
- 1 big red onion, cut into wedges
- 2 tablespoons olive oil
- Black pepper to the taste

Directions:
In a small bowl, mix sugar with coconut aminos and whisk. Heat up a pan with half of the oil over medium-high heat, add cauliflower and onion, stir and cook for 10 minutes. Put the salmon in a baking dish, drizzle the rest of the oil, add coconut aminos, toss a bit, season with black pepper, introduce in the oven and bake at 400 degrees F for 10 minutes. Divide the salmon and the cauliflower mix between plates and serve.
Enjoy!

Nutrition: calories 220, fat 3, fiber 3, carbs 12, protein 9

Salmon and Peaches Mix

Preparation time: 10 minutes
Cooking time: 10 minutes
Servings: 4

Ingredients:

- 1 tablespoon balsamic vinegar
- 1 teaspoon thyme, chopped
- 1 tablespoon ginger, grated
- 4 tablespoons olive oil
- Black pepper to the taste
- 2 red onions, cut into wedges
- 3 peaches cut into wedges
- 4 salmon steaks

Directions:
In a small bowl, combine vinegar with ginger, thyme, 3 tablespoons olive oil and black pepper and whisk. In another bowl, mix onion with peaches, 1-tablespoon oil and pepper and toss. Season salmon with black pepper, place on preheated grill over medium heat, cook for 5 minutes on each side and divide between plates. Put the peaches and onions on the same grill, cook for 4 minutes on each side, divide next to the salmon, drizzle the vinegar mix and serve.
Enjoy!

Nutrition: calories 200, fat 2, fiber 2, carbs 3, protein 2

Salmon and Beans Mix

Preparation time: 10 minutes
Cooking time: 20 minutes
Servings: 4

Ingredients:

- 2 tablespoons coconut aminos
- ½ cup olive oil
- 1 and ½ cup low-sodium chicken stock
- 6 ounces salmon fillets
- 2 garlic cloves, minced
- 1 tablespoon ginger, grated
- 1 cup canned black beans, no-salt-added, drained and rinsed
- 2 teaspoons balsamic vinegar
- ¼ cup radishes, grated
- ¼ cup carrots, grated
- ¼ cup scallions, chopped

Directions:

In a bowl, combine the aminos with half of the oil and whisk. Put the salmon in a baking dish, pour add coconut aminos and the stock, toss a bit, leave aside in the fridge for 10 minutes, introduce in preheated broiler and cook over medium-high heat for 4 minutes on each side. Heat up a pan with the rest of the oil over medium heat, add garlic, ginger and black beans, stir and cook for 3 minutes. Add vinegar, radishes, carrots and scallions, toss and cook for 5 minutes more. Divide fish and the black beans mix between plates and serve.
Enjoy!

Nutrition: calories 220, fat 4, fiber 2, carbs 12, protein 7

Salmon and Pomegranate Mix

Preparation time: 20 minutes
Cooking time: 10 minutes
Servings: 4

Ingredients:

- 1 tablespoon olive oil
- 4 salmon fillets, skinless and boneless
- 4 tablespoons sesame paste
- Juice of 1 lemon
- 1 lemon, cut into wedges
- ½ cucumber, chopped
- Seeds from 1 pomegranate
- A bunch of parsley, chopped

Directions:

Heat up a pan with the oil over medium heat, add salmon, cook for 5 minutes on each side and divide between plates. In a bowl, mix sesame paste and lemon juice and whisk. Add cucumber, parsley and pomegranate seeds and toss. Divide this over the salmon and serve...
Enjoy!

Nutrition: calories 254, fat 3, fiber 6, carbs 9, protein 14

Salmon and Veggie Mix

Preparation time: 10 minutes
Cooking time: 30 minutes
Servings: 6

Ingredients:

- 3 red onions, cut into wedges
- ¾ cup green olives, pitted
- 3 red bell peppers, cut into strips
- ½ teaspoon smoked paprika
- Black pepper to the taste
- 5 tablespoons olive oil
- 6 salmon fillets, skinless and boneless
- 2 tablespoons parsley, chopped

Directions:
Spread bell peppers, onions and olives on a lined baking sheet, add smoked paprika, black pepper and 3 tablespoons olive oil, toss to coat, bake in the oven at 375 degrees F for 15 minutes and divide between plates. Heat up a pan with the rest of the oil over medium-high heat, add the salmon, season with black pepper, cook for 5 minutes on each side, divide next to the bell peppers and olives mix, sprinkle parsley on top and serve.
Enjoy!

Nutrition: calories 221, fat 2, fiber 3, carbs 8, protein 10

Greek Salmon

Preparation time: 10 minutes
Cooking time: 15 minutes
Servings: 4

Ingredients:

- 4 medium salmon fillets, skinless and boneless
- 1 fennel bulb, chopped
- Black pepper to the taste
- ¼ cup low-sodium veggie stock
- 1 cup non-fat yogurt
- ¼ cup green olives pitted and chopped
- ¼ cup chives, chopped
- 1 tablespoon olive oil
- 1 tablespoon lemon juice

Directions:
Arrange the fennel in a baking dish, add salmon fillets, season with black pepper, add stock, bake in the oven at 390 degrees F for 10 minutes and divide everything between plates. In a bowl, mix yogurt with chives, olives, lemon juice, olive oil and black pepper and whisk well. Top the salmon with this mix and serve.
Enjoy!

Nutrition: calories 252, fat 2, fiber 4, carbs 12, protein 9

Creamy Salmon and Asparagus Mix

Preparation time: 10 minutes
Cooking time: 10 minutes
Servings: 6

Ingredients:
- 1 tablespoon lemon zest, grated
- 1 tablespoon lemon juice
- Black pepper to the taste
- 1 cup coconut cream
- 1 pound asparagus, trimmed
- 20 ounces salmon, skinless and boneless
- 1-ounce parmesan cheese, grated

Directions:
Put some water in a pot, add a pinch of salt, bring to a boil over medium heat, add asparagus, cook for 1 minute, transfer to a bowl filled with ice water, drain and put in a bowl. Heat up the pot with the water again over medium heat, add salmon, and cook for 5 minutes and drain. In a bowl, mix lemon peel with cream and lemon juice and whisk Heat up a pan over medium-high heat, asparagus, cream and pepper, cook for 1 more minute, divide between plates, add salmon and serve with grated parmesan.
Enjoy!

Nutrition: calories 354, fat 2, fiber 2, carbs 2, protein 4

Easy Salmon and Brussels sprouts

Preparation time: 10 minutes
Cooking time: 20 minutes
Servings: 6

Ingredients:
- 2 tablespoons brown sugar
- 1 teaspoon onion powder
- 1 teaspoon garlic powder
- 1 teaspoon smoked paprika
- 3 tablespoons olive oil
-
- 1 and ¼ pounds Brussels sprouts, halved
- 6 medium salmon fillets, boneless

Directions:
In a bowl, mix sugar with onion powder, garlic powder, smoked paprika and 2-tablespoon olive oil and whisk well. Spread Brussels sprouts on a lined baking sheet, drizzle the rest of the olive oil, toss to coat, introduce in the oven at 450 degrees F and bake for 5 minutes. Add salmon fillets brush with sugar mix you have prepared introduce in the oven and bake for 15 minutes more. Divide everything between plates and serve.
Enjoy!

Nutrition: calories 212, fat 5, fiber 3, carbs 12, protein 8

Salmon and Beets Mix

Preparation time: 10 minutes
Cooking time: 35 minutes
Servings: 4

Ingredients:

- 1 pound medium beets, sliced
- 6 tablespoons olive oil
- 1 and ½ pounds salmon fillets, skinless and boneless
- Black pepper to the taste
- 1 tablespoon chives, chopped
- 1 tablespoon parsley, chopped
- 3 tablespoon shallots, chopped
- 1 tablespoon lemon zest, grated
- ¼ cup lemon juice

Directions:
In a bowl, mix beets with ½-tablespoon oil and toss to coat, season with black pepper, spread on a lined baking sheet and bake in the oven at 450 degrees F for 20 minutes. Add salmon, brush it with the rest of the oil, introduce in the oven and bake for 15 minutes more. In a bowl, combine the chives with the parsley, shallots, lemon zest and lemon juice and toss. Divide the salmon and the beets between plates, drizzle the chives mix on top and serve.
Enjoy!

Nutrition: calories 272, fat 6, fiber 2, carbs 12, protein 9

Fresh Shrimp Mix

Preparation time: 10 minutes
Cooking time: 10 minutes
Servings: 4

Ingredients:

- 1 pound shrimp, deveined and peeled
- 2 teaspoons olive oil
- 6 tablespoons lemon juice
- 3 tablespoons dill, chopped
- 1 tablespoon oregano, chopped
- 2 garlic cloves, chopped
- Black pepper to the taste
- ¾ cup non-fat yogurt
- ½ pounds cherry tomatoes, halved

Directions:
Heat up a pan with the oil over medium-high heat, add the shrimp and cook for 3 minutes. Add lemon juice, dill, oregano, garlic, black pepper, yogurt and tomatoes, toss, cook for 5 minutes more, divide into bowls and serve.
Enjoy!

Nutrition: calories 253, fat 6, fiber 6, carbs 10, protein 17

Salmon and Potatoes Mix

Preparation time: 10 minutes
Cooking time: 10 minutes
Servings: 4

Ingredients:

- 1 and ½ pounds potatoes, chopped
- 1 tablespoon olive oil
- 4 ounces smoked salmon, chopped
- 1 tablespoon chives, chopped
- 2 teaspoons prepared horseradish
- ¼ cup coconut cream
- Black pepper to the taste

Directions:

Heat up a pan with the oil over medium heat, add potatoes and cook for 10 minutes. Add salmon, chives, horseradish, cream and black pepper, toss, cook for 1 minute more, divide between plates and serve.
Enjoy!

Nutrition: calories 233, fat 6, fiber 5, carbs 9, protein 11

Cod Salad

Preparation time: 12 minutes
Cooking time: 12 minutes
Servings: 4

Ingredients:

- 4 medium cod fillets, skinless and boneless
- 2 tablespoons mustard
- 1 tablespoon tarragon, chopped
- 1 tablespoon capers, drained
- 4 tablespoons olive oil+ 1 teaspoon
- Black pepper to the taste
- 2 cups baby arugula
- 1 small red onion, sliced
- 1 small cucumber, sliced
- 2 tablespoons lemon juice

Directions:

In a bowl, mix mustard with 2 tablespoons olive oil, tarragon and capers and whisk. Heat up a pan with 1 teaspoon oil over medium-high heat, add fish, season with black pepper to the taste, cook for 6 minutes on each side and cut into medium cubes. In a salad bowl, combine the arugula with onion, cucumber, lemon juice, cod and mustard mix, toss and serve.
Enjoy!

Nutrition: calories 258, fat 12, fiber 6, carbs 12, protein 18

Cheesy Shrimp Mix

Preparation time: 10 minutes
Cooking time: 30 minutes
Servings: 10

Ingredients:

- ½ pound shrimp, already peeled and deveined
- 1 cup avocado mayonnaise
- ½ cup low-fat mozzarella cheese, shredded
- 3 garlic cloves, minced
- ¼ teaspoon hot sauce
- 1 tablespoon lemon juice
- A drizzle of olive oil
- ½ cup scallions, sliced

Directions:

In a bowl, mix mozzarella with mayo, hot sauce, garlic and lemon juice and whisk well. Add scallions and shrimp, toss, pour into a baking dish greased with the olive oil, introduce in the oven at 350 degrees F and bake for 30 minutes. Divide into bowls and serve.
Enjoy!

Nutrition: calories 275, fat 3, fiber 5, carbs 10, protein 12

Smoked Salmon and Radishes

Preparation time: 10 minutes
Cooking time: 0 minutes
Servings: 8

Ingredients:

- 3 tablespoons beet horseradish, prepared
- 1 pound smoked salmon, skinless, boneless and flaked
- 2 teaspoons lemon zest, grated
- 4 radishes, chopped
- ½ cup capers, drained and chopped
- 1/3 cup red onion, roughly chopped
- 3 tablespoons chives, chopped

Directions:

In a bowl, combine the salmon with the beet horseradish, lemon zest, radish, capers, onions and chives, toss and serve cold.
Enjoy!

Nutrition: calories 254, fat 2, fiber 1, carbs 7, protein 7

Trout Spread

Preparation time: 10 minutes
Cooking time: 0 minutes
Servings: 8

Ingredients:

- 4 ounces smoked trout, skinless, boneless and flaked
- ¼ cup coconut cream
- 1 tablespoon lemon juice
- 1/3 cup non-fat yogurt
- 1 and ½ tablespoon parsley, chopped
- 3 tablespoons chives, chopped
- Black pepper to the taste
- A drizzle of olive oil

Directions:

In a bowl, mix trout with yogurt, cream, black pepper, chives, lemon juice and the dill and stir. Drizzle the olive oil at the end and serve.
Enjoy!

Nutrition: calories 204, fat 2, fiber 2, carbs 8, protein 15

Shrimp and Mango Mix

Preparation time: 10 minutes
Cooking time: 0 minutes
Servings: 4

Ingredients:

- 3 tablespoons balsamic vinegar
- 3 tablespoons coconut sugar
- 6 tablespoons avocado mayonnaise
- 3 mangos, peeled and cubed
- 3 tablespoons parsley, finely chopped
- 1 pound shrimp, peeled, deveined and cooked

Directions:

In a bowl, mix vinegar with sugar and mayo and whisk. In another bowl, combine the mango with the parsley and shrimp; add the mayo mix, toss and serve.
Enjoy!

Nutrition: calories 204, fat 3, fiber 2, carbs 8, protein 8

Spring Salmon Mix

Preparation time: 10 minutes
Cooking time: 0 minutes
Servings: 4

Ingredients:
- 2 tablespoons scallions, chopped
- 2 tablespoons sweet onion, chopped
- 1 and ½ teaspoons lime juice
- 1 tablespoon chives, minced
- 1 tablespoon olive oil
- 1 pound smoked salmon, flaked
- 1 cup cherry tomatoes, halved
- Black pepper to the taste
- 1 tablespoon parsley, chopped

Directions:
In a bowl, mix the scallions with sweet onion, limejuice, chives, oil, salmon, tomatoes, black pepper and parsley, toss and serve.
Enjoy!

Nutrition: calories 200, fat 8, fiber 3, carbs 8, protein 6

Salmon and Green Beans Mix

Preparation time: 10 minutes
Cooking time: 0 minutes
Servings: 4

Ingredients:
- 3 tablespoons balsamic vinegar
- 2 tablespoons olive oil
- 1/3 cup kalamata olives, pitted and minced
- 1 garlic clove, minced
- Black pepper to the taste
- ½ teaspoon lemon zest, grated
- 1 pound green beans, blanched and halved
- ½ pound cherry tomatoes, halved
- ½ fennel bulb, sliced
- ½ red onion, sliced
- 2 cups baby arugula
- ¾ pound smoked salmon, flaked

Directions:
In a bowl, combine the green beans with cherry tomatoes, fennel, onion, arugula and salmon and toss. Add vinegar, oil, olives, garlic, black pepper and lemon zest, toss and serve.
Enjoy!

Nutrition: calories 212, fat 3, fiber 3, carbs 6, protein 4

Saffron Shrimp

Preparation time: 10 minutes
Cooking time: 30 minutes
Servings: 4

Ingredients:

- 1 teaspoon lemon juice
- Black pepper to the taste
- ½ cup avocado mayo
- ½ teaspoon sweet paprika
- 3 tablespoons olive oil
- 1 fennel bulb, chopped
- 1 yellow onion, chopped
- 2 garlic cloves, minced
- 1 cup canned tomatoes, no-salt-added and chopped
- 1 and ½ pounds big shrimp, peeled and deveined
- ¼ teaspoon saffron powder

Directions:

In a bowl, combine the garlic with lemon juice, black pepper, mayo and paprika and whisk. Add the shrimp and toss. Heat up a pan with the oil over medium-high heat, add the shrimp, fennel, onion and garlic mix, toss and cook for 4 minutes. Add tomatoes and saffron, toss, divide into bowls and serve.
Enjoy!

Nutrition: calories 210, fat 2, fiber 5, carbs 8, protein 4

Cold Crab and Watermelon Soup

Preparation time: 4 hours
Cooking time: 0 minutes
Servings: 4

Ingredients:

- ¼ cup basil, chopped
- 2 pounds tomatoes
- 5 cups watermelon, cubed
- ¼ cup red wine vinegar
- 1/3 cup olive oil
- 2 garlic cloves, minced
- 1 zucchini, chopped
- Black pepper to the taste
- 1 cup crabmeat

Directions:

In your food processor, mix tomatoes with basil, vinegar, 4 cups watermelon, garlic, 1/3 cup oil and black pepper to the taste, pulse, pour into a bowl and keep in the fridge for 1 hour. Divide this into bowls, add zucchini, crab and the rest of the watermelon and serve.
Enjoy!

Nutrition: calories 231, fat 3, fiber 3, carbs 6, protein 8

Shrimp and Orzo

Preparation time: 10 minutes
Cooking time: 30 minutes
Servings: 4

Ingredients:

- 1 pound shrimp, peeled and deveined
- Black pepper to the taste
- 3 garlic cloves, minced
- 1 tablespoon olive oil
- ½ teaspoon oregano, dried
- 1 yellow onion, chopped
- 2 cups low-sodium chicken stock
- 2 ounces orzo
- ½ cup water
- 4 ounces canned tomatoes, no-salt-added and chopped
- Juice of 1 lemon

Directions:

Heat up a pan with the oil over medium-high heat, add onion, garlic and oregano, stir and cook for 4 minutes. Add orzo, stir and cook for 2 more minutes. Add stock and the water, bring to a boil, cover, reduce heat to low and cook for 12 minutes. Add lemon juice, tomatoes, black pepper and shrimp, introduce in the oven and bake at 400 degrees F for 15 minutes. Divide between plates and serve.
Enjoy!

Nutrition: calories 228, fat 4, fiber 3, carbs 7, protein 8

Spanish Mussels Mix

Preparation time: 10 minutes
Cooking time: 23 minutes
Servings: 4

Ingredients:

- 3 tablespoons olive oil
- 2 pounds mussels, scrubbed
- Black pepper to the taste
- 3 cups canned tomatoes, crushed
- 1 shallot, chopped
- 2 garlic cloves, minced
- 2 cups low-sodium veggie stock
- 1/3 cup cilantro, chopped

Directions:

Heat up a pan with the oil over medium-high heat, add shallot, stir and cook for 3 minutes. Add garlic, stock, tomatoes and black pepper, stir, bring to a simmer and cook for 10 minutes. Add mussels and cilantro, toss, cover the pan, cook for another 10 minutes, divide into bowls and serve.
Enjoy!

Nutrition: calories 210, fat 2, fiber 6, carbs 5, protein 8

Scallops and Quinoa Salad

Preparation time: 10 minutes
Cooking time: 20 minutes
Servings: 6

Ingredients:

- 12 ounces sea scallops
- 4 tablespoons olive oil+ 2 teaspoons
- 4 teaspoons coconut aminos
- 1 and ½ cup quinoa, already cooked
- 2 teaspoons garlic, minced
-

- 1 cup snow peas, sliced
- 1/3 cup balsamic vinegar
- 1 cup scallions, sliced
- 1/3 cup red bell pepper, chopped
- ¼ cup cilantro, chopped

Directions:

In a bowl, mix scallops with half of the aminos and toss. Heat up a pan with 1-tablespoon olive oil over medium heat, add quinoa, stir and cook for 8 minutes. Add garlic and snow peas, stir, cook for 5 more minutes and take off heat. Meanwhile, in a bowl, mix 3 tablespoons olive oil with the rest of the coconut aminos and vinegar, whisk well, add the quinoa mix, scallions and bell pepper and toss. Heat up another pan with 2 teaspoons olive oil over medium-high heat, add scallops, cook for 1 minute on each side, add over the quinoa mix, toss a bit, sprinkle cilantro on top and serve.
Enjoy!

Nutrition: calories 221, fat 5, fiber 2, carbs 7, protein 8

Salmon and Veggies Soup

Preparation time: 10 minutes
Cooking time: 22 minutes
Servings: 6

Ingredients:

- 2 tablespoon olive oil
- 1 leek, chopped
- 1 red onion, chopped
- Black pepper to the taste
- 2 carrots, chopped
- 4 cups low-stock veggie stock

- 4 ounces salmon, skinless, boneless and cubed
- ½ cup coconut cream
- 1 tablespoon dill, chopped

Directions:

Heat up a pan with the oil over medium heat, add leek and onion, stir and cook for 7 minutes. Add black pepper, add carrots and stock, stir, bring to a boil and cook for 10 minutes. Add salmon, cream and dill, stir, boil everything for 5-6 minutes more, ladle into bowls and serve.
Enjoy

Nutrition: calories 232, fat 3, fiber 4, carbs 7, protein 12

Salmon Salsa

Preparation time: 10 minutes
Cooking time: 0 minutes
Servings: 12

Ingredients:
- 3 yellow tomatoes, seedless and chopped
- 1 pound smoked salmon, boneless, skinless and flaked
- 1 red tomato, seedless and chopped
- Black pepper to the taste
- 1 cup watermelon, seedless and chopped
- 1 red onion, chopped
- 1 mango, peeled, seedless and chopped
- 2 jalapeno peppers, chopped
- ¼ cup parsley, chopped
- 3 tablespoons lime juice

Directions:
In a bowl, mix all the tomatoes with mango, watermelon, onion, salmon, black pepper, jalapeno, parsley and limejuice, toss and serve cold.
Enjoy!

Nutrition: calories 123, fat 2, fiber 4, carbs 5, protein 5

Salmon and Cucumber Salad

Preparation time: 10 minutes
Cooking time: 0 minutes
Servings: 4

Ingredients:
- 2 cucumbers, cubed
- 2 teaspoons lemon juice
- 4 ounces non-fat yogurt
- 1 teaspoon lemon zest, grated
- Black pepper to the taste
- 2 teaspoons dill, chopped
- 8 ounces smoked salmon, flaked

Directions:
In a bowl, the cucumbers with the lemon juice, lemon zest, black pepper, dill, salmon and yogurt, toss and serve cold.
Enjoy!

Nutrition: calories 242, fat 3, fiber 4, carbs 8, protein 3

Tuna Pate

Preparation time: 10 minutes
Cooking time: 0 minutes
Servings: 10

Ingredients:
- 6 ounces canned tuna, drained and flaked
- 3 teaspoons lemon juice
- 1 teaspoon onion, minced
- 8 ounces low-fat cream cheese
- ¼ cup parsley, chopped

Directions:
In a bowl, mix tuna with cream cheese, lemon juice, parsley and onion, stir really well and serve cold.
Enjoy!

Nutrition: calories 172, fat 2, fiber 3, carbs 8, protein 4

Shrimp and Avocado Salad

Preparation time: 10 minutes
Cooking time: 0 minutes
Servings: 2

Ingredients:
- 2 green onions, chopped
- 2 avocados, pitted, peeled and cut into medium chunks
- 2 tablespoons cilantro, chopped
- 1 cup shrimp, already cooked, peeled and deveined
- A pinch of salt and black pepper

Directions:
In a salad bowl, mix shrimp with avocado, green onions, cilantro, salt and pepper, toss and serve cold.
Enjoy!

Nutrition: calories 160, fat 2, fiber 3, carbs 10, protein 6

Shrimp and Cilantro Sauce

Preparation time: 10 minutes
Cooking time: 4 minutes
Servings: 2

Ingredients:

- 1 pound shrimp, peeled and deveined
- 3 tablespoons cilantro, chopped
- 3 tablespoons olive oil
- 1 tablespoon pine nuts
- Zest of 1 lemon, grated
- Juice of ½ lemon

Directions:
In your blender, combine the cilantro with 2 tablespoons oil, pine nuts, lemon zest and lemon juice and pulse well. Heat up a pan with the rest of the oil over medium-high heat, add the shrimp and cook for 3 minutes. Add the cilantro mix, toss, cook for 1 minute, divide between plates and serve with a side salad.
Enjoy!

Nutrition: calories 210, fat 5, fiber 1, carbs 8, protein 12

Citrus Calamari

Preparation time: 10 minutes
Cooking time: 5 minutes
Servings: 4

Ingredients:

- 1 lime, sliced
- 1 lemon, sliced
- 2 pounds calamari tubes and tentacles, sliced
- Black pepper to the taste
- ¼ cup olive oil
- 2 garlic cloves, minced
- 3 tablespoons lemon juice
- 1 orange, peeled and cut into segments
- 2 tablespoons cilantro, chopped

Directions:
In a bowl, mix calamari with black pepper, lime slices, lemon slices, orange slices, garlic, oil, cilantro and lemon juice and toss. Heat up a pan over medium-high heat, add calamari mix, cook for 5 minutes, divide into bowls and serve.
Enjoy!

Nutrition: calories 190, fat 2, fiber 1, carbs 11, protein 14

Mussels Curry

Preparation time: 10 minutes
Cooking time: 10 minutes
Servings: 4

Ingredients:

- 2 and ½ pounds mussels, scrubbed
- 14 ounces canned coconut milk
- 3 tablespoons red curry paste
- 1 tablespoon olive oil
- Black pepper to the taste
- ½ cup low-sodium chicken stock
- Juice of 1 lime
- Zest of 1 lime, grated
- ¼ cup cilantro, chopped
- 3 tablespoons basil, chopped

Directions:
Heat up a pan with the oil over medium-high heat, add curry paste, stir and cook for 2 minutes. Add stock, black pepper, coconut milk, limejuice, lime zest and mussels, toss, cover the pan and cook for 10 minutes. Divide this into bowls, sprinkle cilantro and basil on top and serve. Enjoy!

Nutrition: calories 260, fat 12, fiber 2, carbs 10, protein 12

Salmon Casserole

Preparation time: 10 minutes
Cooking time: 1 hour
Servings: 4

Ingredients:

- 8 sweet potatoes, sliced
- 4 cups salmon, cooked and flaked
- 1 red onion, chopped
- 2 carrots, chopped
- Black pepper to the taste
- 1 celery stalk, chopped
- 2 cups coconut milk
- 3 tablespoons olive oil
- 2 tablespoons chives, chopped
- 2 garlic cloves, minced

Directions:
Heat up a pan with the oil over medium heat, add garlic, stir and cook for 1 minute. Add coconut milk, black pepper, carrots, celery, chives, onion and salmon, stir and take off heat. Arrange a layer of potatoes in a baking dish, add the salmon mix, top with the rest of the potatoes, introduce in the oven and bake at 375 degrees F for 1 hour. Slice, divide between plates and serve.
Enjoy!

Nutrition: calories 220, fat 9, fiber 6, carbs 8, protein 12

Scallops and Cauliflower Mix

Preparation time: 10 minutes
Cooking time: 10 minutes
Servings: 4

Ingredients:
- 12 sea scallops
- 3 garlic cloves, minced
- Black pepper to the taste
- 2 cups cauliflower florets, chopped
- 2 tablespoons olive oil
- 2 cups sweet potatoes, chopped
- 1 tablespoon thyme, chopped
- ¼ cup pine nuts, toasted
- 1 cup low-sodium veggie stock
- 2 tablespoons chives, finely chopped

Directions:
Heat up a pan with the oil over medium-high heat, add thyme and garlic, stir and cook for 2 minutes. Add scallops, cook them for 2 minutes, season them black pepper, add cauliflower, sweet potatoes and the stock, toss and cook for 5 minutes more. Divide the scallops mix between plates, sprinkle chives and pine nuts on top and serve.
Enjoy!

Nutrition: calories 200, fat 10, fiber 4, carbs 9, protein 10

Spiced Salmon

Preparation time: 10 minutes
Cooking time: 10 minutes
Servings: 4

Ingredients:
- 4 salmon fillets
- 2 tablespoons olive oil
- 1 teaspoon cumin, ground
- 1 teaspoon sweet paprika
- 1 teaspoon onion powder
- 1 teaspoon chili powder
- ½ teaspoon garlic powder
- A pinch of salt and black pepper

Directions:
In a bowl, combine the cumin with paprika, onion powder, chili powder, garlic powder, salt and black pepper, toss and rub the salmon with this mix. Heat up a pan with the oil over medium-high heat, add the salmon, cook for 5 minutes on each side, divide between plates and serve with a side salad.
Enjoy!

Nutrition: calories 220, fat 10, carbs 8, fiber 12, protein 10

Smoked Salmon and Tomatoes Salad

Preparation time: 10 minutes
Cooking time: 0 minutes
Servings: 2

Ingredients:

- 4 cups cherry tomatoes, halved
- 1 red onion, sliced
- 8 ounces smoked salmon, thinly sliced
- 4 tablespoons olive oil
- ½ teaspoon garlic, minced
- 2 tablespoons lemon juice
- 1 tablespoon oregano, chopped
- Black pepper to the taste
- 1 teaspoon balsamic vinegar

Directions:
In a salad bowl, combine the tomatoes with the onion, salmon, oil, garlic, lemon juice, oregano, black pepper and vinegar, toss and serve cold.
Enjoy!

Nutrition: calories 159, fat 8, fiber 3, carbs 7, protein 7

Coconut Cream Shrimp

Preparation time: 10 minutes
Cooking time: 0 minutes
Servings: 2

Ingredients:

- 1 pound shrimp, cooked, peeled and deveined
- 1 tablespoon coconut cream
- ¼ teaspoon jalapeno, chopped
- ½ teaspoon lime juice
- 1 tablespoon parsley, chopped
- A pinch of black pepper

Directions:
In a bowl, mix the shrimp with the cream, jalapeno, limejuice, parsley and black pepper, toss, divide into small bowls and serve.
Enjoy!

Nutrition: calories 183, fat 5, fiber 3, carbs 12, protein 8

Salmon and Mushroom Mix

Preparation time: 30 minutes
Cooking time: 10 minutes
Servings: 4

Ingredients:

- 8 ounces salmon fillets, boneless
- 2 tablespoons olive oil
- Black pepper to the taste
- 2 ounces white mushrooms, sliced
- ½ shallot, chopped
- 2 tablespoons balsamic vinegar
- 2 teaspoons mustard
- 3 tablespoons parsley, chopped

Directions:
Brush salmon fillets with 1-tablespoon olive oil, season with black pepper, place on preheated grill over medium heat, cook for 4 minutes on each side and divide between plates. Heat up a pan with the rest of the oil over medium-high heat, add mushrooms, shallot and some black pepper, stir and cook for 5 minutes. Add the mustard, the vinegar and the parsley, stir, cook for 2-3 minutes more, add over the salmon and serve.
Enjoy!

Nutrition: calories 220, fat 4, fiber 8, carbs 6, protein 12

Cod Sweet Potato Chowder

Preparation time: 10 minutes
Cooking time: 20 minutes
Servings: 4

Ingredients:

- 3 cups sweet potatoes, cubed
- 4 cod fillets, skinless and boneless
- 1 cup celery, chopped
- 1 cup onion, chopped
- Black pepper to the taste
- 2 tablespoons garlic, minced
- 2 tablespoons olive oil
- 2 tablespoons tomato paste, no-salt-added
- 3 cups veggie stock
- 1 and ½ cups tomatoes, chopped
- 1 and ½ teaspoons thyme

Directions:
Heat up a pot with the oil over medium heat, add tomato paste, celery, onion and garlic, stir and cook for 5 minutes. Add tomatoes, tomato paste, potatoes and pepper, stir, bring to a boil, reduce heat and cook for 10 minutes. Add thyme and cod, stir, cook for 5 minutes more, ladle into bowls and serve.
Enjoy!

Nutrition: calories 250, fat 6, fiber 5, carbs 7, protein 12

Simple Cinnamon Salmon

Preparation time: 10 minutes
Cooking time: 10 minutes
Servings: 2

Ingredients:

- 2 salmon fillets, boneless and skin-on
- Black pepper to the taste
- 1 tablespoon cinnamon powder
- 1 tablespoon olive oil

Directions:
Heat up a pan with the oil over medium heat, add pepper and cinnamon and stir well. Add salmon, skin side up, cook for 5 minutes on each side, divide between plates and serve with a side salad.
Enjoy!

Nutrition: calories 220, fat 8, fiber 4, carbs 11, protein 8

Scallops and Strawberry Mix

Preparation time: 10 minutes
Cooking time: 6 minutes
Servings: 2

Ingredients:

- 4 ounces scallops
- ½ cup Pico de gallo
- ½ cup strawberries, chopped
- 1 tablespoon lime juice
- Black pepper to the taste

Directions:
Heat up a pan over medium heat, add scallops, cook for 3 minutes on each side and take off heat, in a bowl, mix strawberries with limejuice, Pico de gallo, scallops and pepper, toss and serve cold.
Enjoy!

Nutrition: calories 169, fat 2, fiber 2, carbs 8, protein 13

Baked Haddock

Preparation time: 10 minutes
Cooking time: 30 minutes
Servings: 4

Ingredients:

- 1 pound haddock, boneless
- 3 teaspoons water
- 2 tablespoons lemon juice
- A pinch of salt and black pepper
- 2 tablespoons avocado mayonnaise
- 1 teaspoon dill, chopped
- Cooking spray

Directions:
Spray a baking dish with some cooking oil, add fish, water, lemon juice, salt, black pepper, mayo and dill, toss, introduce in the oven and bake at 350 degrees F for 30 minutes. Divide between plates and serve.
Enjoy!

Nutrition: calories 264, fat 4, fiber 5, carbs 7, protein 12

Basil Tilapia

Preparation time: 10 minutes
Cooking time: 10 minutes
Servings: 4

Ingredients:

- 4 tilapia fillets, boneless
- Black pepper to the taste
- ½ cup low-fat parmesan, grated
- 4 tablespoons avocado mayonnaise
- 2 teaspoons basil, dried
- 2 tablespoons lemon juice
- ¼ cup olive oil

Directions:
Grease a baking dish with the oil, add tilapia fillets, black pepper, spread mayo, basil, drizzle lemon juice and top with the parmesan, introduce in preheated broiler and cook over medium-high heat for 5 minutes on each side. Divide between plates and serve with a side salad.
Enjoy!

Nutrition: calories 215, fat 10, fiber 5, carbs 7, protein 11

Salmon Meatballs

Preparation time: 10 minutes
Cooking time: 30 minutes
Servings: 4

Ingredients:
- Cooking spray
- 2 garlic cloves, minced
- 1 yellow onion, chopped
- 1 pound wild salmon, boneless and minced
- ¼ cup chives, chopped
- 1 egg
- 2 tablespoons Dijon mustard
- 1 tablespoon coconut flour
- A pinch of salt and black pepper

Directions:
In a bowl, mix onion with garlic, salmon, chives, coconut flour, salt, pepper, mustard and egg, stir well, shape medium meatballs, arrange them on a baking sheet, grease them with cooking spray, introduce in the oven at 350 degrees F and bake for 25 minutes. Divide the meatballs between plates and serve with a side salad.
Enjoy!

Nutrition: calories 211, fat 4, fiber 1, carbs 6, protein 13

Tuna Cakes

Preparation time: 10 minutes
Cooking time: 10 minutes
Servings: 12

Ingredients:
- 15 ounces canned tuna, drain well and flaked
- 3 eggs
- ½ teaspoon dill, dried
- 1 teaspoon parsley, dried
- ½ cup red onion, chopped
- 1 teaspoon garlic powder
- A pinch of salt and black pepper
- Olive oil for frying

Directions:
In a bowl, mix tuna with salt, pepper, dill, parsley, onion, garlic powder and eggs, stir and shape medium cakes out of this mix. Heat up a pan with oil over medium-high heat, add tuna cakes, cook for 5 minutes on each side, divide between plates and serve with a side salad.
Enjoy!

Nutrition: calories 210, fat 2, fiber 2, carbs 6, protein 6

Indian Cod Mix

Preparation time: 10 minutes
Cooking time: 25 minutes
Servings: 4

Ingredients:
- 4 cod fillets, skinless and boneless
- ½ teaspoon mustard seeds
- A pinch of black pepper
- 2 green chilies, chopped
- 1 teaspoon ginger, grated
- 1 teaspoon curry powder
- ¼ teaspoon cumin, ground
- 4 tablespoons olive oil
- 1 teaspoon turmeric powder
- 1 red onion, chopped
- ¼ cup cilantro, chopped
- 1 and ½ cups coconut cream
- 3 garlic cloves, minced

Directions:
Heat up a pot with half of the oil over medium heat, add mustard seeds, ginger, onion and garlic, stir and cook for 5 minutes. Add turmeric, curry powder, chilies and cumin, stir and cook for 5 minutes more. Add coconut milk, salt and pepper, stir, bring to a boil and cook for 15 minutes. Heat up another pan with the rest of the oil over medium heat, add fish, stir, cook for 3 minutes, add over the curry mix, also add cilantro, toss, cook for 5 minutes more, divide into bowls and serve.
Enjoy!

Nutrition: calories 200, fat 14, fiber 7, carbs 6, protein 9

Italian Shrimp

Preparation time: 10 minutes
Cooking time: 22 minutes
Servings: 4

Ingredients:
- 8 ounces mushrooms, chopped
- 1 asparagus bunch, cut into medium pieces
- 1 pound shrimp, peeled and deveined
- Black pepper to the taste
- 2 tablespoons olive oil
- 2 teaspoons Italian seasoning
- 1 yellow onion, chopped
- 1 teaspoon red pepper flakes, crushed
- 1 cup low-fat parmesan cheese, grated
- 2 garlic cloves, minced
- 1 cup coconut cream

Directions:
Put water in a pot, bring to a boil over medium heat, add asparagus, steam for 2 minutes, transfer to a bowl with ice water, drain and put in a bowl. Heat up a pan with the oil over medium heat, add onions and mushrooms, stir and cook for 7 minutes. Add pepper flakes, Italian seasoning, black pepper and asparagus, stir and cook for 5 minutes more. Add cream, shrimp, garlic and parmesan, toss, cook for 7 minutes, divide into bowls and serve.
Enjoy!

Nutrition: calories 225, fat 6, fiber 5, carbs 6, protein 8

Shrimp, Bamboo and Snow Peas Soup

Preparation time: 10 minutes
Cooking time: 10 minutes
Servings: 4

Ingredients:
- 4 scallions, chopped
- 1 and ½ tablespoons olive oil
- 1 teaspoon garlic, minced
- 8 cups low-sodium chicken stock
- ¼ cup coconut aminos
- 5 ounces canned bamboo shots, no-salt-added sliced
- Black pepper to the taste
- 1 pound shrimp, peeled and deveined
- ½ pound snow peas

Directions:
Heat up a pot with the oil over medium heat, add scallions and ginger, stir and cook for 2 minutes. Add coconut aminos, stock and black pepper, stir and bring to a boil. Add shrimp, snow peas and bamboo shots, stir, cook for 5 minutes, ladle into bowls and serve.
Enjoy!

Nutrition: calories 200, fat 3, fiber 2, carbs 4, protein 14

Lemony Mussels

Preparation time: 5 minutes
Cooking time: 5 minutes
Servings: 4

Ingredients:
- 2 pound mussels, scrubbed
- 2 garlic cloves, minced
- 1 tablespoon olive oil
- Juice of 1 lemon

Directions:
Put some water in a pot, add mussels, bring to a boil over medium heat, cook for 5 minutes, discard unopened mussels and transfer them to a bowl. In another bowl, mix the oil with garlic and lemon juice, whisk well, and add over the mussels, toss and serve.
Enjoy!

Nutrition: calories 140, fat 4, fiber 4, carbs 8, protein 8

Dash Diet Dessert Recipes

Fresh Parfait

Preparation time: 10 minutes
Cooking time: 0 minutes
Servings: 6

Ingredients:
- 4 cups non-fat yogurt
- 3 tablespoons stevia
- 2 tablespoons lime juice
- 2 teaspoons lime zest, grated
- 4 grapefruits, peeled and chopped
- 1 tablespoon mint, chopped

Directions:
In a bowl, combine the yogurt with the stevia, limejuice, lime zest and mint and stir. Divide the grapefruits into small cups, add the yogurt mix in each and serve.
Enjoy!

Nutrition: calories 200, fat 3, fiber 4, carbs 15, protein 10

Delicious Peach Pie

Preparation time: 10 minutes
Cooking time: 20 minutes
Servings: 4

Ingredients:
- 2 peaches, peeled and sliced
- ½ cup raspberries
- ½ teaspoon coconut sugar
- 3 eggs, whisked
- 1 tablespoon avocado oil
- ½ cup almond milk
- ½ cup whole flour
- ¼ cup non-fat yogurt

Directions:
In a bowl, combine the peaches with sugar and raspberries. In another bowl, combine the eggs with milk and flour and whisk. Grease a pie pan with the oil, add eggs mixture, then peaches mix, spread, bake in the oven at 400 degrees F for 20 minutes, slice and serve.
Enjoy!

Nutrition: calories 199, fat 4, fiber 3, carbs 12, protein 9

Simple Brownies

Preparation time: 10 minutes
Cooking time: 30 minutes
Servings: 8

Ingredients:
- 6 ounces dark chocolate, chopped
- 4 egg whites
- ½ cup hot water
- 1 teaspoon vanilla extract
- 2/3 cup coconut sugar
- 1 and ½ cups whole flour
- ½ cup walnuts, chopped
- Cooking spray
- 1 teaspoon baking powder

Directions:
In a bowl, combine the chocolate and the hot water and whisk really well. Add vanilla extract and egg whites and whisk well again. In another bowl, combine the sugar with flour, baking powder and walnuts and stir. Combine the 2 mixtures, stir well, pour this into a cake pan greased with cooking spray, spread well, bake in the oven for 30 minutes, cool down, slice and serve. Enjoy!

Nutrition: calories 144, fat 4, fiber 4, carbs 9, protein 8

Apple Tart

Preparation time: 10 minutes
Cooking time: 25 minutes
Servings: 8

Ingredients:
- 4 apples, cored, peeled and sliced
- ¼ cup natural apple juice
- ½ cup cranberries, dried
- 2 tablespoons cornstarch
- 2 teaspoons coconut sugar
- 1 teaspoon vanilla extract
- ¼ teaspoon cinnamon powder

For the crust:
- 1 and ¼ cup whole wheat flour
- 2 teaspoons sugar
- 3 tablespoons coconut oil, melted
- ¼ cup cold water

Directions:
In a bowl, combine the cranberries with the apple juice. In another bowl, combine the apples with cornstarch, toss and add the cranberries mix. Stir everything, add vanilla and cinnamon and stir everything again. In a separate bowl, mix the flour with the sugar, oil and cold water and stir until you obtain a dough. Transfer the dough to a working surface, flatten well, roll into a circle and transfer to a tart pan. Press the crust well into the pan, add the apples mix over the crust, introduce in the oven, bake at 375 degrees F for 25 minutes, cool it down, slice and serve. Enjoy!

Nutrition: calories 182, fat 5, fiber 4, carb 15, protein 5

Easy Chocolate Cake

Preparation time: 10 minutes
Cooking time: 25 minutes
Servings: 10

Ingredients:
- 3 cups whole wheat flour
- 1 cup coconut sugar
- 1 tablespoon vanilla extract
- 3 tablespoons cocoa powder
- 2 tablespoons vinegar
- 2 and ½ teaspoons baking soda
- 2 cups hot water
- ½ cup coconut oil, melted

Directions:
In a bowl, combine the flour with the baking soda, sugar, flour and cocoa powder and stir. Put this into a baking pan, make 3 holes in this mix, add the vanilla extract in one, the oil in another and the vinegar in the third one. Add the water over the mix from the pan, whisk everything for 2 minutes, introduce in the oven at 350 degrees F, bake for 25 minutes, and leave the cake to cool down, slice and serve.
Enjoy!

Nutrition: calories 200, fat 4, fiber 2, carbs 12, protein 6

Apple Pancakes

Preparation time: 10 minutes
Cooking time: 10 minutes
Servings: 4

Ingredients:
- ½ cup brown rice flour
- ½ cup sweet rice flour
- ¼ cup almond flour
- 1 teaspoon baking soda
- 1 teaspoon baking powder
- 2 tablespoons flaxseeds
- ½ teaspoon cinnamon powder
- 2 tablespoons maple syrup
- ½ cup natural apple sauce
- ¼ cup water
- Cooking spray
- 2 apples, cored, peeled and chopped

Directions:
In a bowl, combine the brown rice flour with sweet rice flour, almond flour, baking soda, baking powder, flaxseeds, cinnamon, maple syrup, applesauce, water and apples and stir well. Heat up a pan over medium-high heat, grease with cooking spray, drop some of the batter, spread, cook the pancake until it is golden on both sides and transfer to a plate. Repeat with the rest of the batter and serve your pancakes warm.
Enjoy!

Nutrition: calories 232, fat 4, fiber 6, carbs 12, protein 4

Easy Fudge

Preparation time: 2 hours
Cooking time: 7 minutes
Servings: 12

Ingredients:
- 1 cup non-fat milk
- ½ cup low-fat butter
- 2 cups coconut sugar
- 12 ounces dark chocolate, chopped
- 1 teaspoon vanilla extract

Directions:
Heat up a pan with the milk over medium heat, add the sugar and the butter, stir and cook everything for 7 minutes. Take this off heat, add the chocolate and whisk everything. Pour this into a lined square pan, spread well, keep in the fridge for 2 hours, cut into small squares and serve.
Enjoy!

Nutrition: calories 154, fat 5, fiber 5, carbs 16, protein 3

Fruit Salad

Preparation time: 10 minutes
Cooking time: 0 minutes
Servings: 8

Ingredients:
- 1 watermelon, peeled and chopped
- 1 teaspoon vanilla extract
- 1 cup strawberries, chopped
- 1 cup kiwis, peeled and chopped
- 1 cup blueberries
- 1 teaspoon coconut sugar
- 8 ounces non-fat yogurt
- 8 ounces low-fat cream cheese

Directions:
In a bowl, combine the watermelon with the vanilla, strawberries, kiwis, blueberries, sugar, yogurt and cream cheese, toss, divide into small cups and serve cold.
Enjoy!

Nutrition: calories 143, fat 4, fiber 6, carb 12, protein 5

Black Bean Brownies

Preparation time: 10 minutes
Cooking time: 20 minutes
Servings: 12

Ingredients:

- 1 and ½ cups canned black beans, no-salt-added, drained and rinsed
- 2 tablespoons coconut sugar
- ½ cup quick oats
- 2 tablespoons cocoa powder
- 1/3 cup maple syrup
- ¼ cup coconut oil, melted
- ½ teaspoon baking powder
- 2 teaspoons vanilla extract
- Cooking spray

Directions:

In your food processor, combine the black beans with coconut sugar, oats, cocoa powder, maple syrup, oil, baking powder and vanilla extract and pulse well. Grease a square pan with cooking spray, add the black beans mix, spread, introduce in the oven, and bake at 350 degrees F for 20 minutes, leave aside to cool down, slice and serve.
Enjoy!

Nutrition: calories 200, fat 3, fiber 3, carbs 14, protein 4

Banana Cake

Preparation time: 10 minutes
Cooking time: 25 minutes
Servings: 8

Ingredients:

- 2 cups whole wheat flour
- ¼ cup cocoa powder
- 1 banana, peeled and mashed
- ½ teaspoon baking soda
- ½ cup coconut sugar
- ¾ cup almond milk
- ¼ cup coconut oil, melted
- 1 egg
- 1 egg white
- 1 teaspoon vanilla extract
- 1 tablespoon lemon juice
- Cooking spray

Directions:

In a bowl, combine the flour with the cocoa powder, baking soda and sugar and stir. Add banana, milk, oil, egg, and egg white, vanilla and lemon juice and stir really well. Grease a cake pan with cooking spray, pour the cake mix, spread, bake in the oven at 350 degrees F for 25 minutes, cool down, slice and serve.
Enjoy!

Nutrition: calories 165, fat 1, fiber 4, carbs 17, protein 4

Chocolate Pudding

Preparation time: 10 minutes
Cooking time: 10 minutes
Servings: 4

Ingredients:
- 2 tablespoons coconut sugar
- 3 tablespoons cornstarch
- 2 tablespoons cocoa powder
- 2 cups almond milk
- 1/3 cup chocolate chips, unsweetened
- ½ teaspoon vanilla extract

Directions:
Put the cornstarch in a pan, add cocoa, sugar and milk, whisk well and heat up over medium heat for 5 minutes. Take this off heat, add vanilla and chocolate chips, whisk well, pour into small cups and serve cold.
Enjoy!

Nutrition: calories 182, fat 5, fiber 3, carbs 16, protein 6

Coconut Mousse

Preparation time: 10 minutes
Cooking time: 0 minutes
Servings: 12

Ingredients:
- 2 and ¾ cup coconut milk
- 1 teaspoon coconut extract
- 1 teaspoon vanilla extract
- 4 teaspoons coconut sugar
- 1 cup coconut, toasted

Directions:
In a bowl, combine the coconut milk with the coconut extract, vanilla extract, coconut and sugar, whisk well, divide into small cups and serve cold.
Enjoy!

Nutrition: calories 152, fat 5, fiber 1, carbs 11, protein 3

Mango Pudding

Preparation time: 10 minutes
Cooking time: 50 minutes
Servings: 4

Ingredients:

- 1 cup brown rice
- 2 cups water
- 1 mango, peeled and chopped
- 1 cup coconut milk
- 2 tablespoons coconut sugar
- 1 teaspoon vanilla extract
- ½ teaspoon cinnamon powder

Directions:

Put the water in a pan and bring to a boil over medium heat. Add rice, stir, cover the pan and cook for 40 minutes. Add milk, sugar, vanilla, cinnamon and mango, stir, cover the pan again, cook for 10 minutes more, divide into bowls and serve.
Enjoy!

Nutrition: calories 251, fat 3, fiber 4, carbs 16, protein 7

Rhubarb Pie

Preparation time: 10 minutes
Cooking time: 25 minutes
Servings: 12

Ingredients:

- 2 cups whole wheat flour
- 1 cup low-fat butter, melted
- 1 cup pecans, chopped
- 1 and ¼ cup coconut sugar
- 4 cups rhubarb, chopped
- 1 cup strawberries, sliced
- 8 ounces low-fat cream cheese

Directions:

In a bowl, combine the flour with the butter, pecans and ¼-cup sugar and stir well. Transfer this to a pie pan, press well into the pan, introduce in the oven and bake at 350 degrees F for 20 minutes. In a pan, combine the strawberries with the rhubarb, cream cheese and 1-cup sugar, stir well and cook over medium heat for 4 minutes. Spread this over the piecrust and keep in the fridge for a few hours before slicing and serving.
Enjoy!

Nutrition: calories 162, fat 5, fiber 5, carbs 15, protein 6

Fruit Skewers

Preparation time: 10 minutes
Cooking time: 0 minutes
Servings: 10

Ingredients:

- 5 strawberries, halved
- ¼ cantaloupe, cubed
- 2 bananas, cut into chunks
- 1 apple, cored and cut into chunks

Directions:
Thread strawberry, cantaloupe, bananas and apple chunks alternately onto skewers and serve them cold.
Enjoy!

Nutrition: calories 76, fat 1, fiber 1, carbs 10, protein 2

Berries Mix

Preparation time: 10 minutes
Cooking time: 10 minutes
Servings: 6

Ingredients:

- 2 teaspoons lemon juice
- 1 pound blackberries
- 1 pound strawberries
- 4 tablespoons coconut sugar

Directions:
In a pan, combine the strawberries with blackberries and sugar, stir, bring to a simmer over medium heat and cook for 10 minutes. Divide into cups and serve cold.
Enjoy!

Nutrition: calories 120, fat 2, fiber 3, carbs 4, protein 4

Blueberry Compote

Preparation time: 10 minutes
Cooking time: 15 minutes
Servings: 6

Ingredients:
- 5 tablespoons coconut sugar
- 1-ounce orange juice
- 1 pound blueberries

Directions:
In a pot, combine the sugar with the orange juice and blueberries, toss, bring to a boil over medium heat, cook for 15 minutes, divide into bowls and serve cold.
Enjoy!

Nutrition: calories 120, fat 2, fiber 3, carbs 6, protein 9

Summer Strawberry Stew

Preparation time: 10 minutes
Cooking time: 10 minutes
Servings: 6

Ingredients:
- 16 ounces strawberries, halved
- 2 tablespoons water
- 2 tablespoons coconut sugar
- 2 tablespoons lemon juice
- 2 tablespoons cornstarch
- ¼ teaspoon almond extract

Directions:
In a pot, combine the strawberries with the water, sugar, lemon juice, cornstarch and almond extract, toss well, cook over medium heat for 10 minutes, divide into bowls and serve.
Enjoy!

Nutrition: calories 160, fat 2, fiber 2, carbs 6, protein 6

Lemon Apple Mix

Preparation time: 10 minutes
Cooking time: 15 minutes
Servings: 6

Ingredients:
- 6 apples, cored and roughly chopped
- 4 tablespoons coconut sugar
- 2 teaspoons vanilla extract
- 2 teaspoons lemon juice
- 2 teaspoons cinnamon powder

Directions:
In a small pan, combine the apples with the sugar, vanilla, lemon juice and cinnamon, toss, heat up over medium heat, cook for about 10-15 minutes, divide between small dessert plates and serve.
Enjoy!

Nutrition: calories 210, fat 4, fiber 3, carbs 8, protein 5

Minty Rhubarb

Preparation time: 10 minutes
Cooking time: 10 minutes
Servings: 4

Ingredients:
- 1/3 cup water
- 2 pound rhubarb, roughly chopped
- 3 tablespoons coconut sugar
- 1 tablespoon mint, chopped

Directions:
Put the water in a small pot, heat up over medium heat, add the sugar and whisk well. Add rhubarb and mix, toss, cook for 10 minutes, divide into bowls and serve.
Enjoy!

Nutrition: calories 160, fat 2, fiber 4, carbs 8, protein 5

Nigella Mango Sweet Mix

Preparation time: 10 minutes
Cooking time: 10 minutes
Servings: 8

Ingredients:

- 1 and ½ pounds mango, peeled and cubed
- 1 teaspoon nigella seeds
- 3 tablespoons coconut sugar
- ½ cup apple cider vinegar
- 1 teaspoon cinnamon powder

Directions:
In a small pot, combine the mango with the nigella seeds, sugar, vinegar and cinnamon, toss, bring to a simmer over medium heat, cook for 10 minutes, divide into bowls and serve.
Enjoy!

Nutrition: calories 160, fat 3, fiber 4, carbs 8, protein 3

Blueberry Curd

Preparation time: 10 minutes
Cooking time: 10 minutes
Servings: 4

Ingredients:

- 2 tablespoons lemon juice
- 2 tablespoons coconut oil, melted
- 3 tablespoons coconut sugar
- 12 ounces blueberries
- 2 eggs

Directions:
Put the oil in a pot, heat up over medium heat, add lemon juice and coconut sugar and whisk well. Add the blueberries and the eggs whisk well, cook for 10 minutes, divide into small cups and serve cold.
Enjoy!

Nutrition: calories 201, fat 3, fiber 2, carbs 6, protein 3

Lemon Cream

Preparation time: 10 minutes
Cooking time: 15 minutes
Servings: 4

Ingredients:
- 3 cups coconut milk
- Juice of 2 lemons
- Lemon zest of 2 lemons, grated
- ½ cup maple syrup
- 3 tablespoons coconut oil
- 1 egg
- 2 tablespoons gelatin
- 1 cup water

Directions:
In your blender, mix coconut milk with lemon juice, lemon zest, maple syrup, coconut oil, egg and gelatin and pulse really well. Divide this into small jars and seal them. Put the jars in a pan, add the water, introduce in the oven and cook at 380 degrees F for 15 minutes. Serve the cream cold.
Enjoy!

Nutrition: calories 161, fat 3, fiber 5, carbs 6, protein 4

Almond Peach Mix

Preparation time: 10 minutes
Cooking time: 10 minutes
Servings: 4

Ingredients:
- 4 cups water
- 1 peach, chopped
- 2 cups rolled oats
- 1 teaspoon vanilla extract
- 2 tablespoons flax meal
- ½ cup almonds, chopped

Directions:
In a pan, combine the water with the oats, vanilla extract, flax meal, almonds and peach, stir, bring to a simmer over medium heat, cook for 10 minutes, divide into bowls and serve.
Enjoy!

Nutrition: calories 161, fat 3, fiber 3, carbs 7, protein 5

Fruits Stew

Preparation time: 10 minutes
Cooking time: 10 minutes
Servings: 4

Ingredients:
- 1 plum, pitted and chopped
- 1 pear, cored and chopped
- 1 apple, cored and chopped
- 2 tablespoons coconut sugar
- ¼ cup coconut, shredded
- ½ teaspoon cinnamon powder
- 3 tablespoons coconut oil, melted
- ¼ cup pecans, chopped

Directions:
In a pan, combine the oil with coconut, cinnamon and sugar, stir and heat up over medium heat. Add plum, pear, apple and pecans, stir, cook for 8 minutes, divide into bowls and serve cold. Enjoy!

Nutrition: calories 142, fat 4, fiber 4, carbs 14, protein 7

Easy Pomegranate Mix

Preparation time: 10 minutes
Cooking time: 5 minutes
Servings: 2

Ingredients:
- 1 cup steel cut oats
- 2 cup pomegranate juice
- Seeds of 1 pomegranate

Directions:
In a small pot, combine the pomegranate juice with pomegranate seeds and oats, toss, cook over medium heat for 5 minutes, divide into bowls and serve cold. Enjoy!

Nutrition: calories 172, fat 4, fiber 5, carbs 10, protein 5

Black Rice Pudding

Preparation time: 10 minutes
Cooking time: 20 minutes
Servings: 4

Ingredients:

- 6 and ½ cups water
- 1 cup coconut sugar
- 2 cups black rice, washed and rinsed
- 2 teaspoons cinnamon powder
- ½ cup coconut, shredded

Directions:
Put the water in a pan, heat up over medium-high heat, add sugar, rice and coconut, stir, bring to a simmer, reduce heat to medium and cook for 20 minutes. Add cinnamon, toss, divide into bowls and serve cold.

Nutrition: calories 220, fat 4, fiber 4, carbs 10, protein 6

Peach Stew

Preparation time: 10 minutes
Cooking time: 10 minutes
Servings: 6

Ingredients:

- 5 cups peaches, peeled and cubed
- 3 tablespoons coconut sugar
-
- 1 teaspoon ginger, grated
- 2 cups water

Directions:
In a pot, combine the peaches with the sugar, ginger and water, toss, bring to a boil over medium heat, cook for 10 minutes, divide into bowls and serve cold.
Enjoy!

Nutrition: calories 142, fat 1, fiber 2, carbs 7, protein 2

Coconut Cream

Preparation time: 1 hour
Cooking time: 10 minutes
Servings: 4

Ingredients:

- 2 cups coconut cream
- 1 teaspoon cinnamon powder
- 3 eggs, whisked
-

- 5 tablespoons coconut sugar
- Zest of 1 lemon, grated

Directions:

In a small pan, combine the cream with cinnamon, eggs, sugar and lemon zest, whisk well, simmer over medium heat for 10 minutes, divide into ramekins and keep in the fridge for 1 hour before serving.
Enjoy!

Nutrition: calories 130, fat 5, fiber 2, carbs 8, protein 6

Strawberries and Avocado Salad

Preparation time: 5 minutes
Cooking time: 0 minutes
Servings: 2

Ingredients:

- 1 banana, peeled and sliced
- 2 cups strawberries, halved
- 3 tablespoons mint, chopped

- 2 avocados, pitted and peeled

Directions:

In a bowl, combine the banana with the strawberries, mint and avocados, toss and serve cold.
Enjoy!

Nutrition: calories 150, fat 4, fiber 4, carbs 8, protein 6

Blueberry Cream

Preparation time: 5 minutes
Cooking time: 0 minutes
Servings: 1

Ingredients:
- ¾ cup blueberries
- 1 tablespoon low-fat peanut butter
- ¾ cup almond milk
- 1 banana, peeled
- 2 dates

Directions:
In a blender, combine the blueberries with peanut butter, milk, banana and dates, pulse well, divide into small cups and serve cold.
Enjoy!

Nutrition: calories 120, fat 3, fiber 3, carbs 6, protein 7

Apple Coconut Cupcakes

Preparation time: 10 minutes
Cooking time: 22 minutes
Servings: 12

Ingredients:
- 4 tablespoons coconut butter
- ½ cup natural applesauce
- 4 eggs
- 1 teaspoon vanilla extract
- ¾ cup almond flour
- 2 teaspoons cinnamon powder
- ½ teaspoon baking powder
- 1 apple, cored and sliced

Directions:
Heat up a pan with the butter over medium heat, add applesauce, vanilla and eggs, stir, heat up for 2 minutes, take off heat, cool down, add almond flour, baking powder and cinnamon, stir, divide into a lined cupcake pan, introduce in the oven at 350 degrees F and bake for 20 minutes. Leave the cupcakes to cool down, divide between dessert plates and top with apple slices.
Enjoy!

Nutrition: calories 200, fat 4, fiber 4, carbs 12, protein 5

Cinnamon Apples

Preparation time: 10 minutes
Cooking time: 20 minutes
Servings: 4

Ingredients:
- 4 big apples, cored
- 4 tablespoons raisins
- 1 tablespoon cinnamon powder

Directions:
Stuff the apples with the raisins, sprinkle the cinnamon, arrange them in a baking dish, introduce in the oven at 375 degrees F, bake for 20 minutes and serve cold.
Enjoy!

Nutrition: calories 200, fat 3, fiber 4, carbs 8, protein 5

Pumpkin Bars

Preparation time: 10 minutes
Cooking time: 15 minutes
Servings: 14

Ingredients:
- 2 and ½ cups almond flour
- ½ teaspoon baking soda
- 1 tablespoon flax seed
- 3 tablespoons water
- ½ cup pumpkin flesh, mashed
- ¼ cup coconut sugar
- 2 tablespoons coconut butter
- 1 teaspoon vanilla extract

Directions:
In a bowl, mix flax seed with water and stir. In another bowl, mix flour with, baking soda, flax meal, pumpkin, coconut sugar, coconut butter and vanilla, stir well, spread on a baking sheet, press well, bake in the oven at 350 degrees F for 15 minutes, leave aside to cool down, cut into bars and serve.
Enjoy!

Nutrition: calories 210, fat 2, fiber 4, carbs 7, protein 8

Cold Cashew and Berry Cake

Preparation time: 5 hours
Cooking time: 0 minutes
Servings: 6

Ingredients:

For the crust:
- ½ cup dates, pitted
- 1 tablespoon water
- ½ teaspoon vanilla
- ½ cup almonds, chopped

For the cake:

- 2 and ½ cups cashews soaked overnight and drained
- 1 cup blackberries
- ¾ cup maple syrup
- 1 tablespoon coconut oil, melted

Directions:

In your food processor, mix dates with water, vanilla and almonds, pulse well, transfer this to a working surface, flatten it and press on the bottom of a round pan. In your blender, mix maple syrup with coconut oil, cashews and blackberries, blend well, spread evenly over the crust, and keep in the freezer for 5 hours, slice and serve.
Enjoy!

Nutrition: calories 230, fat 4, fiber 4, carbs 12, protein 8

Cold Carrot and Mandarins Cake

Preparation time: 3 hours
Cooking time: 0 minutes
Servings: 6

Ingredients:
- 3 carrots, grated
- 1/3 cup dates, pitted
- 4 mandarins, peeled
- A handful walnuts, chopped
- 8 tablespoons coconut oil, melted
- 1 cup cashews, soaked for 2 hours
- Juice of 2 lemons
- 2 tablespoons coconut sugar
- 2 tablespoons water

Directions:

In your food processor, mix carrots with dates, walnuts, mandarins and half of the coconut oil, blend very well, pour into a cake pan and spread well. Add cashews to your food processor, also add lemon juice, stevia, water and the rest of the oil and blend some more. Add this over the carrots mix, spread, and keep in the fridge for 3 hours, slice and serve.
Enjoy!

Nutrition: calories 170, fat 2, fiber 4, carbs 11, protein 8

Green Tea Cream

Preparation time: 2 hours
Cooking time: 5 minutes
Servings: 6

Ingredients:
- 14 ounces coconut milk
- 2 tablespoons green tea powder
- 14 ounces coconut cream
- 3 tablespoons coconut sugar

Directions:
Put the milk in a pan, add sugar and green tea powder, stir, bring to a simmer, cook for 2 minutes, take off heat, cool down, add coconut cream, whisk well, divide into small bowls and keep in the fridge for 2 hours before serving.
Enjoy!

Nutrition: calories 160, fat 3, fiber 3, carbs 7, protein 6

Coconut Figs

Preparation time: 6 minutes
Cooking time: 5 minutes
Servings: 4

Ingredients:
- 2 tablespoons coconut butter
- 12 figs, halved
- ¼ cup coconut sugar
- 1 cup almonds, toasted and chopped

Directions:
Put butter in a pot, heat up over medium heat, add sugar, whisk well, also add almonds and figs, toss, cook for 5 minutes, divide into small cups and serve cold.
Enjoy!

Nutrition: calories 150, fat 4, fiber 5, carbs 7, protein 4

Lemony Banana Mix

Preparation time: 10 minutes
Cooking time: 0 minutes
Servings: 4

Ingredients:
- 4 bananas, peeled and chopped
- 5 strawberries, halved
- Juice of 2 lemons
- 4 tablespoons coconut sugar

Directions:
In a bowl, combine the bananas with the strawberries, lemon juice and sugar, toss and serve cold.
Enjoy!

Nutrition: calories 172, fat 7, fiber 5, carbs 5, protein 5

Cocoa Banana Dessert Smoothie

Preparation time: 5 minutes
Cooking time: 0 minutes
Servings: 2

Ingredients:
- 2 medium bananas, peeled
- 2 teaspoons cocoa powder
- ½ big avocado, pitted, peeled and mashed
- ¾ cup almond milk

Directions:
In your blender, combine the bananas with the cocoa, avocado and milk, pulse well, divide into 2 glasses and serve.
Enjoy!

Nutrition: calories 155, fat 3, fiber 4, carbs 6, protein 5

Kiwi Bars

Preparation time: 30 minutes
Cooking time: 0 minutes
Servings: 4

Ingredients:

- 1 cup olive oil
- 1 and ½ bananas, peeled and chopped
- 1/3 cup coconut sugar
- ¼ cup lemon juice
- 1 teaspoon lemon zest, grated
- 3 kiwis, peeled and chopped

Directions:

In your food processor, mix bananas with kiwis, almost all the oil, sugar, lemon juice and lemon zest and pulse well. Grease a pan with the remaining oil, pour the kiwi mix, spread, keep in the fridge for 30 minutes, slice and serve,
Enjoy!

Nutrition: calories 207, fat 3, fiber 3, carbs 4, protein 4

Black Tea Bars

Preparation time: 10 minutes
Cooking time: 35 minutes
Servings: 12

Ingredients:

- 6 tablespoons black tea powder
- 2 cups almond milk
- ½ cup low-fat butter
- 2 cups coconut sugar
- 4 eggs
- 2 teaspoons vanilla extract
- ½ cup olive oil
- 3 and ½ cups whole wheat flour
- 1 teaspoon baking soda
- 3 teaspoons baking powder

Directions:

Put the milk in a pot, heat it up over medium heat, add tea, stir, take off heat and cool down. Add butter, sugar, eggs, vanilla, oil, flour, baking soda and baking powder, stir well, pour into a square pan, spread, introduce in the oven, bake at 350 degrees F for 35 minutes, cool down, slice and serve.
Enjoy!

Nutrition: calories 220, fat 4, fiber 4, carbs 12, protein 7

Green Pudding

Preparation time: 2 hours
Cooking time: 5 minutes
Servings: 6

Ingredients:

- 14 ounces almond milk
- 2 tablespoons green tea powder
- 14 ounces coconut cream
- 3 tablespoons coconut sugar
- 1 teaspoon gelatin powder

Directions:
Put the milk in a pan, add sugar, gelatin, coconut cream and green tea powder, stir, bring to a simmer, cook for 5 minutes, divide into cups and keep in the fridge for 2 hours before serving. Enjoy!

Nutrition: calories 170, fat 3, fiber 3, carbs 7, protein 4

Lemony Plum Cake

Preparation time: 1 hour and 20 minutes
Cooking time: 40 minutes
Servings: 8

Ingredients:

- 7 ounces whole wheat flour
- 1 teaspoon baking powder
- 1-ounce low-fat butter, soft
- 1 egg, whisked
- 5 tablespoons coconut sugar
- 3 ounces warm almond milk
- 1 and ¾ pounds plums, pitted and cut into quarters
- Zest of 1 lemon, grated
- 1-ounce almond flakes

Directions:
In a bowl, combine the flour with baking powder, butter, egg, sugar, milk and lemon zest, stir well, transfer dough to a lined cake pan, spread plums and almond flakes all over, introduce in the oven and bake at 350 degrees F for 40 minutes. Slice and serve cold.
Enjoy!

Nutrition: calories 222, fat 4, fiber 2, carbs 7, protein 7

Lentils Sweet Bars

Preparation time: 10 minutes
Cooking time: 25 minutes
Servings: 14

Ingredients:

- 1 cup lentils, cooked, drained and rinsed
- 1 teaspoon cinnamon powder
- 2 cups whole wheat flour
- 1 teaspoon baking powder
- ½ teaspoon nutmeg, ground
- 1 cup low-fat butter
- 1 cup coconut sugar
- 1 egg
- 2 teaspoons almond extract
- 1 cup raisins
- 2 cups coconut, unsweetened and shredded

Directions:
Put the lentils in a bowl, mash them well using a fork, add cinnamon, flour, baking powder, nutmeg, butter, sugar, egg, almond extract, raisins and coconut, stir, spread on a lined baking sheet, introduce in the oven, bake at 350 degrees F for 25 minutes, cut into bars and serve cold. Enjoy!

Nutrition: calories 214, fat 4, fiber 2, carbs 5, protein 7

Lentils and Dates Brownies

Preparation time: 10 minutes
Cooking time: 15 minutes
Servings: 8

Ingredients:

- 28 ounces canned lentils, no-salt-added, rinsed and drained
- 12 dates
- 1 tablespoon coconut sugar
- 1 banana, peeled and chopped
- ½ teaspoon baking soda
- 4 tablespoons almond butter
- 2 tablespoons cocoa powder

Directions:
Put lentils in your food processor, pulse, add dates, sugar, banana, baking soda, almond butter and cocoa powder, pulse well, pour into a lined pan, spread, bake in the oven at 375 degrees F for 15 minutes, leave the mix aside to cool down a bit, cut into medium pieces and serve. Enjoy!

Nutrition: calories 202, fat 4, fiber 2, carbs 12, protein 6

Rose Lentils Ice Cream

Preparation time: 30 minutes
Cooking time: 1 hour and 20 minutes
Servings: 4

Ingredients:
- ½ cup red lentils, rinsed
- Juice of ½ lemon
- 1 cup coconut sugar
- 1 and ½ cups water
- 3 cups almond milk
- Juice of 2 limes
- 2 teaspoons cardamom powder
- 1 teaspoon rose water

Directions:
Heat up a pan over medium-high heat with the water, half of the sugar and lemon juice, stir, bring to a boil, add lentils, stir, reduce heat to medium-low and cook for 1 hour and 20 minutes. Drain lentils, transfer them to a bowl, add coconut milk, the rest of the sugar, limejuice, cardamom and rose water, whisk everything, transfer to your ice cream machine, process for 30 minutes and serve.
Enjoy!

Nutrition: calories 184, fat 4, fiber 3, carbs 8, protein 5

Mandarin Pudding

Preparation time: 10 minutes
Cooking time: 30 minutes
Servings: 8

Ingredients:
- 1 mandarin, peeled and sliced
- Juice of2 mandarins
- 4 ounces low-fat butter, soft
- 2 eggs, whisked
- ¾ cup coconut sugar+ 2 tablespoons
- ¾ cup whole wheat flour
- ¾ cup almonds, ground

Directions:
Grease a loaf pan with some of the butter, sprinkle 2 tablespoons sugar on the bottom and arrange mandarin slice inside. In a bowl, combine the butter with the rest of the sugar, eggs, almonds, flour and mandarin juice and whisk using a mixer. Spoon mix over mandarin slices, introduce in the oven, bake at 350 degrees F for 30 minutes, divide into bowls and serve
Enjoy!

Nutrition: calories 202, fat 3, fiber 2, carbs 12, protein 6

Cherry Stew

Preparation time: 10 minutes
Cooking time: 10 minutes
Servings: 6

Ingredients:
- ½ cup cocoa powder
- 1 pound cherries, pitted
- ¼ cup coconut sugar
- 2 cups water

Directions:
In a pan, combine the cherries with the water, sugar and the cocoa powder, stir, cook over medium heat for 10 minutes, divide into bowls and serve cold.
Enjoy!

Nutrition: calories 207, fat 1, fiber 3, carbs 8, protein 6

Spiced Rice Pudding

Preparation time: 10 minutes
Cooking time: 45 minutes
Servings: 6

Ingredients:
- ½ cup basmati rice
- 4 cups almond milk
- ¼ cup raisins
- 3 tablespoons coconut sugar
- ½ teaspoon cardamom powder
- ¼ teaspoon cinnamon powder
- ¼ cup walnuts, chopped
- 1 tablespoon lemon zest, grated

Directions:
In a pan, mix sugar with milk, stir, bring to a boil over medium-high heat, add rice, raisins, cardamom, cinnamon, walnuts and lemon zest, stir, cover the pan, reduce heat to low, cook for 40 minutes, divide into bowls and serve cold.
Enjoy!

Nutrition: calories 200, fat 4, fiber 5, carbs 8, protein 3

Apple Loaf

Preparation time: 10 minutes
Cooking time: 35 minutes
Servings: 6

Ingredients:

- 3 cups apples, cored and cubed
- 1 cup coconut sugar
- 1 tablespoon vanilla
- 2 eggs
- 1 tablespoon apple pie spice
- 2 cups almond flour
- 1 tablespoon baking powder
- 1 tablespoon coconut oil, melted

Directions:
In a bowl, mix apples with coconut sugar, vanilla, eggs, apple pie spice, almond flour, baking powder and oil, whisk, pour into a loaf pan, introduce in the oven and bake at 350 degrees F for 35 minutes. Serve cold.
Enjoy!

Nutrition: calories 180, fat 6, fiber 5, carbs 12, protein 4

Cauliflower Pudding

Preparation time: 10 minutes
Cooking time: 20 minutes
Servings: 6

Ingredients:

- 1 tablespoon coconut oil, melted
- 7 ounces cauliflower rice
- 4 ounces water
- 16 ounces coconut milk
- 3 ounces coconut sugar
- 1 egg
- 1 teaspoon cinnamon powder
- 1 teaspoon vanilla extract

Directions:
In a pan, combine the oil with the rice, water, milk, sugar, egg, cinnamon and vanilla, whisk well, bring to a simmer, cook for 20 minutes over medium heat, divide into bowls and serve cold.
Enjoy!

Nutrition: calories 202, fat 2, fiber 6, carbs 8, protein 7

Rhubarb Stew

Preparation time: 10 minutes
Cooking time: 5 minutes
Servings: 3

Ingredients:
- Juice of 1 lemon
- 1 teaspoon lemon zest, grated
- 1 and ½ cup coconut sugar
- 4 and ½ cups rhubarbs, roughly chopped
- 1 and ½ cups water

Directions:
In a pan, combine the rhubarb with the water, lemon juice, lemon zest and coconut sugar, toss, bring to a simmer over medium heat, cook for 5 minutes, and divide into bowls and serve cold. Enjoy!

Nutrition: calories 108, fat 1, fiber 4, carbs 8, protein 5

Almond Pumpkin Pudding

Preparation time: 1 hour
Cooking time: 0 minutes
Servings: 4

Ingredients:
- 1 and ½ cups almond milk
- ½ cup pumpkin puree
- 2 tablespoons coconut sugar
- ½ teaspoon cinnamon powder
- ¼ teaspoon ginger, grated
- ¼ cup chia seeds

Directions:
In a bowl, combine the milk with pumpkin, sugar, cinnamon, ginger and chia seeds, toss well, divide into small cups and keep them in the fridge for 1 hour before serving. Enjoy!

Nutrition: calories 145, fat 7, fiber 7, carbs 11, protein 9

Cashew Lemon Fudge

Preparation time: 2 hours
Cooking time: 0 minutes
Servings: 4

Ingredients:
- 1/3 cup natural cashew butter
- 1 and ½ tablespoons coconut oil, melted
- 2 tablespoons coconut butter
- 5 tablespoons lemon juice
- ½ teaspoon lemon zest
- 1 tablespoons coconut sugar

Directions:
In a bowl, mix cashew butter with coconut butter, oil, lemon juice, lemon zest and sugar and stir well. Line a muffin tray with some parchment paper, scoop 1 tablespoon of lemon fudge mix in a lined muffin tray, keep in the fridge for 2 hours and serve
Enjoy!

Nutrition: calories 142, fat 4, fiber 4, carbs 8, protein 5

Seeds Bars

Preparation time: 30 minutes
Cooking time: 0 minutes
Servings: 6

Ingredients:
- ¼ cup cocoa nibs
- 1 cup almonds, soaked for at least 3 hours
- 2 tablespoons cocoa powder
- ¼ cup hemp seeds
- ¼ cup goji berries
- ¼ cup coconut, shredded
- 8 dates, pitted and soaked

Directions:
In your food processor, combine the cocoa with almonds, cocoa powder, hemp seeds, goji berries, coconut and dates, pulse well, press this on a lined baking sheet, and keep in the fridge for 30 minutes, slice and serve.
Enjoy!

Nutrition: calories 170, fat 6, fiber 3, carbs 7, protein 7

Chocolate Pomegranate Fudge

Preparation time: 2 hours
Cooking time: 5 minutes
Servings: 6

Ingredients:
- ½ cup coconut milk
- 1 teaspoon vanilla extract
- 1 and ½ cups dark chocolate, chopped
- ½ cup almonds, chopped
- ½ cup pomegranate seeds

Directions:
Put milk in a pan, heat up over medium-low heat, add chocolate, stir well, cook for 5 minutes, take off heat, combine with the vanilla extract, half of the pomegranate seeds and half of the almonds, stir well, spread on a lined baking sheet, sprinkle the rest of the almonds and pomegranate seeds, keep in the fridge for 2 hours, cut and serve.
Enjoy!

Nutrition: calories 148, fat 3, fiber 4, carbs 6, protein 5

Pumpkin Cream

Preparation time: 10 minutes
Cooking time: 1 hour
Servings: 6

Ingredients:
- 1 and ½ cups pumpkin puree
- 2/3 cup coconut sugar
- 1 cup coconut milk
- 2 tablespoons chia seeds, ground
- 1 tablespoon baking powder
- 2 teaspoons pumpkin pie spice
- 1 teaspoon cinnamon powder
- ½ teaspoon vanilla extract

Directions:
In a bowl, mix pumpkin puree with coconut milk, sugar, chia seeds, baking powder, pumpkin pie spice, cinnamon and vanilla, whisk well, pour into 6 ramekins, place them all on a baking tray filled halfway with hot water, introduce in the oven at 325 degrees F and bake for 1 hour. Serve the cream cold.
Enjoy!

Nutrition: calories 200, fat 5, fiber 2, carbs 6, protein 6

Green Apple Bowls

Preparation time: 10 minutes
Cooking time: 0 minutes
Servings: 3

Ingredients:

- 3 big green apples, cored and cubed
- 1 cup strawberries, halved
- 1 tablespoon coconut sugar
- ½ teaspoon cinnamon powder
- ½ teaspoon vanilla extract

Directions:
In a bowl, combine the apples with strawberries, sugar, cinnamon and vanilla, toss and serve.
Enjoy!

Nutrition: calories 205, fat 1, fiber 3, carbs 8, protein 4

Minty Grapefruit Stew

Preparation time: 10 minutes
Cooking time: 10 minutes
Servings: 6

Ingredients:

- 1 cup water
- 1 cup coconut sugar
- ½ cup mint, chopped
- 4 grapefruits, peeled and roughly chopped

Directions:
Put the water in a pan, add sugar, mint and grapefruits, toss, bring to a simmer over medium heat, cook for 10 minutes, divide into bowls and serve cold.
Enjoy!

Nutrition: calories 120, fat 1, carbs 2, fiber 4, protein 6

Conclusion

You have to give the Dash diet a chance! This amazing lifestyle will change your life forever and it will transform you into a happier and healthier person in no time!
All you have to do is to respect this diet's principles and you will soon see its wonderful benefits!

The Dash diet is actually easy to follow once you understand it!
That's why we are here today! If you have decided to opt for this great diet, this cookbook will come in hand for sure!
We've gathered the best 500 Dash diet recipes just for you! You can try something new each day!
You can enjoy a textured and rich Dash diet recipe at any time! All you have to do is to get your hands on a copy and start your new Dash lifestyle right away!

Recipe Index